Adrian Vickers is Professor of Southeast Asian Studies at the University of Sydney, and is also Director of the university's Australian Center for Asian Art and Archaeology and Asian Studies Program. Originally from Tamworth, New South Wales, his interest in Bali began when studying Indonesian language at High School, especially after travelling there as part of a school group in 1972/73. He went on to study Indonesian, Balinese, Old Javanese, and Dutch at the University of Sydney, where he was awarded a PhD in 1987. He has also worked at the University of New South Wales and the University of Wollongong, and held visiting positions at the University of Indonesia, Udayana University Bali, and Leiden University.

Adrian has carried out research in Bali since 1978, living at different times in the villages of Kamasan and Batuan, as well as Sanur. He has since travelled extensively in Southeast Asia.

Adrian is author of many articles and books on Indonesian history, culture and society, including *A History of Modern Indonesia* (Cambridge, 2005). He is a sought-after speaker, commentator and analyst on the subject of Indonesia. His book *Balinese Art: Paintings and Drawings of Bali 1800-2010* will be published by Tuttle in mid 2012.

T0160624

BALI

A PARADISE CREATED

Second Edition

ADRIAN VICKERS

TUTTLE Publishing
Tokyo | Rutland, Vermont | Singapore

Published by Tuttle Publishing, an imprint of Periplus Editions (HK) Ltd.

www.tuttlepublishing.com

First edition published by Penguin Books Australia in 1989 and Periplus Editions (HK) Limited in 1990.

Copyright © 2012 by Adrian Vickers

Library of Congress Catalog No. 2007308206

ISBN 978-0-8048-4260-0

Distributed by

North America, Latin America & Europe
Tuttle Publishing
364 Innovation Drive
North Clarendon, VT 05759-9436 U.S.A.
Tel: 1 (802) 773-8930; Fax: 1 (802) 773-6993
info@tuttlepublishing.com; www.tuttlepublishing.com

Japan
Tuttle Publishing
Yaekari Building, 3rd Floor
5-4-12 Osaki, Shinagawa-ku
Tokyo 141-0032
Tel: (81) 3 5437-0171; Fax: (81) 3 5437-0755
sales@tuttle.co.jp; www.tuttle.co.jp

Asia Pacific
Berkeley Books Pte. Ltd.
61 Tai Seng Avenue, #02-12, Singapore 534167
Tel: (65) 6280-1330; Fax: (65) 6280-6290
inquiries@periplus.com.sg; www.periplus.com

Indonesia
PT Java Books Indonesia
Kawasan Industri Pulogadung
Jl. Rawa Gelam IV No. 9, Jakarta 13930
Tel: (62) 21 4682-1088; Fax: (62) 21 461-0206
crm@periplus.co.id; www.periplus.com

16 15 14 13   10 9 8 7 6 5 4 3 2

Printed in Singapore   1305MP

Contents

Contents

Acknowledgements

While a vast amount has been published about Bali, it tends to divide very clearly. There is the general—often too-general—popular or travel writing, mainly based on rehashing or republishing works from the 1930s, and inaccessible academic work. This book is designed to bridge the gap between the two, and to bring to a wider audience important scholarship on Bali.

In carrying out this task I need to apologize most of all to Professor James A. Boon, Dr. Henk Schulte Nordholt, and Dr. Michel Picard, whose territory I have ventured onto in order to draw together the various strands of Balinese cultural history. Besides these three, I only have space to thank a few of those in Bali or engaged in the study of Bali who have influenced this work: Drs I Putu Budiastra; Professor Linda Connor; Professor Hildred Geertz; Dr. Jean-Francois Guermonprez; Professor H. I. R. Hinzler; Professor Mark Hobart; Dr. Douglas Miles; I Nyoman Mandra; Ida Bagus Pidada Kaot; Dr. Stuart Robson; Dr. Raechelle Rubinstein; John Stowell (particularly for very detailed criticism of the original book); Dr. David Stuart-Fox; Associate Professor Carol Warren, John Wilkinson, and Professor P. J. Worsley. In revising the original book, I benefitted from the research of and discussions with Barbara Bicego, Leo Haks, Laura Noszlopy, Dr. Nyoman Darma Putra, Dr. Graeme MacRae, Degung Santikarma, and Dr. Agnieszka Sobocinska. Sadly many of the people who profoundly affected my view of Bali are no longer alive: Professor I Gusti Ngurah Bagus, Professor Anthony Forge, Drs B. Joseph, I Ktut Kantor, Anak Agung Kompiang Gedé,

Dr. Barbara Lovric, Ratu Dalem Pemayun, I Gusti Madé Deblog, Ida Bagus Putu Gedé (Pedanda Batuan), I Madé Kanta, Mangku Mura, Pan Seken, Dalang Ktut Rinda, and Ida Bagus Madé Togog.

I owe a great debt to Professor Alfred McCoy who, as series editor, came up with the original idea for the book, helped relieve me of the boring aspects of my academic style, and shaped the nature of this book. Thanks also to Dr. Ian Black and Professor John Ingleson who provided all kinds of support to see me through 1988. Of the many staff in the school of History at the University of New South Wales, Libi Nugent and Shayne Sarantos in particular helped with the important material details of writing, and Mark Hutchinson with miscellaneous computer assistance. Dr. Kathy Robinson provided interest and encouragement. Hazel and Emma Vickers have lived with Bali for many years, and illuminated my own understandings of the island. Hazel's editorial work has also been vital in updating the book.

The original illustrations for this book were funded by a Special Research Grant from the University of New South Wales. Deborah Hill provided the photographs on pp. 272 and 208 from her photographic expeditions to Bali. I would also like to acknowledge the assistance of the various copyright holders for the illustrations to this book: Mitchell Library, State Library of New South Wales, Sydney for illustrations from C. de Houtman, *Verhael vande Reyse ...Naer Oost Indien*, Middleburgh: Barent Langhencs, 1597 edition (p. 28) and 1598 edition (p. 30); from Cornelis de Bruin, *Voyages de Corneille le Brun*. Amsterdam: Wetstein, 1718 (original edn 1711) (p. 32); from F. Valentijn, *Nederlands Indie Oud en Nieuw*, Dordrecht: van Braam, 1724-26 (p. 37); the Tropen Museum, Amsterdam (pp. 102 and 186); the Royal Institute for Linguistics and Anthropology, Leiden, the Netherlands, for the phtographs on pp. 55, 56, 105, and 195 from their photograph archive; Ernst Drissen for the photographs by Thilly Weissenborn, originally from the Studio "Lux," Garut, Java (pp. 147 and 191); Stichting Walter Spies for the photograph on p. 150; Lois Bateson for the painting from the Bateson-Mead collection on p. 204; and Mary Catharine Bateson for permission to quote from the Bateson-Mead archives and for the photograph of Ida Bagus Madé Jatasura from G. Bateson and M. Mead, *Balinese*

Character: A Photographic Analysis, New York: New York Academy of Sciences, 1942 (p. 223); Alfred A. Knopf Inc for illustration from M. Covarrubias, *Island of Bali,* New York: Alfred A. Knopf, 1937 (p. 163); Doubleday for the illustration from B. Hope and Bob Thomas, *The Road to Hollywood,* London: W. H. Allen, 1977 (p. 183); and Louise and Robert Koke for the drawings and photographs from L. Koke, *Our Hotel in Bali,* Wellington: January Books, 1987 (pp. 129 and 170, and the photographs on p. 174), with thanks to the late Hugh Mabbett for his assistance with the illustrations from the Kokes' book. The whereabouts of the copyright holders of Tyra de Kleen with P. de Kat Angelino, *Mudras op Bali,* The Hague: Adi Poestaka, 1922 (p. 122); images from The Island of Bare Breasts, 1930s tourist postcard (p. 141) and W.O.J Nieuwenkamp, *Zweftochen op Bali* (p. 137) are unknown.

Photograph on p. 177 courtesy of Laura Rosenberg; cartoons on pp. 291 and 293 courtesy of Ida Bagus Surya Darma and Kadek Jango Pramartha.

Preface to the Second Edition

Bali: A Paradise Created has been in print for over twenty years. Since the book's original publication, the island has undergone profound changes due to both the steady intensification of tourism and the problems of having become a target of international terrorism with the 2002 and 2005 bombings. At the time that the book was written, Bali had yet to feel the impact of Indonesia's economic deregulation. When I returned to island in 1989 after a three-year absence, I found the island radically changed by this move, as the scale of development increased massively, the streets suddenly became clogged with traffic, and poor itinerant workers from surrounding islands poured into Bali. The more up-beat conclusion of the original edition has had to be substantially modified in this new version of *Bali: A Paradise Created*.

Bali: A Paradise Created is concerned with the changing image of Bali, particularly the dialectic between indigenous perceptions and Western imaginings of the island. It is not solely a simplistic account of the Western image of Bali, as some readers have thought, since the focus of my research for this and other books has been on how the Balinese see themselves. This book was always meant to give expression to the multiple voices of the experience of Bali. Although it is a cultural history of Bali, in writing it I did not want to give the kind of "everything you always wanted to know but were too bored to ask" account that many people seem to think constitutes the writing of history. I have, however, been surprised at how often readers fail to detect irony. Many of the purveyors of romantic ideas of Bali that this book criticizes have taken what I wrote as validation of their idealization and stereotyping.

After writing *Bali: A Paradise Created*, I had the opportunity to compile a selection of writings about Bali, mainly travel essays, published in 1994 under the title *Traveling to Bali: Four Hundred Years of Journeys*.[1] Just before that book was published, I also worked with Kerry Negara in the making of her film, *Done Bali* (Negara Film and Television Productions, 1993), which dealt with many of the issues covered in *Bali: A Paradise Created*. During the 1990s, through a grant from the Australian Research Council, my colleague Carol Warren and I had an opportunity to carry out research on modern Bali. As part of that research we organized the collection of oral history interviews with Balinese, and material from this Bali Oral History Project have informed the revision of this book.

A variety of other writers have also ventured into the same territory of image-making. An important product of this is the compilation of writings and images by Balinese, *Bali: Living in Two Worlds*[2], which is an apt complement to my book. Other Balinese have sought to counter what they consider to be unfair treatment in the stereotyping of Bali, most notably Luh Ketut Suryani's rebuttals of Margaret Mead's psychologizing.[3] Mark Hobart has produced an erudite series of studies of the knowledge of Bali.[4] Probably the most significant attempt to deal with the problem of images of Bali since the 1990s has been Michael Hitchcock's and I Nyoman Darma Putra's joint book which, like many of the recent studies already mentioned, demonstrates the importance of Western-Balinese collaborations.[5]

In revising this book I have not wanted to overcook the narrative,

---

1. Traveling *to Bali. Four Hundred Years of Travel Writing*, Kuala Lumpur: Oxford University Press.

2. Urs Ramseyer and I Gusti Raka Pañji Tisna (ed.), *Bali: Living in Two Worlds. A Critical Self-Portrait*, Basel: Museum der Kulturen and Verlag Schwabe & Co., 2001.

3. Gordon D. Jensen and Luh Ketut Suryani, *The Balinese People: A Reinvestigation of Character*, Singapore: Oxford University Press, 1992.

4. Mark Hobart, *After Culture: Anthropology as Radical Metaphysical Critique*, Yogyakarta: Duta Wacana University Press, 2000.

5. Michael Hitchcock and I Nyoman Darma Putra, *Tourism, Development and Terrorism in Bali*, Aldershot: Ashgate, 2007.

to make it either fall apart or become unpalatably tough with extra information. Rather, I have focused on the rapid changes to the image of Bali; to that end, minimal updating of the earlier chapters has been done, and a new chapter added. The changes to Bali's image in the last decade have come about because of the clash between official Balinese policy to maintain the island's Cultural Tourism, and the pressures of an international industry that defines the island in terms of resort tourism. At the same time, Bali's image as a terrorist target has complicated the narratives of development and growth. It is becoming harder and harder to tell the story of Bali, as the island is torn in different directions by overdevelopment, competition from other tourist "paradises," over-population, and the changing nature of the Indonesian state.

Introduction to the
Japanese Edition of 1996

When this book was first written I had no idea that it would ever be translated into Japanese. I wrote with Western (primarily Australian and European) and Indonesian readers in mind, so Japanese readers may find aspects of what I have written both unfamiliar and familiar. What may be unfamiliar is the fact that so much of the interaction I describe is concerned with sets of images: changing Western images of Bali. What may be familiar is the way in which Western images of Bali are part of processes of creating an image of the Orient, since Japan featured in the Western imagination as a great and inscrutable power in this Orient.

The Japanese translation of this book made me aware of how little I knew of Japanese ideas about Bali. We know from McPhee's *House in Bali*[1] that there were Japanese photographers and shopkeepers in Bali in the 1930s, and K'tut Tantri[2], who worked closely with the Japanese and the Resistance, is a valuable source on Bali during World War II. But much remains undocumented, so that for example it is only recently that I discovered that the main camp for "Comfort Women" during that same period was in Wongaya, Dénpasar[3], and through asking about it was able to elicit many responses from older Balinese concerning the Japanese period.

1. Colin McPhee, *A House in Bali*. Repr., Oxford: Singapore, 1979, p.14.

2. K'tut Tantri, *Revolt in Paradise*. London: Heinemann, 1960.

3. George Hicks, *The Comfort Women: Sex Slaves of the Japanese Imperial Forces*. St Leonards: Allen and Unwin, 1995.

Geoffrey Robinson, in his recent political history of Bali from the 1920s to 1965[4], has produced an excellent account of the major features of the period, but we still await a Japanese historian to provide both the Japanese perspective and much of the detail of the interaction of Balinese and Japanese. Likewise Post-War Japanese investment in Indonesia is a vast and unanalysed area for English-speaking audiences.

Since its original publication this book has drawn many reactions: Australians have asked why there is not more on Australian perceptions of Bali (indeed there was a chapter on this topic originally intended for the book, much of which was published as a separate article[5]), and Balinese reactions have run the full spectrum from pleasure to offence. Balinese who rankle at having to live up to the expectation of the tourist image of the island have been pleased to see it dissected, while others have not been pleased to have the past existence of institutions of slavery intrude into the respectability of modernity. Others have felt that I have misrepresented them or their families, or not given enough emphasis to the roles of particular royal families or regions of Bali.

Histories are not written to please, or at least they should not be. However one of my intentions was always to present Balinese history as multiple, not just as a single narrative. For that reason the chapters have been organized as a set of discontinuous and overlapping narratives. In so doing my representation of Balinese histories is still only partial: there are as many histories of Bali as there are Balinese, and lacking the literary dexterity of Salman Rushdie in his great work *Midnight's Children*, I can only simplify, not do justice to that profusion of histories. Likewise this book was written for a general audience, so many of my academic colleagues find some of the discussions unsatisfying, for example the account of Gèlgèl history in Chapter 2 deserves far more thorough examination of sources.[6]

---

4. Geoffrey Robinson, *The Dark Side of Paradise. Political Violence in Bali.* Ithaca: Cornell University Press, 1995.

5. Adrian Vickers, "A Paradise Bombed," *Griffith Review* 1 (Spring 2003): 105-113.

6. See Helen Creese, "Balinese *Babad* as Historical Sources: A Reinterpretation of the Fall of Gèlgèl," *Bijdragen tot de Taal-, Land- en Volkenkunde* 147 (1991): 236-60.

Being partial, a history such as this can only be uneven, and in many ways the emphases in this book come out of my own academic pursuits. The last chapter* in particular does not describe the most recent developments: it was written in 1988, based on experiences of Bali from the late 1970s to the mid-1980s, and since then Bali's tourism has ballooned in a way that makes me now much less optimistic about the forces of commercialization and environmental destruction which are the obverse of rapid tourist development.

* Chapter 5 of the 2012 edition

Introduction

Bali is the "enchanted isle," "the last paradise,"one of the world's great romantic dreams. Tahiti called to Gauguin with the beauty, beaches and tropical climate of the South Seas; India lured travelers with its Eastern mystery and Hinduism; but Bali's image combines all these attractions. The South Pacific disappoints—visitors there find it expensive, westernized by way of the missionaries, and without much to offer tourists beyond leis and kava. India is just too vast and overwhelming. Asia and the Pacific meet in Bali, which remains open, accessible, compact—its cultural riches on display, ready to be appreciated by the tourist just off the Qantas jet from Sydney, Perth or Melbourne.

Over the last century writers have enriched the idea of Bali, praising "its extreme fertility, its endless beauty, and the artistry and charm of its people."[1] Colin McPhee, the writer and musicologist, found in 1930s Bali a many-sided natural treasure-house. For him, each part of the day had a quality that revealed a particular aspect of the island. For the morning it was "a golden freshness" when the island "dripped and shone with moisture like a garden in a florist's window." In mid-day day Bali "had become hard and matter-of-fact." In the afternoon and the evening its qualities shone through, as it "grew unreal, lavish and theatrical like old-fashioned opera scenery."[2] The natural fertility and

1. Robert Blackwood, *Beautiful Bali,* Melbourne: Hampden Hall, 1970, p. 1.

2. Colin McPhee, *A House in Bali,* Kuala Lumpur: Oxford University Press, 1979, p. 18.

beauty of Bali seem to go hand-in-hand with its cultural fecundity.

For another writer from the 1930s, Hickman Powell, the attractions were more physical. He described the movement from the urbanized and colonized north of Bali to what for him was the real Bali of the south. As he drove towards it, the real Bali came to meet him in the form of "a solitary female figure, swinging toward us." The erotic promise of the island revealed itself to him at the moment when, "a scarf fell carelessly from a shoulder, and the bronze bowls of maiden breasts projected angular, living shadows." This woman became a metaphor for the island, "a part of a vast spreading wonderland, embodied dreams of pastoral poets." The south of Bali was "a teeming, pregnant woman, and in her eyes burned afterglow of fallen empires."[3]

Such is the island's image of crowded splendor; an artistic people in harmony with nature; a vibrant, erotic atmosphere; and an exotic ancient history. It is indeed a beautiful island, overflowing with colors, smells and sounds that assault the newly-arrived traveler with the same force as the hot, humid air. More than any other tropical island, Bali has become the most exotic of exotic locations, a fantasy of all the splendors of the Orient and the beauties of the Pacific. Over three centuries the West has constructed a complex and gorgeous image of the island that has come to take over even Balinese thought.

The image now seems so definite and permanent, but it has not always been so. In the nineteenth century Bali failed to charm, was in fact positively threatening. As one Dutch visitor said: "The Balinese are a fierce, savage, perfidious, and bellicose people, loath to do any work, and so they dislike agriculture. They are also very poor, and subsist only on rice that the fruitful island of Lombok provides."[4] Many commentators of those times considered the Balinese as dangerous, both liable to run amuk and adherents of such barbarous practices as widow burning. People in the nineteenth century wrote about Bali as part of a region of the world where the

---

3. Hickman Powell, *The Last Paradise*, London: Jonathan Cape, 1930, p. 6.

4. Dirk van Hogendorp, *Bericht van den Tegenwoordigen Toestand der Bataafsche Bezittingen in Oost-Indiëen den Handel op Dezelve*, 2nd edn, Delft: Roelofswaert, 1800, vol. 1, p. 191.

natives were lazy, the level of civilization was inferior to that of Europe, and proper forms of government were entirely lacking. The intention, of course, was to bring "proper" government to the island in the form of European colonization.

This "wild" Bali was not fully tamed by colonialism until the twentieth century. Only in 1908 was the whole of the island forced to acknowledge Dutch control after a long and bloody struggle. But, in the process of taming the island the Dutch came to appreciate Balinese culture. Not only did they come to see Bali as a museum of the classical culture of ancient Java, but they also became interested in the community life of the ordinary peasant.

It was during the 1920s and 1930s that the image of Bali as the island paradise really took hold. Eager to have the world forget its ruthless conquest of the island, the Dutch government began promoting Bali as a tourist destination. In so doing they made Balinese culture and village life central preoccupations of writing about the island, so shifting attention to aspects of Bali overlooked in earlier times. Suddenly wild Bali became a tame and attractive "Island Eden."

Most of what is said and thought about Bali today goes back to that period; the earlier perceptions of the island have been forgotten. Bali's image became one of a Utopia where tired Europe could refresh itself and find spiritual harmony. In the 1930s the rich and famous made Bali an extension of the salons of Paris, Berlin, and New York. For young homosexual men in particular the gentle nature of the island provided a marked contrast to the strict norms of Europe.

Even in the 1930s people were aware that tourist clichés had arisen about the island, but in the 1950s the image of Bali as paradise became fixed. In combating the image of the island of bare breasts, writers simply substituted more complex images of cultural and artistic wealth. Gradually the American film industry took the elements of Bali known from the 1930s and rearranged them. The famous 1950s film, *South Pacific,* relocated Bali as the beautiful "Bali-Hai," the dream island of American servicemen; the respite from the jungle battlefields of the Pacific. Hollywood, never worried about geographical niceties, made Bali the paradise of paradises by combining all the ideals of the South Seas into one.

During the 1950s, after the traumas of war, Bali was discovered anew, but this time not just by Europeans. When Pandit Nehru, first prime minister of India and hero of the newly-emerging non-aligned nations, called Bali "the morning of the world" he coined the most memorable of all the praises heaped on the island. Bali's image was not simply the province of Europeans and Americans who belonged to the world powers, it was international property.

Indonesians endorsed this fascination with Bali's image. President Sukarno, the charismatic demagogue who united the thousands of islands and hundreds of cultures of the Indies into Indonesia, had a Balinese mother. It was natural for him then, to focus attention on Balinese culture. In Sukarno's Indonesia the image of Bali from the 1920s and 1930s was given new life, as the President established a palace there and held court regularly, entertained by Balinese dancers, his walls hung with Balinese paintings. Although foreign tourists were not particularly welcome, Bali in the 1950s became a tourist destination for Indonesians emulating their flamboyant President.

At the end of the 1960s the destruction of the Indonesian Communist Party and the birth of the New Order government of General Suharto brought a new phase of tourism. First to come were the hippy travelers on the "Asian Highway," rediscovering the "Bali-Hai" of their childhood, and adding hallucinogenic magic mushrooms and good surf to the island's qualifications. Gradually more and more hotels opened, and formal planning was needed. The Indonesian government's five-year development schemes took up that planning, and ensured that Bali would take center-stage in Indonesian tourism. All this provided an added stimulus to the image of Bali as a paradise. International travel agencies produced new literature about the island's charms, and the former generation of expatriate residents from the 1930s wrote books about Bali or had their earlier works republished. It was convenient for the tourism industry to use the old image, since this image suited the new purpose so well. In the language of travel agencies this became the real Bali.

Decades of tourist promotion, travel and academic writing bear down on the island, making the image almost irrefutable. *National Geographic,* presidents, prime ministers, anthropologists, film-makers, and poets are all too much to argue with. Bali could not be anything else but a rich ancient culture, "a forgotten Medieval community where sun-bronzed women dress as Eve, a land where nobody hurries, and all is peace,"[5] a spiritual community of "care-free islanders... as happy as mortals can be,"[6] where everyone you meet is a dancer or an artist, where every day begins and ends with the splendors of nature: "as near an approach this side of heaven to a poet's dream."[7]

Image making

The nineteenth-century sailor who was challenged in the market of north Bali by kris-wielding warriors, and the twentieth-century tourist who watched astounding dances in the Bali Beach Hotel both experienced something of the real Bali. While both experiences may have been part of very different images of the island, it would not be fair to say that when people like these wrote about Bali they simply made it up as they went along; they wrote to tell us about the "truth" of Bali. How then did the overall picture of Bali come to change so much?

When Nehru went to Bali and called it "the morning of the world" he did not go there with a completely blank view. He had heard about the island from others, and probably read some of the travelers' accounts of Bali from the 1930s. When he got to Bali he was guided by his host, President Sukarno, who organized dances for him and took him to see the most beautiful spots on this illustrious island. Nehru then gave an informed opinion that, not surprisingly, confirmed the opinions of most others.

By such means personal experiences became part of a more widely-held image. The word about Bali has been passed from mouth to mouth, book to book, and has accumulated the perspectives of thousands of people. Each writer about Bali begins by thinking he or she is presenting a new view of the island, and turns out a work very similar to most others. This happens because the weight of the information available puts limits on what can be new in what is said

---

5. Helen Eva Yates, *Bali: Enchanted Isle,* London: Allen & Unwin, 1933, p. 19.

6. Dan Davies-Moore, "The Girls of Bali," *Inter-Ocean* 9 (1928): 485-9.

7. Elliot Napier, travel account from *Sydney Morning Herald* 20 Oct. 1934. My thanks to David Walker and John Ingleson for providing this quotation from their own research on Australian images of Asia.

about Bali. Direct experiences have to be incorporated into expectations of what Bali should be like.

The most surprising thing about the romantic image of Bali is that it has been slowly built up, layer upon layer, as each new writer has taken something from earlier works and developed it. There have always been writers, artists, scholars or politicians who have been particularly influential in forming and spreading cultural images. By virtue of their personalities, talents or positions they became authorities to whom others deferred. In the history of images of Bali there have been a number of these key figures: Margaret Mead, one of this century's best-known anthropologists, who put Bali on the map of international scholarship; President Sukarno himself, patron of the arts, who made Bali the mother culture of Indonesia; Walter Spies, the gifted yet doomed artist of the 1930s, who added Romantic depth to Bali's image; and Sir Thomas Stamford Raffles, the energetic British administrator who founded Singapore in 1819 after running the Netherlands East Indies for five years, and who was one of the first to take Bali's culture seriously.

The story of Bali's images is the story of the impact and influences of these and other characters. Their writings made it seem as if the image of Bali was the only reality because they were so intensely personal in their views. Some people added new elements, others took existing views and gave them greater currency, but gradually individual perceptions have been compounded and frozen. Yet the more Bali's packaging is unwrapped the more complicated contributions to these images become. While these images may be simplified and called "western" images, their collective authors incorporated many different ideas into them, for example Northern European Protestantism, the values of the Enlightenment, German Romanticism, or American egalitarianism. Direct experiences were always filtered through these influences, so that experiences were reconciled with the backgrounds of those who wrote about, spoke of, painted or otherwise showed Bali to the rest of the world.

This book is an attempt to unwrap the packaging of Bali. Each section of the book looks at the changing western images of Bali, and contrasts them with Balinese self-images, exploring the underlying social and cultural forces. This play of images of Bali—western against Balinese—culminates in the modern image of Bali shared by Balinese, other Indonesians and the rest of the world.

The Balinese images have been different in kind from the western images of Bali. These Balinese images were images first of social order: kings at the top, presiding with high priests over a caste system. This social order revolved around images of courtly life in which the aristocracy presented themselves as handsome princes constantly pursuing political goals through love and war, and always with the adoration of loyal subjects. Underpinning ideas of the courtly life were images of ties to the ancestors, which became important in competitions for status between clans. The themes of caste, courtly splendor and ancestry all worked together to place the peasantry at the bottom of the social order, but at least in Balinese images the lives of these ordinary men and women were presented in great detail, whereas in western images the peasant simply became an idealized figure with no real identity.

Individual Balinese have had just as strong a role in the image-making process as the characters of western history. The only difference is that the Balinese names have been less often recorded: Baturènggong, the sixteenth-century emperor whose reign was a golden age for Bali; his descendant, the "Virgin Queen" of east Bali who had a Dutch general assassinated; or the two Sukawati princes of central Bali who molded the cultural center of Ubud into an international tourist destination. Each of these is as deserving of attention as the American, Dutch, and British image-makers.

At times the western and Balinese images have been in tune, at other times one has contradicted the others. It was important for Dutch sailors to see Bali as Hindu, not Islamic, in the seventeenth century, at the same time as it was important for Balinese that Bali was the center of a great empire taking in parts of Java and the islands of Eastern Indonesia. In the eighteenth century the Dutch saw it as a backwater of the slave trade, yet the Balinese were mainly preoccupied with the creation of new kingdoms by dynamic princes. In the nineteenth century Bali was chaotic and violent to the English and Dutch colonists, yet to the Balinese it was a domain in which a struggle for status and hierarchy was taking place. In the twentieth century Bali became harmonious and artistic for generations of tourists, at the same time as it was experienced by Balinese as an island of crisis.

This period of four hundred years when the different Balinese images that make up modern Bali emerged was a time of social and cultural change. Dutch colonial conquest and rule accelerated that change, and in the process speeded up the interaction of Balinese and western images. During the Dutch period western images predominated because they complemented colonial power. Since the end of colonialism another stage of the complex interaction of images has emerged, the Balinese promotion of the idea of Bali as a paradise. The context of tourism and international relations in the contemporary world makes it harder to separate Balinese and western images, and so the final chapters of this book will examine this last stage of the image-making process, the way the different types of images have become intertwined.

Ultimately there is no single, "real" Bali. When the package is unwrapped we are left with something of a Pandora's box of political struggles, individual glory and suffering, optimism and frustration—in short, both a nightmare and a "day-dream of a summer's afternoon."

What is it that is so unique about Bali that it should be the subject of all these images? The special qualities of Bali have developed over many centuries from the key elements of high population density and complex social structure, which have been especially conducive to increasing artistic diversity. Contrasting periods of prosperity and social tension have given depth to this culture, a depth upon which the many rulers of Bali have elaborated as the patrons of painting, sculpture, architecture, poetry, theater and music.

Bali is small: 144 kilometers at its widest, 80 kilometers from north to south. For all its size it has been one of the most densely populated parts of the earth for centuries. In the sixteenth century the population density was almost forty people per square kilometer. Since then it has grown to ten times that figure. By the year 2000 the island reached a population of 3,000,000.

The heart of Bali is in the south where the present capital, Dénpasar, lies. A dramatic range of volcanoes splits the island in two, and orients it around its most visible peak, Mount Agung in the east.

The mountains spring out of nowhere. When your plane lands on the small tip of the south you look up from the flat beaches, through the palm trees, to these cloud-shrouded peaks.

One of the many stories of Bali is ecological. Such a dense population has always needed an intensive method of food production to sustain it. Rice, as elsewhere in Asia, has been Bali's staple food for thousands of years. The lowlands in the south were a natural place to set up a complex wet-rice growing system, where the rivers that run off the mountains could be turned into an intricate system of channels and terraces.

Civilization came early to this ecological niche. By the tenth century CE Bali had kings who were producing inscriptions in the Indian language, Sanskrit, which had come to Bali with Hinduism in the preceding centuries. Both came via Bali's much larger neighbor, Java, as did most other aspects of Bali's civilization.

While Java eventually switched to Islam, Bali has maintained its Hindu religion. It has mixed Hindu beliefs with Buddhism and elements from local rituals to create its own unique style of worship and ceremony. Today Hindus from South India would find little in Bali to recognize as their own religion. They would find a belief in Siva as the major deity, and a version of Indian caste, but also strong devotion to ancestors, and a belief in a high god or Supreme Being called Sang Hyang Widhi.

Economically Bali has had much to offer the outside world. Even in recent times Bali has been one of the main exporters of pigs to Singapore. At other times it has exported rice, cotton, and coffee, but in the seventeenth and eighteenth centuries the slave trade was all-important. Balinese slaves went not only to the Dutch center of Batavia (now Jakarta), but to the West Indies, South Africa, and many of the islands in the Pacific and Indian Oceans.

In the seventeenth century the strong central kingdom of Bali ruled from the southern capital of Gèlgèl broke down. From an empire that stretched from east Java to the island of Sumbawa, it was transformed by the end of the eighteenth century into nine small warring kingdoms, each in competition with the other, each its own special cultural center. The kingdom of Gèlgèl, which preceded the nine kingdoms, laid the foundations for the development of modern

Balinese culture. The subsequent increase in the number of courts, each elaborating and extending the varieties of ritual, art, theater and music on the island, deepened that culture.

This is the Bali that the Dutch, motivated by economic interests and a desire to tidy up the imperial map of the Netherlands East Indies, finally conquered in the nineteenth century. They struggled to gain control of the island from 1846 to 1908 and it took them seven separate military expeditions to fully defeat the Balinese kings and puzzle out the political system.

Dutch rule over the whole of Bali only lasted thirty-four years. Then came World War II, and after it the slow birth of the Republic of Indonesia from 1945 to 1949. During the Indonesian Revolution Bali returned briefly to Dutch hands, but in 1950 it became fully a part of Sukarno's new Republic. This transition heightened many tensions in the island; especially between the younger generation of revolutionaries, and the old rulers whom they called "feudal." The conflict was transformed into one about social order, culture and power, climaxing in a split between adherents of the Communist and Nationalist Parties of Indonesia. After a so-called coup in Jakarta on 30 September 1965 the Nationalists and the military killed an estimated 100,000 Communists and suspected Communists on Bali. This was a time when the rivers literally ran with blood and the graveyards overflowed.

Since the inauguration of Suhoarto's New Order government in the wake of the killings, Bali has been a center of mass tourism. The government inherited the idea of Bali as a paradise from the Dutch and from Sukarno, and used it to boost revenue and restore the bankrupt economy that Sukarno had also left them. Bali's role as a paradise has been vital for the development of the Indonesian national economy. In the 1980s about 400,000 tourists a year visited Bali—more than the whole population of the island in the sixteenth century. Of these over one-quarter were Australians out for a good time on the beach at Kuta, or in search of the riches promised by Bali's image. Although that image was severely dented by the Bali terrorist bombings of 2002 and 2006, the intensification of tourism has continued into the twenty first century.

CHAPTER ONE

Savage Bali

There is much that has been forgotten in the world's image of Bali. Early European writers once saw it as full of menace, an island of theft and murder, symbolized by the wavy dagger of the Malay world, the kris. Although the twentieth-century image of the island as a lush paradise drew on the earlier writings about Bali, these were only selectively referred to, when they did not contradict the idea of the island Eden. The overall negative intent of most of the earlier western writings about Bali has been discarded.

From the first western encounters with Bali at the end of the sixteenth century until the first decades of the twentieth century, one image of Bali has predominated: its warlike image. This image has gone through at least three stages. Initially, from the end of the sixteenth century, it was part of a very positive idea of Bali as an exotic place of eastern bounty and strange Hinduism. From the mid-seventeenth century slave trading made Bali both appealing and threatening, a place to acquire useful females, but where male slaves showed a temperament that made them rebellious. In this period Bali became a more dangerous place, somewhere wild and untamed, where Europeans were loath to go. The beginning of the nineteenth century saw the first steps towards the abolition of the slave trade, at the same time as a new phase in Bali's image began. Bali remained warlike and threatening as it resisted European colonization, but added the attractions of a culture that gave its menace a "civilized" edge. European powers saw it as their mission to tame the wild Bali.[1]

A Hindu Corner of an Islamic World

Cornelis de Houtman discovered Bali in 1597 as leader of the first Dutch expedition to the East Indies; 300,000 Balinese and a considerable number of other inhabitants of the Indies were not really so surprised to hear that there was a Bali, nor were the Portuguese sailors and missionaries, and the English privateer, Sir Francis Drake, who had preceded de Houtman.[2] This Dutch discovery of Bali came at a time of religious war in Europe, war which made the Dutch and other Europeans see all conflicts in religious terms as they tried to force their way into the area. Bali's image at this time was largely a product of these European preoccupations and policies.

In the sixteenth-century, as now, Islam was the great enemy of the Christian faith. To these Europeans Bali was a religiously-oriented island, a Hindu outpost in a sea of Islam. It overflowed with the tropical wonders of the Indies, and was controlled by a sumptuous ruler surrounded by the military signs of power and wealth. De Houtman was an adventurer of his day, charged with opening up the lucrative spice trade of Maluku, the Spice Islands, to the Dutch. He was therefore an enemy of the Catholic Spanish and Portuguese, and a stout Protestant, as were most of his Northern European countrymen. Like other Protestants he was opposed not only to the Papists who had ruled the Low Countries, but also to Islam. The book that described de Houtman's journey to the rest of Europe was reprinted and adapted many times, and in different languages. In accordance with the

---

1. For an analysis of parts of Bali's images, see James A. Boon, *The Anthropological Romance of Bali,* Cambridge: Cambridge University Press, 1977; and Henk Schulte Nordholt, *Bali: Colonial Conceptions and Political Change 1700-1940, From Shifting Hierarchies to "Fixed Order,"* Rotterdam: Comparative Asian Studies Programme 15, 1986, p. 3. For an uncritical summary of some of the European material on Bali, see Willard A. Hanna, *Bali Profile: People, Events, Circumstances, 1001-1976,* New York: American Universities Field Staff, 1976 (republished as *Bali Chronicles*, Singapore: Periplus, 2004). My major disagreement with Boon is that he emphasises continuity in the idea of Bali, whereas I see massive shifts in the images, for which his analysis does not account.

2. On de Houtman's "discovery," see G. P. Rouffaer & J. W. IJzerman, *De Eerst Schipvaart der Nederlanders naar Oost-Indiëonder Cornelis de Houtman, 1595-1597,* vols 7, 25, 32, The Hague: Lindschoten Vereeniging, 1915, 1925, 1929. For one of the journals also quoted in Rouffaer & IJzerman, see Aernout Lintgensz, "Bali 1597," *BKI* 1 (1856): 203-34.

The king of Bali in 1597: The magnificence of Balinese kingship as seen by the Dutch in the rare first edition of the account of the first Dutch expedition of the East Indies.

scientific standards of the day it presented a summary of the peoples, natural produce and ecology encountered on the journey from the harbor of Amsterdam to the Spice Islands. Its images came to have a central place in Northern European thinking about the Indies.

Bali in that book was a counter to the hostile world of Islam, for throughout their voyage de Houtman and his men had encountered Islamic kingdoms. Against the Muslim kings, the Moors and Turks, de Houtman's book announced the discovery of a friendly "Heathen" kingdom, by which he meant a Hindu kingdom, Hinduism being something Europe had been familiar with since the days of Alexander the Great. In the first edition of the book there were just a few illustrations, and only two were of kings—a Muslim king from Sumatra, and Bali's "Heathen" or Hindu king.[3]

Bali's description bespoke wealth and luxury. The Dutch, who

---

3. In later editions more images compounded the scheme of things, more meanings were added. For an analysis attuned to the German and English elaborations of de Houtman's representations of Bali, see Boon, *Anthropological Romance,* pp. 10-19. On European religious conflicts and Bali, see James A. Boon, *Other Tribes, Other Scribes,* Cambridge: Cambridge University Press, 1982, pp. 156-77.

did not have a proper king at the time, and who thus had a unique perspective on the role of kingship in the state, were fascinated with the king of Bali. The accompanying illustration in the first edition of the book showed the king half-naked in a splendid ox-cart, surrounded by his bodyguards, who were armed with gold-tipped spears and blowpipes. The bodyguards represented both a display of subjects and the promise of violence inherent in any interactions between foreign nations. The backdrop was one of rice fields and the other produce of nature's tropical bounty, the abundant wealth that made the picture an invitation to trade in the Indies.[4]

Bali's attractions invited comparison with Holland. The island was irrigated, but most importantly was more densely populated than its neighbors, and was located astride a major trade route (although this last aspect of Bali's attractions is hard to remember now because the Dutch very quickly changed the major trade routes of the region and put Bali on the periphery).[5] The Dutch saw Bali as very promising—the king and his minister were friendly, they were not Moors, and they had much to trade. The island was militarily strong and exotically rich, attributes that were symbolized by the handle of the king's dagger or kris, a bejeweled and sculpted piece of gold weighing two pounds, and carried by a bearer. This beautiful object was the first and foremost of many krisses that became emblems of Bali's wealth and savagery.

Widow burning compounded the fascination of Bali's Hinduism. This practice of *satia* or "sutee" was already known to the Europeans from India, and remained a major motif of Bali into the twentieth century. The first Dutch illustrations of widow sacrifice in India were used to show the Balinese version, but in written accounts some of the local variants in the practice were explained.

One of the first such accounts dwelt on the sacrifice of twenty-two female slaves during the cremation of a queen of Bali. After the ritual offerings were made and the slaves, dressed only in white, positioned, it explained, they were held and prepared for execution.

---

4. See also A. Vickers, "The King of Bali," in W. Eisler (ed.), *Terra Australis: The Furthest Shore,* Sydney: Art Gallery of NSW, 1988, pp. 51-2.

5. On the comparison between Bali and Holland, see Boon, *Anthropological Romance,* pp. 15-16.

A (somewhat fanciful) Dutch view of widow-sacrifice in Bali, from the 1598 edition of the account of the first Dutch voyage to the East Indies.

The kris was an important part of the execution, for, "some of the most courageous demanded the kris themselves, which they received in the right hand, passing it into the left, after respectfully kissing the weapon." The writer paid great attention to the gorier aspects of the ritual, describing how those about to die, "wounded their right arms, sucked the blood which flowed from the wound, and stained their lips with it, making with the point of the finger a bloody mark on their foreheads." The climax came as the women returned the krisses to the executioners, and, "received a first stab between the false ribs and the second, from the shoulder downwards, in a slanting direction towards the heart."[6]

The women's willingness to kill themselves and the mechanics of

---

6. Translated in A. van der Kraan, "Human Sacrifice in Bali: Sources, Notes, and Commentary," *Indonesia* 40 (1985): 89-121, especially pp. 92-5. Although, as van der Kraan rightly points out, these cases were not always the sacrifice of widows, they have become known as "widow sacrifice" in most of the literature, and I have retained this term as a translation of the two Balinese terms *mabela* (self-stabbing as an act of loyalty to the dead), and *masatia* (throwing oneself into the funeral pyre as an act of loyalty). Van der Kraan confuses these two terms. Linda Connor and Mary Ida Bagus have carried out subsequent research on the various accounts and oral history that shows that, more often than not, low-ranking servants and concubines were the ones who died.

sacrifice were not so much abominable as fascinating to the Dutch. At home, in the terrible wars and brutal justice of Europe, they would probably have been witness to events as horrible, but the fact that these women were so willing to die added a special exoticism and excitement to "Heathen" religion.

Through witnessing cremations and widow sacrifices these European observers were convinced of the power of Hinduism. Such a religion, linked with symbols of Balinese military prowess, like the kris, would greatly help the Dutch against their Muslim enemies. Although Bali was exotic, it was considered still civilized, not "brutish" as were some of the islands of the Indies. Therefore Bali was an appropriate ally for Holland.

The Dutch East India Company had great hopes for the island, a promise that was not to be fulfilled. Over the next forty years trading expeditions, missionary groups and embassies touched on the island, but the hopes of political alliances between Protestants and Hindus against the Moors came to nothing.

A Dutch embassy of 1633 seeking allies against the Javanese sultanate of Mataram floundered on the fact that the Balinese did not shape their political enmities solely on the basis of religion.[7] Except for occasional exchanges of letters and gifts, this was the extent of Balinese-Dutch political relations for the next 160 years. Not even letters written on gold could induce the Company to get mixed up in Balinese politics, which were in any case becoming increasingly confusing to outside observers. The largely positive, though savagely exotic, image of Bali that began European relations with Bali was to gradually fade into a more negative image. It would be another 250 years before Bali came back into the positive light of European gaze.

Despotic Decadence

By the middle of the seventeenth century both the Dutch and the Balinese economies were thriving. The Dutch were experiencing their golden age as a major world economic power, and Bali was

---

7. P. A. Leupe, "Het Gezantschap naar Bali onder Gouverneur-Generaal Hendrik Brouwer in 1633," *BKI* 5 (1859): 1-71.

Balinese slave of Batavia, *c.*1700

entering an era in which slavery would become both its chief export earner and the main vehicle by which it would be known to the rest of the world. In Dutch eyes during this period the Hindu civilization known from the end of the sixteenth century was gradually replaced by slave-trading despotism. Bali became known as an island of arbitrary brutality, where the peasants were sold for the profits of kings and merchants, or had to flee the relentless warfare that gripped the region. It was arbitrary too for the way the character of the Balinese predisposed them to swift anger and running amuk.

During this period Europe and Asia became more closely linked through trade. By the early 1600s the Dutch East India Company had succeeded in creating its network of trading forts or "factories" from the southern tip of Africa to Japan, with its Javanese post of Batavia at the center of this trading empire. Amsterdam housed the greatest stock exchange in the world, and the broad middle class of the Netherlands lived prosperously. The Dutch reorganized trade in the Indies to suit themselves, and in doing so drastically lessened Bali's role as a staging post in the trade with the Spice Islands of Maluku. As their monopolistic grip tightened, the Dutch created another opening for Bali—in the expansion of its slave trade.

Bali had sold its own and other Eastern Indonesian slaves since the tenth century, but the creation of Batavia and new trading conditions allowed the slave trade to flourish until the Balinese were selling up to two thousand men, women, and children a year.[8] From Bali slaves went throughout the world following the networks of Dutch trade, but especially to Batavia—where in the seventeenth century Balinese slaves numbered between 8000 and 10,000 out of a total slave population of 15,000 to 18,000.[9]

In this age of trade empires the concept of colonialism proper

---

8. On the size and impact of the slave trade, see Henk Schulte Nordholt, Macht, Mensen en Middelen: Patronen van Dynamic in de Baiische Politiek ± 1700-1940 (unpub. MA thesis), Amsterdam: Vrije Universiteit, 1980; A. van der Kraan, "Bali: Slavery and Slave Trade," in A. Reid (ed.), *Slavery, Bondage and Dependency in Southeast Asia,* St Lucia: University of Queensland Press, 1983, pp. 315-40; and for the first records of slavery and Bali, see Jan Wisseman Christie, "Negara, Mandala, and Despotic State: Images of Early Java," in D. G. Marr and A. C. Milner (eds.), *Southeast Asia in the 9th to 14th Centuries,* pp. 65-73, Singapore: Institute of Southeast Asian Studies/ Research School of Pacific Studies, Australian National University, 1986, p. 71. Boon's omission of slavery is a major weakness in his *Anthropological Romance.*

9. On the Balinese in Batavia, see C. Lekkerkerker, "De Baliers van Batavia," *Indische Gids* 40 (1918): 409-31, and van der Kraan, "Bali: Slavery and Slave Trade."

did not yet exist. European servants of the Company in Batavia had few prejudices against accommodating themselves to local norms. Batavia was very much a Mestizo or hybrid society; traders, sailors, soldiers and clerks from the various European countries married women of the Indies and allowed their households to take on a mixed style, combining European and Asian elements.[10]

Bali's women were most highly prized. They were sought as wives by the section of the Chinese community most important to the Company, the entrepreneurs who connected Java with the lucrative trade to China. The reason for the women's desirability was obvious, and had little to do with the rosy image of Balinese sexuality that grew up later.[11] The Chinese liked eating pork, and Muslim wives who abhorred the flesh of the pig would neither cook for them nor eat with them. Balinese Hindus with a cultivated taste for pork would. The idea that Balinese made good wives for more erotic reasons came as an embellishment on their culinary skills. Balinese women were also sometimes taken as mistresses by Dutch men and the Balinese second person pronoun for a woman of low status, *nyai,* became the word used in Indies society for a native mistress of a Dutchman.

A Slave Trader and a Potentate

Jan Troet, one of the more prominent slave traders in the archipelago, was particularly influential in contributing to the image of Bali as a place of brutality. His legacy was his letters of complaint and reports to the Company, rather than any comprehensive account of Bali or Balinese slaves, but it was for the way he died on Bali for which he was immortalized. Troet was born in Ambon in the Spice Islands and, like the other free citizens or *burgers,* he had a special status in the Dutch trading empire that set him above other natives in the eyes of both the Dutch and himself. This, and his origins in the first and favored outpost of the Dutch meant that he felt free to

---

10. See Jean Gelman Taylor, *The Social World of Batavia: European and Eurasian in Dutch Asia,* Madison: University of Wisconsin Press, 1983; on Batavia as a Chinese city, see L. Blussé, *Strange Company: Chinese Settlers, Mestizo Women and the Dutch in VOC Batavia,* Dordrecht: Foris, 1986.

11. See Lekkerkerker, "De Baliers van Batavia," p. 415.

travel throughout the archipelago and to treat it as his proper area of trade. Again, like the other entrepreneurs of his day he had his finger in many pies, trading not only slaves but in the important textiles and porcelain that kept the economy of Asia going at that time. It was important for him both to know local conditions and to try to establish good relations with local rulers.

In 1661 Troet sent a protest to the Company about male Balinese slaves. A whole boatload had "run amuk" and taken his ship, leaving him (and his cargo) stranded on Sumatra.[12] This was one of the first of many complaints about the tendency of Balinese slaves to run amuk, a threat to trade from the Dutch point of view, but hardly unreasonable from the Balinese point of view, for these people were, after all, being sold as goods against their will.

The Company eventually received so many of these reports that in 1665 it put a ban on its employees owning Balinese slaves, and in 1688 banned the import of Balinese slaves altogether in favor of others who were less likely to show resistance.[13] This did not completely eliminate Bali's slave trade. But as Europeans built up an image of the whole Malay "race" as liable to run amuk for no apparent reason, they kept in mind these stories of the arbitrary nature of the Balinese.

Originally the term *amuk* referred to the indigenous form of warfare where leading warriors on each side would dress in white and go berserk at the head of their troops in a series of hand-to-hand skirmishes at the beginning of battle. This aristocratic show of strength and bravery was designed to intimidate the enemy and perhaps end a battle without the need to engage the main bodies of troops. Over time the proper meaning was lost, and "amuk" in English has come to mean a kind of crazed bloodlust.

The Balinese were still militarily formidable at this time, and in 1664 a Dutch sailor, Hoornbeek, and a trader, Andries Hardy, were at the receiving end of Balinese blowpipes. The Company did not let this incident affect them too much; the losses were mitigated by the fact that King Pañji Sakti, the newly emergent king of northern

---

12. See A. Kumar, *Surapati: Man and Legend,* Leiden: Brill, 1976, p. 366.
13. ibid., p. 19. See also Lekkerkerker, "De Baliers van Batavia."

Bali, was very apologetic and willing to keep up good trading relations with them. The deaths, however, were another contribution to the image of the Balinese as fierce and warlike.

At this time the dangerous side of Bali was still seen as secondary to Bali's role in trade. Despite his complaint about Balinese slaves Jan Troet certainly did not let the incident stop him trading with Bali. Along with a number of Dutch traders Troet was on intimate terms with King Pañji Sakti, forming an ongoing and mutually beneficial relationship.

Troet called the king "elder brother" and "he never came to Bali but he was feted by the king at home."[14] In return, besides trading in slaves, he kept the king well supplied with arms. Pañji Sakti had two Dutch harbor masters in his service in the late 1660s, Mossel and Michiel, and was vitally interested in western technology.[15] As a kind of *parvenu* king he was dependent on the slave trade and access to western military technology for his power.[16] The king even paid restitution when two of Troet's ships were wrecked and their contents claimed as a gift from the sea by the inhabitants of northern Bali, a tradition which was to get the Balinese in trouble in the nineteenth century.

It was singularly unusual for a king to acknowledge such cases, as shipwrecks were usually considered to be the workings of the magical forces of the sea, bad luck for the owner of the ship and its cargo. In 1672 or 1673 the relationship between this dynamic king and his slave-trading, gun-running associate dramatically changed. François Valentijn, prelate and major writer about the Indies in the early eighteenth century, heard from Troet's widow herself how the king's lords poisoned their relationship with "knavish counsel." Troet, accused of wanting to make "an assault" on the king's state and life, was cruelly murdered on his last return to the island.[17]

Valentijn placed great credence in the story: after all, the woman

---

14. Francois Valentijn, *Oud en Nieuw Oost Indien,* vol. III, pt 2, Dordrecht: J. van Braam, 1726, pp. 252-9. On Valentijn (1666-1721) see Rob Nieuwenhuys, *Oost-Indische Spiegel,* Amsterdam: Querido, 1978, pp. 48-53; and Jörg Fisch, *Hollands Ruhm in Asien,* Stuttgart: Steiner, 1986.

15. H. J. de Graaf, "Goesti Pandji Sakti, Vorst van Boeleleng," *TBG* 83,1 (1949):59-82.

16. See Schulte Nordholt, Macht, Mensen en Middelen, pp. 49-54.

17. Valentijn, *Oud en Nieuw Oost Indien.*

Bali *c.* 1720 as seen by Dutch cartographers. This map is from Valentijn's study of the Indies, and is a copy of earlier maps. The mapmaker has included the villages mentioned in Valentijn's text but placed them almost at random.

who told it had been his landlady in Ambon. He added other complementary information from the most reliable of sources, Henrik Leydekker, the greatest Bible translator of his day. Leydekker told how Pañji Sakti, who gave him a silver-inlaid and bejeweled kris (which was later given to Valentijn), was not only a great womanizer, but also a "great sodomite" who surrounded himself with transvestites.[18]

Troet's tale was immortalized in Valentijn's great encyclopedia of the Company's trading empire at its height. It found a place next to an impressive map and lengthy descriptions of the major locations and cultural features of Bali, including Balinese music. Valentijn was particularly interested in trade, and gave prices for the Balinese slaves of the day: 70 to 80 Spanish "pieces of eight" (the international currency of the day, one of which was worth

18. ibid.

approximately £1 in the nineteenth century), for an unskilled man, 100 to 150 for a skilled one, and 70 to 80 coins for a woman, going up to 130 if she was particularly beautiful or skilled at weaving. In summarizing all the previous information on the island, including Troet's story, Valentijn ensured that images of Bali were part of the mainstream of western images of the Indies. In this version of the image of Bali, not only were the people liable to run amuk, but the aristocracy consisted of decadent and licentious potentates, totally untrustworthy and arbitrary, but wealthy. From this time onwards, after slavery, Balinese royal despotism was to be a key feature in Dutch thinking about the island.

Slave to King

The image of Bali as a place of great ferociousness owes much to the reputation of one man, a slave named Surapati. Combining charisma and fighting skills into an extraordinary story of social mobility, Surapati moved from slave to mercenary to king. His origins are somewhat mysterious, but most of the sources say he was born on Bali. Surapati's story reveals the tensions that underlay the nature of slavery in the Indies. He was sold as a young man, and suffered servitude and maltreatment from the Dutch. However he maintained his independent spirit, and according to the stories associated with him devoted himself to mystical exercises, which served to bolster his reputation as a leader.

Surapati was unbending and recalcitrant when he served in his youth as a slave to one of the Company's high traders in Batavia.[19] In keeping with the reputation of the Balinese to run amuk rather than surrender to slavery, he escaped and was pursued by the Dutch. The Company, however, recognized that his free spirit and military brilliance could be put to their use, and hired him and his followers to serve in their irregular forces. This did not satisfy Surapati, and in central Java he became part of the palace guard of the Sultan. In a complicated plot he murdered the Company's envoy to the court and fled to Pasuruhan, in east Java, where he made himself king and

---

19. For what may be a portrait of Surapati with his master and mistress, see Blusse, *Strange Company,* p. 180.

with his sons was known as the scourge of the Company from the end of the seventeenth century.[20]

In October 1706 the Company sent an expedition to Surapati's kingdom of Pasuruhan to ease their frustrations at his hindrance of their control over Java. Surapati's kingdom survived the attack, but the king himself was wounded, and, as a result, died the next month.[21]

The Company became less and less interested in Bali as the eighteenth century progressed. By 1755 Java was well and truly under Dutch control: Mataram, the premier kingdom, had been pacified, reduced and finally divided into smaller principalities. For around a century the Balinese kingdoms were simply a nuisance, interfering in Javanese politics and creating confusion on Java and Madura in alliance with other enemies of the Company.

In the Balinese-controlled part of eastern Java known as the Eastern Salient, renegades from South Sulawesi, Javanese refugees from the Company's control, Chinese, and even English traders roamed freely. This easy movement and massing of military and economic resources was always a threat to the Company's economic and political interests. Finally in the 1760s the Company "cleaned up" what it regarded as smugglers, bandits and pirates, which meant a virtual depopulation of this whole region.[22] After this Bali ceased to have a role in Javanese politics, and hence in the Company's thoughts.

For the rest of the eighteenth century it was mainly known as one of the principal indigenous producers of rifles, a tribute to the craftsmanship that would later earn Bali more gentle fame.[23] The reputation of this rifle-making confirmed the idea of warlike Bali already present in the European interest in Balinese krisses and blowpipes.

Slavery and warfare created the western image of Bali in the eighteenth century. Vestiges of the earlier image of Hindu Bali remained, but as the Dutch came to see religion as less important than

---

20. See Kumar, *Surapati.*

21. ibid., pp. 35-7.

22. See A. Kumar, "Javanese Historiography in and of the 'Colonial Period': A Case Study," in A. Reid & D. Marr (eds), *Perceptions of the Past in Southeast Asia,* Singapore:Heinemann/ Asian Studies Association of Australia, 1979, pp. 187-206.

23. See A. Reid, *Europe and Southeast Asia: The Military Balance,*Townsville: James Cook University, Center for Southeast Asian Studies Occasional Paper no. 16, 1982, p. 4.

trade they began to look upon Bali with less respect. The ideas of military strength, of widow sacrifice, and of luxury were maintained as elements of Bali's despotic decadence.

New Age, Old Images

At the end of the eighteenth century it was not Bali that was in trouble but the Company itself. Corruption, declining markets and fundamental changes in the world economy saw the rise of the British and the emergence of Calcutta as Asia's major trade center. The Company went bankrupt, and the Dutch Government had to take over the running of the Indies.

This did not last long. The Netherlands fell to Napoleon and in 1808 a representative of the new Napoleonic regime, Governor-General Herman Willem Daendels (1762-1818), the energetic and single-minded "Iron Marshal," arrived in the Indies. Daendels was the harbinger of new European attitudes, stemming from a radical shift in thinking that introduced conceptions of rationalization and progress into the world. In the pursuit of rational government he was ruthless, dealing with Indonesians and Europeans alike in accordance with his nickname.

Gone were the days of Company employees making themselves rich by siphoning off the profits of their employers. Daendels pursued with vigor the task of turning the network of Dutch trading posts into a proper colony. The motley crew of sailors, traders, adventurers and pastors who were the employees of the Company had to be replaced by civil servants.

Daendels had only three years to carry out his plan. In this time he made the old roads of Java into a major highway, thus improving communications and control immensely; he reformed the nature of Dutch Indies government, setting the foundations for a civil service, and attempted to end the fine Company traditions of corruption and embezzlement. Daendels also corresponded with the many kings and sultans of the Indies in order to make European power the center of politics in the archipelago. He sent a representative to Bali for that purpose, but this man found it more profitable to hire himself out as a mercenary to the kings of south Bali.

In 1811 the most successful of the imperialist nations, the English, took control, on behalf of the Dutch Government in exile in London. During their five-year reign the English, through their dynamic overseer of the colony, not only entrenched the new age of imperialism, they also introduced new elements into European thinking about Bali. They did this while maintaining the images of the fierceness of the Balinese and the despotic nature of their rulers. The new elements in British images of Bali included the idea of the village as the basis of Balinese culture, and an awareness of the civilization of Bali inherited from ancient Java.

The British appointed a lieutenant-governor to run the Indies, a promising young man of thirty, who was later to found the trading city of Singapore: Sir Thomas Stamford Raffles (1781-1826). Raffles was an even more energetic rationalizer than Daendels, if that was possible, and this appointment was his big break. He had leapt up the English East India Company structure, and served his time in the new English outpost of Penang, in what is now Malaysia, where he attracted his Calcutta-based superiors' attention. Although later writers tend to idolize him as an example of imperialism, he took much from the Dutch, but made their work his own.

Raffles's trade experience combined with a passion for the theories of the most exciting source of ideas in England at the time, the academic group known as the Political Economists, whose chief proponent was Adam Smith. These writers were to establish the idea of a proper and free running economy as the basis of a prosperous society. The ideas of the Political Economists with their advocacy of free exchange of goods, based on the enlightened capacity of all people to achieve according to their labors, lay behind the new rationalism of colony building. They introduced the concept of "progress" into the vocabulary of Europe, and defined that progress in terms of the scientific knowledge of the world by which all irrational elements, especially those elements which interfered with the free process of trade, would be overcome. Once such hindrances were overcome, society would be improved and the greater good of the population achieved.[24]

---

24. For a discussion of Raffles and his associates and their debt to Political Economy, see H. M. J. Maier, Fragments of Reading: The Malay Hikayat Merong Mahawangsa (diss.), Leiden University, 1985, Alblasserdam: Kanters. On Raffles and Bali, see Boon, *Anthropological Romance,* pp. 20-4.

Raffles did not come to the Indies with the later colonial view that the people were lazy natives, even thought this was an idea the English were to take up in Malaya. He came as a son of the Enlightenment, seeing the natives as potentially enterprising. For him the old political structures of the Indies were a feudal encumbrance on the free exchange of commodities.

As with all colonial ideologies the practice was not as simple as the theory, especially for the peasantry whose labor was so prized by Raffles. He instituted a new form of "land rent" or taxation to replace traditional tributes to rulers, which meant that peasants ended up paying the equivalent of up to 50% of their crops to the English. His "free trade" made British companies central to commerce of the archipelago, and so made the economy of the Dutch East Indies dependent on the British Empire. Ten years after he left the whole colony was in hock to two British firms in Calcutta.

Raffles's disdain for the despotic "feudal" kings of the Indies was partly derived from earlier European images of Oriental despotism based on experiences in India and the Middle East. Raffles brought key ideas from India to the Indies, the most enduring of which was the concept that the basis of society was the autonomous village. The "feudal" aristocracy was seen as extrinsic to that reality of Asian society.[25]

To Raffles, the Balinese were noble savages, with "a higher cast of spirit, independence, and manliness than belongs to any of their neighbors." He even apologized for them, saying that, "to a stranger their manners appear abrupt, unceremonious, coarse and repulsive; but upon further acquaintance this becomes less perceptible, and their undisguised frankness commands reciprocal confidence and respect." What pleased Raffles most, as a Political Economist, was

---

25. On Raffles's emphasis on the village as the basis of social organization, see A. D. A. de Kat Angelino, *Staatkundig Belied en Bestuurszorg in Nederlandsch Indie,* 2 vols, The Hague: Nijhoff, 1929-30: vol. II, pp. 28-34. For general comments on the Political Economists and their relation to Karl Marx, see M. Foucault, *The Order of Things,* London: Tavistock, pp. 221-6, 253-63. On the way the Political Economists influenced Marx's view of India, see Edward Said, *Orientalism,* London: Routledge & Kegan Paul, 1978, pp. 153-6, and S. N. Mukherjee, The Idea of Feudalism: From the Philosophes to Karl Marx', in E. Leach *et al.* (eds), *Feudalism: Comparative Studies,* Sydney: Sydney Studies in Society and Culture 2, pp. 25-39.

that they were "free from that listlessness and indolence which are observable in the inhabitants of Java." In Bali "the individual retains all the native manliness of his character and all the fire of the savage state."[26]

Raffles looked at the Balinese with eyes of enthusiastic optimism, and saw that even their rulers were not as despotic as the Javanese. He saw in the Balinese a people suited to the new age: "Neither degraded by despotism nor enervated by habits of indolence or luxury, they perhaps promise fairer for a progress in civilization and good government than any of their neighbours."[27]

In Raffles's view of the world the character of the Balinese people predisposed them to enterprise and achievement and was distinct from their despotic government. Such was the vision of the Political Economists that they could look into the eyes of a people and discern their capacity for economic advancement. Advancement was related to civilization or the capacity to achieve civilization, which was in turn related to the "character" of what the Europeans defined as "races."

Raffles associated the civilization of Bali with the ancient civilization of Java. In doing this he implied that the present-day Javanese were degraded or corrupt compared to the promise of that ancient civilization. He based these views on an active interest in the impressive remains of the Hindu temples he examined in central and east Java, and on examples of Old Javanese literature obtained from Bali. He praised this Hinduism above Islam, which, like most other Europeans of his day, he regarded as a threatening and barbaric religion. Bali's Hinduism was important because, "on Java we find Hinduism only among the antiquities of the island. Here it is a living source of action and a universal rule of conduct. The present state of Bali may be considered, therefore, as a kind of commentary on the ancient condition of the natives of Java."[28] Ironically Raffles combined an

26. Sir Thomas Stamford Raffles, *The History of Java,* Kuala Lumpur: Oxford University Press (repr.), 1965 [1817], vol. II, app. K (ccxxxi). On a British expedition against north Bali in 1814 see P. L. van Bloemen Waanders, "Bijdragen tot de Kennis van het Eiland Bali," *TNI* 2 (1868):370-410, especially p. 389.

27. ibid., p. ccxxxii.

28. ibid., p. ccxxxv.

appreciation for the museum-like qualities of Bali with an interest in its capacity for development, a contradictory stance that would be inherited by many later students of Bali.

Raffles's antiquarian interest in Hindu religion and literature as they were preserved on Bali was shared with other orientalists, who were often more interested in the noble past of the East than in what they considered to be its degenerate present.[29] Even though he repeated the barbaric image of widow-burning that fascinated the first European commentators on Bali, he rejected it as the intrinsic image of Bali, in favor of an appreciation of rough manliness and the continuation of achievements now lost to Java.

Raffles's comments show how he fitted his particular ideas of Bali into the framework of economic activity and ideas of race. "Race" as a notion only developed in Europe in the eighteenth century, as part of the dark side of the Enlightenment. For people like Raffles the relationship between economic conditions (which included what we would now call ecology) and race formed the existence of a people.

Raffles Revised

Raffles's image of Bali was to be important to late nineteenth-century commentators, but not because of the high value he placed on the Balinese character. It was the image of Bali as the museum of Javanese culture, which was to be remembered when the Dutch turned a more positive gaze on Bali some seventy years later.

As soon as Raffles left the Indies in 1816 the "noble" part of his "noble savage" image of Bali was rejected. One of the first Dutch envoys to visit the island when the Dutch re-established themselves in 1818, the self-important H. A. van den Broek, also dwelt at length on the Balinese character, which he depicted by detailed descriptions of individual Balinese. He, however, returned to the old "wild" image of the Balinese, mainly because the kings had ignored all his overtures of political relations and given him the run around. To make matters worse, this superior Dutch civil servant complained, he was even jostled and abused when he visited one capital, without

---

29. See Said, *Orientalism.*

any reprimand to the malefactors.[30] The Balinese also persisted in trading with whomever they liked, which the Dutch saw as smuggling, accusing the Balinese of allowing "pirates" from all over the archipelago to use their harbors as bases.

To the missionaries, Bali was seen as one of many sites where the natives could be converted, but the Balinese continued to frustrate the zealous Christians by refusing to give up Hinduism. One nineteenth-century English missionary furthered the bad name of Bali by describing it not simply as heathen, but anti-European as well: "A captain of a vessel who has made fifteen voyages to Bali, told me he has had the crease [kris] frequently drawn on him." According to this source, the attacks came not through the fault of the traders, who were "remonstrating against their deceitful method of weighing goods." What this meant was probably that Balinese, like many others in Southeast Asia, had their own method of trade, which did not accord with the English desires for "free trade." The missionary capped this off with comments that reveal his intentions quite clearly: "I have also experienced impertinent rebuffs, and insulting taunts from them which I never met with from the natives in a European colony..."[31] The inference is that Bali should be colonized, to give the natives manners, and make them more compliant to the wishes of European traders and missionaries. The Balinese committed the crime of not giving Europeans the respect they thought they deserved.

Free commerce and the relationship between trade, religion and the character of races were the issues that had concerned Raffles, and continued to concern writers from the first part of the nineteenth century. Raffles's views did not suit the prevailing Dutch tendency to monopolies trade and oppose recalcitrant native rulers, even though Raffles and the Dutch shared the same ends: European control of the Indies. In the decades after Raffles English writers came around to accepting the negative views of Bali from the Dutch, especially

---

30. [H.A.] van den B[roek], "Verslag Nopens het Eiland Bali," *De Oosterling* 1(1835): 158-236. See also P. H. van den Kemp, "Het Verblijf van Commissaris van den Broek op Bali," *BKI* 50 (1899): 331-91. See Boon, *Anthropological Romance,* pp. 24-30.

31. "A Short Account of the Island of Bali," in J. H. Moor (ed.), *Notices of the Indian Archipelago,* London: Frank Cass, 1968 repr., p. 91.

since Bali did not play the game and welcome increasing European involvement in Southeast Asia.

The Balinese, in fact, even refused to stop their slave trade at a time when the English had convinced the other western powers that slavery should end. This confirmed Dutch and European opinion—that the Balinese, like most non-westerners, were barbarous. By the late 1820s England no longer needed the slave trade to make its mark as a world power; it had the industrialization of its homeland and the trade in more respectable goods such as opium instead. Of course, the arguments were never put in those terms; anti-slavery was considered a humanitarian issue. Initially the Dutch did not bother with the English horror of slavery, and in the late 1820s tried to recruit soldiers for war in Java by buying slaves. At that time there was still a strong trade of Balinese slaves with the French colony of Bourbon (Réunion), and some Balinese slaves found their way to other French and Dutch colonies. Bali came to replace Batavia as the major slave entrepot of the Indies.[32] The Dutch gradually came to accept that slavery was a pernicious breach of the basic liberty that the Enlightenment had shown to be the right of all men. By the 1830s the Dutch had ceased all trade in slaves, although the slave trade in Bali went on until the 1860s.[33]

Reports such as that of a Dutch agent, the trader of Arab descent, Pangeran Saïd Hassan, no doubt played their part in changing Dutch thinking. Saïd Hassan found on Bali ninety pirate vessels from the southern Philippines, and a thriving slave trade, which he described through heart-rending anecdotes, such as the example of the Raja of Bulèlèng, who sold a brother and sister of six and nine years of age to a French captain. The captain refused to buy the mother as well, "on account of her age" (she was about forty), so he "ordered the children to be led away. But the children did not want to be separated from their mother and held her around the neck. The mother, too, did not

---

32. Rodney Needham, *Sumba and the Slave Trade,* Clayton: Monash University, Center of Southeast Asian Studies Working Papers, 1983, p. 40. Note that Needham follows other sources in attributing the 1814 English expedition to north Bali to an attempt to end slavery. While this may have been part of the motivation, Balinese incursions into English territory in East Java, combined with a suspicion that the Balinese rulers were plotting with other rajas and sultans (especially from south Sulawesi) played a larger part in Raffles's thinking.

33. ibid., pp. 23-7.

want to let go of her children and they embraced each other, crying loudly." The European sailors separated them by force, taking the children to their boat. At this point, "the mother fell down onto the beach and lay as if dead for over an hour. When night came she cried and screamed for her children... She remained in this condition for several days. Saïd Hassan added the final comment that "the hearts of those who had brought her into this state were harder than iron."[34]

Such reports shifted the blame for complicity in human suffering to other colonials and to the Balinese themselves. This made it suddenly imperative for the Dutch to get rid of slavery and the other related forms of economic activity that they could not control: "smuggling" (trade between the other islands and Java which did not go through Dutch ports) and "piracy."

In the 1820s and 1830s Bali's trade increased remarkably, particularly with the British colony of Singapore, something which made the Dutch envious and nervous. While Bali remained independent under its many kings, the Dutch had no say in where its growing trade went, and there was always the possibility that the British might be able to make a claim for an independent Bali. The Dutch at first tried to set up trading posts in Kuta, on the southwest coast, one of which was run by a Frenchman called Dubois, who spent most of his time trying to work out what was going on, and trying to avoid the physical attacks of his local competitors.

The Dutch invented international law, and they made good use of it. Free trade was well and good in Dutch eyes, but it was better to be able to keep controls on unruly native princes by binding them to legal agreements. In the 1840s the Dutch made a concerted effort to get all the Balinese kings to sign treaties with the Netherlands government. These treaties were chiefly about the regulation of trade and the safeguarding of Dutch monopolies, but the Dutch couched this in terms of statements about sovereignty.

The signing of the treaties presented some problems for the Dutch government. Bali had eight kings at the time, and the Dutch would have preferred only one king to have signed on behalf of the others, a precedent that went back to the time of their treaty-making

---

34. Unpublished report of Saïd Hassan, 1824, quoted and translated in van der Kraan, "Bali."

in Java with the kingdom of Mataram. Fortunately the kingdoms of Bali were organized into a hierarchy, with the eastern kingdom of Klungkung having the highest status. Despite a lengthy debate amongst the experts in Batavia about what the high status of Klungkung really meant, the government decided that for the purposes of treaty making Klungkung's position was one of "High King and High Priest," with sovereignty over the other kingdoms. Just as the rulers of the former kingdom of Mataram in Java signed over virtually the whole large island over a period of a century and a half, so Klungkung could sign Bali over to the Dutch.[35]

The ruler of Klungkung and the other Balinese kings who signed the treaty did not see themselves as signing away their sovereignty. They denied later that they had ever signed the contracts that the Dutch insisted were binding. For Dutch writers these denials were attempts to avoid responsibility, but in fact the treaties look suspicious on closer examination, and it appears that the Netherlands's agent, Huskus Koopman, desperate to get results, bribed the kings' Malay scribes to make the wording of versions of the contracts in Dutch different from those in Malay in the crucial passages that speak of Bali being owned by the Netherlands East Indies Government.[36]

The Dutch thought they were hard done by. Their agents had little to show for their efforts, and the Balinese kept making impositions on them, such as a request for a rhinoceros. The high king of the state of Klungkung needed a live rhinoceros for one of his rituals, so he sent the Dutch a black horse, such as was ridden by kings, and thought this a fair exchange. It took the Dutch months to get one, and even longer to ship it from Surabaya to their agent at Kuta and thence to Klungkung, mainly because the locals of Kuta refused

---

35. See M. C. Ricklefs, *A History of Modern Indonesia,* Macmillan: London, first edition 1980, pp. 66-100.

36. I owe this insight to Henk Schulte Nordholt (pers. comm.); see his dissertation, *Een Balische Dynastie: Hierarchie en Conflict in de Negara Mengwi 1700-1940,* Vrije Universiteit te Amsterdam, Haarlem: Multi-Print Noord, 1988, p. 154, and it is heavily hinted at (though not in such direct terms) by C. Lekkerkerker, in his "Het Voorspel der Vestiging van de Nederlandsche Macht op Bali en Lombok," *BKI* 70 (1923): 198-322, especially p. 321, where he notes how the rajas said later they had never signed such a clause. In unpublished historical materials collected by V. E. Korn there is a comment made on the suspect nature of the contracts, which all had one form, one date in Arabic, and were not properly ratified (Korn Collection of the KITLV, no. 267).

to have anything to do with a gift for a king who was not their own. The cost of all this was worked out with characteristic thoroughness as f.869.25, and a considerable amount of frustration.[37] All of this helped confirm the Dutch view that Balinese rulers were arbitrary, opium-smoking despots, more trouble than they were worth.

A Place of Prosperity and a Cultural Center

What was even more galling to the Dutch was that the most success-ful European merchant in Bali was a Danish private trader, Bali's own romantic "Lord Jim," Mads Lange (1806-56). After settling in south Bali in 1839, he became one of the most successful capitalists to operate in the region. With his hunger for adventure and wealth, but a sensitivity to local conditions, Lange was the perfect man for mid-nineteenth-century Bali. Like Raffles he thought that the econ-omy determined everything, but in Lange's case this converted into a naïveté about politics, something that Raffles never had. Round-faced, not particularly handsome for a romantic hero, and perhaps nothing like the intellectual giant Raffles was, Lange was one of the private or what was then called "country traders" in an age when the Indies was a kind of "last frontier" for expansionism.

Lange was pragmatic, but made enough money out of Bali to live well and to take an interest in the cultural and social life of south Bali. From his almost fortress-like base at Kuta he worked in style, setting himself up with such important modern fixtures as a snooker table. There he played host to visiting Europeans and Ba-linese aristocrats alike, and ventured out in the style of a Balinese official to walk his pet Dalmatians. Through his flair for making money he became enmeshed in major events that he did not com-pletely understand, and was a key player in the first Dutch attempts to conquer Bali. Lange had earlier worked for Jardine Matheson in the South China Seas, and then he went to the rice-rich island of Lombok, where he did well until he and an English competitor, George King, were forced to take sides in local politics. In 1838 the political situation was resolved in favor of King's patron, and Lange was forced to flee to Bali.

---

37. See Lekkerkerker, "Het Voorspel," p. 249-52.

Lange's knowledge of how to work in the Indies combined with good luck and good timing. He linked up with the Chinese who were the major agents of trade in south Bali, even marrying the daughter of one of the most successful of them. The Dane then formed an alliance with the lord of Kesiman, who was emerging as the strongest power in the kingdom of Badung's contorted royal family. Lange tied his fortunes to Kesiman, and Kesiman recognized the advantages at that time of having a European trader who could do business with Singapore, Hong Kong and the other centers. He made Lange his "servant," although later, for services rendered, elevated him to the status of a minister in his court.

Lange's main advantage was his good timing in arriving in Bali just when it was taking off as a supplier of primary produce to Java. Using links with the trade of China he became a major supplier of the Chinese copper coins that were the major currency in Balinese internal trade. He understood that it was important to connect the overseas trade links with the Balinese market economy, and so he traded with the women from important families who were the backbone of internal trade in Bali.[38]

First Conquest

While Lange was making his fortune, the Netherlands East Indies Government was making plans. They were not interested in the information about Balinese culture filtering in from the scholars working from Lange's base. They wanted to exercise direct control over these fierce Balinese who showed such disrespect to colonial law and economic interests.

The issue of shipwrecks was the pretext the Dutch were waiting for. According to tradition, when one occurred the local people had a right to claim the wreckage, including the cargo, as bounty from Baruna, the god of the sea. The Dutch treaties repudiated this right. Concern that the Balinese were continually infringing the treaties mingled with anxieties about the British making some claim to Bali.

---

38. On Lange in Bali, see Aage K. Nielsen, *Leven en Avonturen van een Oostinjevaarder opBali*, Amsterdam: Querido, 1928; Henk Schulte Nordholt, "The Mads Lange Connection: A Danish Trader on Bali in the Middle of the Nineteenth Century," *Indonesia* 32 (1981): 17-47.

The Dutch looked on Lange as their agent, a role he was probably not entirely sure of, since his fortunes were dependent on his Balinese patron.

In 1846 the government of the Netherlands East Indies brought matters to a head over the shipwreck rights issue by launching what they called an "expedition" against the king of Bulèlèng, the north Balinese state. The Dutch were confident that right and might were on their side, since they saw the Balinese as clearly in violation of international laws.

The result was a humiliation for the Dutch, and a boost to Bali's warlike image. The chief minister of Bulèlèng, north Bali, Gusti Ktut Jlantik, organized fierce resistance to the Dutch. If there was a real romantic hero of that era, then it was Jlantik, the brave, headstrong warrior whose abilities to take the initiative and marshal diverse forces together served his king well when Bulèlèng was expanding to take over areas to the south. The same aggressive qualities were, however, ultimately to destroy Jlantik, his king, and the king's cousin, the ruler of Karangasem.

The Dutch attempted to come to terms with Jlantik through studying his nature. He was described by his enemies as having in appearance "a fine bearing and a well formed oval face, with a regular, not broad, nose." As for his character, "his countenance, although for a moment hinting at subjection, conveyed a strong will and strength of spirit," something which shone through in his actions: "his gaze was cadgey and his gestures lively."[39]

Jlantik said he would only negotiate with his kris, and so the Dutch initiated their first attack on Bali. They began by bombing the royal palace of Bulèlèng, which probably fuelled the resistance of Jlantik and inspired the king's subjects to strengthen their stance against the Dutch. Gusti Jlantik started from the basis of traditional Balinese warfare in building up his battlefield strategy. In any battle the first to come were the shock troops who would run amuk at the head of the most heavily armed troops, those with rifles. Once these shock troops had exhausted their manic charge, the spear-carrying

39. W. P. Wietzel, *De Derde Militaire Expeditie naar het Eiland Bali in 1849,* Gorinchem: Noorduyn, 1859, p. 68.

troops would come out at the head of the mass of troops, arranged in formations that went back to ancient Javanese military traditions. If the opposition were not destroyed by the initial attack, both sides would have to fight it out in bloody hand-to-hand combat. Jlantik backed up his shock troops by establishing impregnable fortifications in the foothills of north Bali, making his army irresistible.

Gusti Jlantik's tactics, which evoked begrudging admiration from the Dutch, sent the Dutch home in defeat, comforted only by a treaty that Lange helped them negotiate. The raja of Bulèlèng and his allies subsequently totally ignored this treaty, leading to a repeat of the events in 1848, when the Dutch were again defeated. In 1849 the full weight of Dutch might was brought to bear on Bali to compensate for their earlier humiliations.

For the third time, Gusti Jlantik and his forces took a stand at Jagaraga, east of the capital of north Bali. At the same time as the Dutch attacked, the neighboring king of Bangli also saw an opportunity to expand his kingdom northwards, and launched a second front against Bulèlèng. This time Jlantik even had twenty native deserters from the Dutch side,[40] but the Dutch managed to find a weak point and break through, forcing the Balinese defenders to flee to the eastern kingdom of Karangasem. The decisive factor in the battle was the desire of another opponent, the Balinese king of Lombok, to make Karangasem part of his empire and usurp the title of Klungkung as supreme kingdom of Bali. The major Balinese opponents of the Dutch, Gusti Jlantik and his king of Bulèlèng, as well as the king of Karangasem, were all killed by Lombok forces, when they took a last stand in a temple and bravely marched to their deaths.

That was not the end of the war, however. Klungkung, the kingdom with the highest status in Bali, stood firm. As an ally of Karangasem, Klungkung was violently opposed to Lombok's pretensions to taking over the whole island of Bali. The female regent of Klungkung saw that she would have to take a stand in 1849, not principally to keep out the Dutch, but to keep Lombok at bay. The Lombok forces did not have a strong enough base in east Bali to launch a major assault, so they had to be content with control over

40. ibid., p. 39.

Karangasem. When the Dutch attempted to open a new front on the coast of Klungkung, the general in charge of the expedition was killed in a night raid ordered by the steadfast Virgin Queen, Déwa Agung Isteri Kanya, another major blow to Dutch morale, and a blow more keenly felt because this general had been the hero of an earlier Dutch conquest in Sumatra.

At this point the other kings of Bali, including Kesiman, gathered in Klungkung, producing a Balinese fighting force of 33,000 men. The Dutch, failing to understand that delicate political struggles were going on to divest the ruler of Klungkung of her power, blundered into the situation by asserting their military might, only to be met by a Balinese show of solidarity that might have resulted in another disaster for the Dutch had not Mads Lange intervened to negotiate a peace treaty to save his interests. The Dutch saw the peace treaty as a defeat for Klungkung, the Balinese saw it as a defeat for the Dutch, and both sides were happy to save face and break off all conflicts. In the reports and books published by Dutch participants in the three wars, great emphasis was laid on the cunning and savagery of Gusti Jlantik, who is equally the heroic figure in Balinese accounts of the wars. The Balinese victories in battle were of course ascribed to the propensity for running amuk, and the people themselves were said to have fought the Dutch mainly because of "their deep respect and slavish subjection to their kings."[41] The wars and the related embargo on trade with Bali enforced by the Dutch brought to an end the prosperity of the 1830s, and hence Mads Lange's trading empire.[42]

Missionaries and Administrators

After 1849 the Dutch would have preferred to have nothing to do with Bali for some time to come. The aftermath of the wars left them in control of the former kingdom of Bulèlèng, which was basically all of Bali north of the mountain range, and included the vassal

41. ibid., p. 34.

42. See Schulte Nordholt, "The Mads Lange Connection," pp. 40-5; Hanna, *Bali Profile,* pp. 41-9. For other accounts of the war, see I Putu Geria, *Rusak Bulèlèng,* Dénpasar: Balimas, 1957; and P. J. Worsley, *Babad Bulèlèng: A Balinese Dynastic Genealogy,* The Hague: Nijhoff, 1972.

state of Jembrana, the underpopulated state of west Bali. At first the Dutch left their conquered territories in the hands of the king of Bangli, the ruler of the central mountain region of the island.

In 1851 on the advice of Lange and other informants, the Dutch decided it would be better to have a Bulèlèng king, a descendant of the famous seventeenth-century ruler Pañji Sakti, running their state for them, and relieved Bangli of its control. In 1854, two years before Lange died in south Bali, probably from poisoning, the Dutch were forced to intervene directly in their north Balinese territories. They argued that the king of Bulèlèng, who had been installed to rule these states on their behalf, was "rebelling" against them and oppressing the people. In that year Bali's first bureaucrat, the first Dutch administrator, P. L. van Bloemen Waanders, arrived to turn Bulèlèng and Jembrana into units of the Netherlands East Indies. He was a member of the new generation of real civil servants, dedicated to the idea of government, not self-aggrandizement. Under him, Bali was to be run along rational (i.e. Dutch) lines, where "barbarous" practices such as slavery and widow sacrifice would not be allowed. Van Bloemen Waanders was pedestrian in his approach to running north Bali, and his lack of imagination meant he was ill equipped to deal with a country run by different cultural suppositions to his own.

In order to govern Bali, it was necessary to know how it worked, and van Bloemen Waanders at first understood little of what was going on. North and west Bali were governed largely in name, and Dutch rule did not extend far beyond the perimeters of the capital city of Singaraja. To his despair he commented that, "In Bulèlèng there is not a trace of an ordered administration... The population has been able to free itself from all constraints, giving rise to a situation contrary to all principles of government."[43] Bulèlèng was lawless and chaotic, but that was part of the transition to colonial rule, presaging the upending of Balinese society in the twentieth century.

Van Bloemen Waanders faced more difficulties than he realized were possible, and was frustrated in most of his attempts to reform

---

43. P. L. van Bloemen Waanders, "Aanteekening omtrent de Zeden en Gebruiken derBalinezen," *TBG* 8 (1859): 105-279, pp. 113-14, transl. in van der Kraan, "Bali," p. 321. On van Bloemen Waanders see Boon, *Anthropological Romance,* pp. 130-4.

Slaves on Bali, including one from Papua called "Brit," 1865

the way north Bali was run. Like other imperialists of the time he maintained that Asian states could be much better run by Europeans than by the "natives" themselves.[44] But in reality, few Balinese were interested in co-operating with him, and even when they did they could not be relied upon to tell him what he wanted.

Balinese continued to rebel against Dutch rule, and in 1858 and 1868 two more Dutch expeditions were sent to north Bali against revolts led by the district heads *(punggawa)* I Nyoman Gempol and Ida Madé Rai. These revolts were direct responses to the undermining of local authority by the Dutch, in a situation where van Bloemen Waanders's understanding of the details of the way in which Balinese rule worked was imperfect at best.

Van Bloemen Waanders did, however, succeed in some reforms: he outlawed slavery and widow sacrifice, the two foci of much of European image-making of Bali. In the former case people were forced to "free" their personal slaves (slaves had not been sold outside of Bali for some time) and received some compensation

---

44. For similar comments on Malay states, see A. C. Milner, *Kerajaan: Malay Political Culture on the Eve of Colonial Rule,* Tucson: University of Arizona Press, 1982.

Gusti Ktut Jlantik, raja of Bulèlèng, north Bali, with his scribe, 1865.

from the Netherlands Indies Government. In many cases the slaves had nowhere to go, since they had been cut off from their villages long before, and had relied on their masters for support. Nevertheless the Dutch saw this as a progressive move, liable to attract Balinese from the "despotic" southern kingdoms with a promise of freedom. In later writings they always contrasted the benevolent Dutch-ruled areas of Bali with the despotic and anarchic independent kingdoms.

The first Dutch to live on Bali contributed greatly to knowledge of the island. Van Bloemen Waanders wrote a number of accounts of Bali, beginning with reports of his journeys around the island, and then going on to deal in depth with various aspects of Balinese history, law and customs. The Dutch were probably no worse, or better, than other European colonial nations, and one of their virtues was their commitment to understanding of the cultures and societies that they sought to incorporate into their empire.

At the same time the first missionary based on Bali, Rutger van Eck, began his work. Van Eck does not seem to have been well-liked by his contemporaries or successors, who spent much of their time disparaging his scholarly writings and the way he surrounded himself with Balinese who spoke "bastardized Malay."[45] For all that he was member of a fanatical missionary society, he only made one convert, and that man subsequently murdered van Eck's successor, causing the government to ban all missionary activity on the island for fifty years. But van Eck did at least make voluminous contributions to the knowledge of Balinese history, society, language and literature, writings which often implicitly supported the views that Balinese kings were personally distasteful and bad rulers, and that ordinary men and women in particular would benefit from Dutch rule.[46]

Ethical Invasion

At the end of the nineteenth century the colonial map was still patchy. Not only the south of Bali, but large portions of the interior of other Indonesian islands remained unconquered, anomalies in imperial thinking. Lombok was one of the first targets in the Dutch desire to clean up the imperial map. They had long had their eyes on the fertile rice fields of the island, which was one of the major producers of this crop in Southeast Asia, and were boosted in their desires by reports of potential mineral wealth. The issue of smuggling and then an uprising by the Muslim Sasaks against their Balinese rulers provided the Dutch with the opportunity to intervene militarily in 1894.[47]

As at Bulèlèng, bloody fighting and amuks once again took place. The rulers of Lombok had large forces and no desire to give

45. R. Nieuwenhuys (ed.), *H. N. van der Tuuk: De Pen in Gal Gedoopt*, Amsterdam: S. A. van Oorschot, 1962, p. 130.

46. See particularly his "Schetsen van het Eiland Bali," *TNI* 7(1878): 85-130, 165-213,325-56, 405-30; 8 (1879): 36-60, 104-34, 286-305, 365-87; 9 (1880): 1-39, 102-32, 195-221, 401-29; pt II: 1-18, 81-96.

47. See A. van der Kraan, *Lombok: Conquest, Colonization and Underdevelopment,* 1870-1940, Singapore: Heinemann, 1980.

up, but this time Dutch military technology was more advanced, and the Dutch had learned heavy lessons of conquest from a particularly horrible sustained guerrilla war in Aceh, north Sumatra. For most of the history of the Netherlands East Indies Islam had been the great enemy of the Dutch, particularly in Aceh, but one of the many ironies of the Lombok war was that the Dutch came in as defenders of Muslims. One of the major lessons of Aceh was to divide and conquer: drive wedges between the enemy groups, and thus overcome them. Besides using the Muslim Sasaks for this, the Dutch also got the ruler of Karangasem, Gusti Gedé Jlantik, on side.

The conquest began with accusations of incest and tyranny against various of the princes of Lombok, and ended with a *puputan,* a fight to the death by the crown prince, in which he and his family marched out dressed in white to be cut down by the Dutch. This was a traditional way to signal the "ending" of a kingdom, and indeed the word *puputan* means "ending." The *puputan* was both a sign to other kings of an end, and a way to achieve liberation of the soul by death in battle. For this reason it was important for the Balinese to die gloriously, and so retainers who joined in the *puputan* had the job of finishing their rulers off with krisses if they did not die immediately. The Dutch knew of these *puputan* from their accounts of wars in the early part of the nineteenth century, and in one account of the 1849 war it was called "another kind of amok which is wholly and exclusively peculiar to their nation."[48] The *puputan* was to assume great importance in Dutch thinking in the next fifteen years.

The conquest of Lombok in 1894 started the flood of Dutch military and diplomatic moves on Bali. The king of Karangasem realized in 1895 that without Lombok he had lost his major source of revenue and power, and ceded control of his state to the Dutch; in return he was allowed to remain as a "regent" in Dutch indirect rule. The Dutch agent sent to tour south Bali and negotiate with "friendly" rulers was a district officer called Schwartz, who sent back detailed descriptions of the palaces and administrations of the rulers, descriptions that were obviously intended for use in setting

---

48. Weitzel, *De Derde Militaire Expeditie,* p. 10.

up new Dutch administrations.[49] The central Balinese state of Gianyar followed Karangasem's example in 1900, largely because its existence was under threat from power-holders within, as well as from Klungkung, and the only way the king of Gianyar could keep his kingdom was to take sides with the most powerful force around, the Dutch. Schwartz then took up uneasy residence with the raja of Gianyar.

The next stage was not as easy, for unlike Karangasem and Gianyar the other Balinese states held out. Klungkung in particular refused to have anything to do with the Dutch, and the king did not even deign to meet Dutch emissaries. In 1906 the shipwreck issue was revived by the Dutch in south Bali. A Chinese trader claimed restitution for the cargo of his vessel, the *Sri Kumala,* which had been wrecked off the coast of Sanur, in the kingdom of Badung. The king's refusal to admit any responsibility in the matter was the excuse for which the Dutch had been waiting, and they initiated military action against another lawless despot.

The king of Badung and his ally and neighbor the king of Tabanan stood firm against the Dutch, and the inevitable military expedition came in September of that year. The Dutch had landed on the beach at Sanur quite easily, and from there they marched first on Kesiman, but the lord there had already been assassinated by a traitor. From there the Dutch moved on the capital of Dénpasar.

On the morning of 20 September the king, his family, and thousands of armed followers, all dressed in white and ready to meet death in battle, marched out to meet the Dutch. Each of the leading royal warriors ran amuk in turn, marching on as if bullets would bounce off their bodies. The Dutch opened fire on "women with weapons in their hands, lance or kris, and children in their arms,"

---

49. H. J. E. F. Schwartz, "Dagverhaal... Kloengkoeng 1898," "Rapport... Bangli 1899," "Dagverhaal,... Tabanan en Badung 1899," "Rapport [Karangasem]," *TBG* 43 (1901): 108-23, 124-31, 132-58, 554-60; "Aanteekeningen omtrent het Landschap Gianjar," *Tijdschrift van het Binnenlandsch Bestuur* 19 (1900): 166-89. The Dutch experts did not have a single view of the details of Balinese state organization nor of how they should change it, because different Balinese states were actually organized in different ways, Gianyar being the most territorially-based of all the states, and Bangli depending most heavily on appanage ties and ricefields to hold it together. See V. E. Korn, *Het Adatrecht van Bali,* The Hague: Naeff, 1932, pp. 227 & 289. Cf. Clifford Geertz, *Negara: The Theatre State in Nineteenth Century Bali,* Princeton University Press, 1980.

who "advanced fearlessly upon the troops and sought death." The Dutch found that this *puputan* could only be settled in death; surrender was impossible: "where an attempt was made to disarm them this only led to an increase in our losses. The survivors were repeatedly called on to lay down arms and surrender, but in vain."[50] The king, his family and followers advanced relentlessly, killing themselves and any Dutch troops who came within range as they went. The Dutch later tried to cover up the death toll, but while it was fairly light on the Dutch side, well over 1000 Balinese were killed.[51]

The Dutch thought that this would make the remaining independent rulers of Klungkung and Bangli give up, but Klungkung proudly held out as a sign of the king's dignity. In 1908 the scene in Badung was repeated, except that it began with a bombardment of the town and a false start, so that when the final march to death came, only 300 were killed, including all but three of the males closely related to the king. The raja of Bangli, who had sent members of his family to support Klungkung, then wisely capitulated.

The massacres of 1906 and 1908, the two *puputans,* were a source of shame and international embarrassment to the Dutch as they tried to present their colonial march in lofty terms. They argued that they had not realized the Balinese would act so suicidally instead of more sensibly submitting to Dutch rule, but this was something of a strange claim considering that the *puputan* tradition had been well documented.

The *puputans* brought together in one spectacular ending the motifs of Bali's image up to that time: the ancient grandeur, the fanatical devotion to battle symbolized by wild amuk with krisses, and the sacrifice of women, for in many ways the *puputan* was a large-scale version of the act of widow sacrifice on the death of a king. Savage Bali had a savage ending.

Here, then, was the grand signal of the end of independent Bali, the act of death that marked the transition to full colonial rule in

---

50. Participant's report of the chief of staff of the expedition, quoted in Nordholt, *Bali: Colonial Conceptions,* p. 5.

51. ibid.

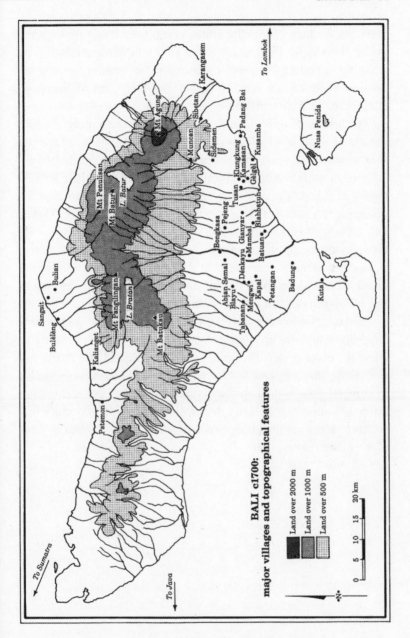

Bali, c. 1700, major villages and topographical features.

1908. In the face of this the Dutch could only try to pick up the pieces. Gradually they fostered the idea of "Museum Bali," by claiming to protect the island's culture. In the decades to come the policies of protection were to lead to another form of European domination of Bali: tourism.

The history of Bali's image up until 1908 was a history of many strands of thought which came together in colonialism. In the period before the nineteenth century there was no one coherently developed or unified attitude to Bali. The views of Bali were formed almost as side products to other concerns: hostility to Islam, and the economic necessity of the slave trade. As imperialism developed into a body of policy and action in the nineteenth century, earlier views could be put to good use against the Balinese, in order to expose the island for conquest. At the same time other sides of the image of Bali developed. Raffles and his associates, in seeking to know Bali scientifically, both contributed to the march of imperialism and provided a more positive view of Bali. In some ways scholarly knowledge was an adjunct to colonialism—it was necessary to know the place in detail in order to take it over and rule it. But not everything that scholars found out about Bali was directly useful in colonial policy-making; they could also appreciate and admire Balinese culture. In the early decades of the twentieth century this positive side of colonial image-making led to the complete rejection of the idea of savage Bali.

CHAPTER TWO

Balinese Images from the Golden Age to Conquest

European images of ferocious Bali tell us little about Balinese images of their own society. The superiority Europeans claimed for themselves was based on the idea that theirs was the only view, and generations of historians have written histories of what we call the Third World based on the premise.[1] Balinese self-images are different from European images—they are part of the way Balinese culture and society are organized—but they have in fact influenced European views of Bali in ways of which the Europeans have not always been aware.

Between the sixteenth century, a golden age of strong kingship for Bali, and the nineteenth century, when European power defeated the kingdoms of Bali, four major Balinese preoccupations emerged, of which the European observers saw only a part. These were: divine kingship; the romance of battle; the veneration of ancestors; and the life of the common people. Each of these preoccupations came to the fore at different times under particular political, economic and cultural circumstances. The early Europeans accepted the idea of kingship and construed it in their own religious terms, and some aspects of the courtly view of warfare they amalgamated into the idea of savage Bali, but they could not appreciate the full import of Balinese cultural identity for Balinese.

---

1. The major representative of this kind of writing in relation to Bali is Willard A. Hanna, *Bali Profile: People, Events, Circumstances,* 1001-1976, New York: American Universities Field Staff, 1976.

Although Balinese cultural history stretches back over two thousand years, the crucial period for the development of modern Balinese culture and cultural institutions has been the last four hundred years. During this period the general ideas of the religious organization of the state and society found throughout Southeast Asia were transformed into these four specifically Balinese cultural preoccupations.

Culture is the accumulated habits of many lifetimes, but more than this it is the way people see themselves and organize their lives according to those perceptions. The most widely known forms of Balinese art, theater and literature manifest the issues and preoccupations which each era of Balinese history has considered most important. Through these artistic manifestations we can go back and understand something of people's experiences, and so the analysis which follows describes the major issues of different eras of Balinese history in terms of the ways predominant images merged with life. The image or images most important in the political and social organization of Bali in one era did not simply die out, but new images were added to them, so that each generation saw itself as continuing the same culture, while at the same time transforming it.

The four Balinese cultural preoccupations mentioned above are all aspects of the self-image of the Balinese as a cultural group. As the concerns of kings, priests and other power-holders, these cultural preoccupations came to dominate aspects of the lives of virtually all Balinese. Everybody knew of the images associated with these preoccupations, because these images were constantly presented through the recitation of elaborate narrative poems, through beautiful paintings, through the flickering shadows of the *wayang* puppet theater, and through spectacular dance-drama. Royalty were patrons of this literature and art, and kings, priests and commoners all participated in writing, painting and performing in them. In doing this they showed that the arts were part of the shared assumptions of Balinese culture, the ideas that everybody took for granted.

In the sixteenth century, when Bali was a single empire, the island already had access to a rich body of symbolism via Java and ultimately Hinduism and Buddhism from India. At that time one of the major features of Balinese self-image was the idea of the World Ruling King. Such a king would venture out from his heavenly palace from time to time to conquer his enemies, and then return in triumph to his beautiful queen. Their marriage formed a mystical union that bestowed order on the state of Bali. To make sure these benefits were properly distributed, the king could call on his chief minister and his court brahman priests to reconcile the earthly running of the state and the divine order of things. The underlying idea of this kingship was that the cosmos and the kingdom were one and that kings and priests had a duty to organize the mundane world, through building palaces, holding rituals, or sponsoring artistic activities, so that it did not clash with the divine world.

The history of Bali from the sixteenth to the nineteenth century is the history of the proliferation of kingdoms, all spreading from the source in the single kingdom of the World Ruler, and adding new symbolic layers to the old. Bali moved from being one kingdom that ruled over parts of the neighboring islands, to being nine separate kingdoms, all in constant competition. As kingdoms multiplied over the centuries, art increased. Royal patronage, carried out through the sponsorship of rituals, ensured that society at large shared in the images of that art and took them for granted as basic assumptions about society and identity.

The distinctive characteristic of Bali's culture is the development of a huge range of cultural and ritual activities over the last four hundred years, so that Balinese culture has become a bewildering array of alternative images and conceptions. As a single kingdom Bali had a dense population and a relatively sophisticated wet-rice irrigation system to feed that population. As Balinese society changed, the images produced in the age of a single kingdom could not completely satisfy the cultural needs of many kingdoms. Each of these new kingdoms was in competition with the other, trying to expand to fit the geographical and symbolic space of the old World Ruler. From this came the impetus for more and more different artistic forms that would express the distinctiveness and the identity of each separate kingdom. Like the Medicis or the Bourbons in Europe, powerful patronage fuelled the engines of cultural dynamism.

By drawing on ancient traditions, Balinese could reconcile these changes with the age-old traditions around which their life was oriented. In the changing circumstances of the 1600s and 1700s, new images were needed to explain how a number of kings could exist in close proximity, and how kings could emerge virtually out of nowhere. The images of this era romanticized the warfare and sexual conquest needed to build new states, turning the *nouveau riche* lords into handsome and brave princes on the up and up. By the end of the eighteenth century a new order had emerged. Kingdoms rose and fell with less regularity, and Bali settled into a pattern in which the island consisted of nine kingdoms. Members of the nine royal families spent much of their time conspiring against their relatives.

As the kingdoms consolidated, each of the families began to turn its attention to its origins, and to try and locate itself in relation to the other royal dynasties of Bali. At the same time power had to be shared in the kingdoms with rising commoner families. So new attention was turned to the daily life of ordinary folk, to how commoners ran their rituals, gained access to religious revelation, or were subject to magical forces. This new attention was part of an attempt to see how such people fitted into the social order and what role they had or should have in the state and society.

The World Ruler: 1500-1651

Modern Balinese government, caste and religion are intimately intertwined, and all date back to one climactic moment in Balinese history, the Golden Age of Gèlgèl when King Baturènggong reigned in partnership with the great priest Nirartha. Since this golden age all Balinese kings have required court priests to provide holy water for them when officiating at their rituals. The kings do the organizing, and provide the manpower and funds to hold the rituals, the commoners provide the basic labor, and the priests carry out the rituals in accordance with the many sacred texts they have studied and preserved.

In the sixteenth century Dalem Baturènggong of Gèlgèl was king of a single Balinese state that stretched from Blambangan and Pasuruhan in east Java to the islands of Lombok and Sumbawa in Eastern Indonesia. The reign of Baturènggong lay at the heart of an epic vision of kingship that all later rulers of Bali were to call upon as the models of their own rules.

Perhaps this golden age, and even Baturènggong himself, may

prove to have been more an image of later times than historical substance. But this is irrelevant to the legacies of the period in Bali's cultural imagination: the existence of a strong, central, World Ruling kingship; the consolidation of a system of social order based on what ancient Java was thought to be like; and a four-caste ideology with the brahman priesthood at its apex. The idea of ancient Java underwent many changes in the next two centuries, but remained important to how Balinese saw their culture. Balinese have continued to recognize their cultural debt to Java's great Hindu empires of the past, and to model their own society on those empires, thus sharing in the glory of their name. Caste has remained a major concern of Balinese social organization, its outlines unchanged, its details changing constantly to suit new circumstances.

The sixteenth and early seventeenth centuries were the age of great kings throughout the Indonesian archipelago. In the late fifteenth century one of the greatest cities in the world had been Melaka (Malacca), the harbor city on the Malay peninsula. The sacking of Melaka in 1511 by the Portuguese preceded the decline of Java's great Hindu-Buddhist kingdom of Majapahit in the next decade. Since the Portuguese, Spanish, and later Dutch and English, were still small competitors amongst the many local powers, the decline of Majapahit allowed other great Southeast Asian powers to rise within the confines of the rich trade of the area. Baturènggong's empire, for example, was bordered by the other great powers of the archipelago at that time—the Muslim kingdoms of Surabaya and Mataram on Java, and of Makassar on Sulawesi.

In the late seventeenth century the Dutch East India Company was able to establish strong control over the trade lanes, the sources of production, and many of the main ports, as well as significant parts of the island of Java. This spelt the beginning of the end for the large powers of Southeast Asia. Paradoxically, up to this point the disruption to the balance of power in Southeast Asia stimulated by the European powers had opened up possibilities of establishing strong and aggressive states to indigenous rulers, such as Baturènggong.

Dalem Baturènggong saw himself as a manifestation of World Ruling Kingship. In art and literature the World Ruler was portrayed as a benevolent and wise man, someone who showed great military might and the ability to conquer all enemies, whether they be lesser kings or fearsome demons. The victorious World Ruler was the incarnation or son of a Hindu god, and for this reason could accomplish things which sometimes even the gods could not. Other kings and subjects would come to render tribute to the World Ruler out of love and would be inspired by his handsome, wise, and benevolent qualities. If they were not, then they would be struck with fear at his terrible strength in battle.

The World Ruler resided at the center of the kingdom in a spectacular palace that encompassed the whole world in symbolic form. Through this symbolism a ruler of a small kingdom could see himself as governing processes that embraced the whole world. The capital of Gèlgèl was the rich heart of the kingdom where all the major state officials resided. The king's palace was located at the center of the city, a huge walled area consisting of grand buildings in numerous separate courtyards. Although no archeological remains have so far been unearthed, we can gain some sense of what the palace of Gèlgèl must have been like from the palaces that succeeded it on Bali, which are supposedly modeled on it. If other courts are truly the lesser reflections of the Gèlgèl palace that they are supposed to be, then the palace of Gèlgèl itself was over 250 meters long by 200 meters wide. Its inner walls of red brick would have been around four meters high, towering over everything around, with beautiful Chinese porcelain plates set into them. At the main entrances a number of mountainous great gates in a kind of pyramid shape topped the walls. These gates were the first of many symbols of the three worlds, heaven, earth and hell. Just outside the main gate was an open yard where the king held audiences and staged theatrical performances. Behind the gates were a series of inner courtyards. The nearest to the entrance of these inner courtyards would have been for the king's menagerie: all kinds of beasts from domestic pigs to horses and deer. Other courtyards near that acted as quarters for the royal slaves and concubines, whose modest pavilions typified the dwellings of most Balinese. Further inside, beyond the lush gardens where ponds enclosed high open pavilions, were the royal quarters with a monumental central building in brick, which was decorated again with porcelain and surrounded by all kinds of statues. Its doors, like the doors of the main gates, were beautifully carved woodwork covered in gold. Like the heroic king Rama's palace in the ancient epic the *Ramayana,* the decorations of the Gèlgèl palace were part of its image of wealth and beauty, they were its treasures which were like white teeth, grinning at the inferior beauty of heaven."[2]

Besides the king, the most important inhabitant of the palace was his first wife, whose importance was greater even than the powerful chief minister. Such a queen was deliberately chosen as first wife of the king from among many subsidiary or lesser wives. Balinese kings needed a large number of wives to ensure that there would be at least one surviving male heir to carry on the dynasty, but also to show that their power extended over the whole kingdom, for the women taken into the court were not only from the aristocracy, but were the sisters and daughters of important leaders on all levels of society. At times polygamy was taken to such lengths that one king of south Bali is remembered as having 800 wives. The women chosen as queens were of royal birth, which meant that they brought their own power, wealth and influence to the court, and created special ties between the king and the other major families of the state. Marriage was as important to politics as war.

The first wife's accomplishments and virtues accorded with the image of femininity presented in art and literature, where the ideal was Sita, the beautiful and loyal wife of Rama in the *Ramayana.* Rama and Sita were the perfect couple, and their sexual union was a mystical ritual that brought fertility, goodness and prosperity to their whole realm. They were also an inseparable pair—the king could not rule without his queen.

Like Sita, a queen had to be prepared to sacrifice herself out of loyalty to her husband. When she had been recaptured from the demon king, Rawana, Sita threw herself into a fire to prove that she had remained loyal to Rama. When she did this, "her mind sparked with anticipation" because she "asked to die out of loyalty... All attachment vanished as, fearless... she dived into the fire." Of course,

---

2. Soewito Santoso, *Ramayana Kakawin,* New Delhi: International Academy for Indian Culture, 1983, p. 39.

"she was not burnt—only the hearts of those who saw her caught fire and turned to ashes." The pyre itself "changed into a golden lotus."[3] Queens were asked to throw themselves on the funeral pyre of their husbands, so that they could remain the perfect couple en route to heaven: unfortunately in practice the flames never seemed to turn into lotus petals. Most frequently lower-ranking servants and concubines killed themselves, often only after being heavily doped up with opium. Such was the "widow sacrifice" that was a source of continuing fascination to European observers.

The inner courtyards behind the gates were closed to all but the king, his wives and family, the chief ministers of state, and the slaves and ubiquitous bodyguards, armed with arrows, spears, blow-pipes and krisses. In front of the main gate the open courtyard was sheltered by a huge banyan tree and surrounded by small pavilions, each of which was mounted with cannons decorated with silver. The palaces of lords of the various areas of Bali were next to the royal palace, and the closest of all was the palace of the major lord of Bali, the lord of Kapal, the region to the west.[4]

The presence in the palace of the different elements of the king-dom, and ultimately of the world, was important to the maintenance of Gèlgèl, the center of the kingdom. In the royal palace there was a great collection of all types of humanity, including albino dwarfs and foreigners, whose strangeness represented the forces of diversity and difference from the norms of Balinese society, forces which the king symbolically harnessed by including their potentially danger-ous presence in the center of his powerful world. Not far to the east of the palace was a Muslim community, which is still there, and these Muslims provided traders for the court as well as interpreters who could speak Malay, the lingua franca of the archipelago.[5] Between

3. ibid., p. 659 (trans, adapted by myself).

4. For some of these details of the palace, see Aernout Lintgensz, "Bali 1597," *BKI* 1 (1856): 203-34. See also G. P. Rouffaer & J. W. IJzerman, *De Eerst Schipvaart der Nederlanders naar Oost-Indië onder Cornelis de Houtman, 1595-1597,* vols 7, 25, 32, The Hague: Lindschoten Vereeniging, 1915, 1925, 1929. The chief remnant of the palace of Kapal is its house-temple, which became the Temple of Jero Kapal or Pancoran, see P. J. Worsley, "E74163," *RIMA* 18,1 (1984): 64-109.

5. On Muslim gravestones from the heart of Gèlgèl's model, Majapahit, see M. C. Ricklefs, *A History of Modern Indonesia,* London: Macmillan, 1980, p. 4.

the Muslim community of Gèlgèl and the former site of the palace is the major temple of Pura Dasar, one of the state temples of the island and a chief place where the king's power was reconciled with the will of the gods. The chief minister of the kingdom resided in part of the massive complex of villages that made up the capital. At one stage he lived a few kilometers to the north of the palace, in what is now the separate village of Jlantik.

To maintain the relationship between ruler and realm the king had to be seen by and to see the people. This was the face-to-face basis of a kingdom where the king and his royal family together with the major lords and all their bodyguards and slaves, would have only numbered a thousand at the most, out of a population of 300,000. The king had to be accessible through audiences in the forecourt of his palace, but he also travelled to different parts of the island making ritual visits to temples, demonstrating that he was a friend of the gods.[6] Kings in Bali had to control or harness the natural and supernatural elements of the world through all possible symbolic means: through having vast palaces which acted as centers of power, through initiating and preserving laws which came from the gods, and through holding vast rituals in which everyone in the state could be involved. This kind of personal contact and participation involving king and subjects formed an emotional and religious bond between the two that made the state work.[7]

The Javanese Origins of Gèlgèl
The sixteenth-century kingdom of Gèlgèl was the culmination of a constellation of Indian and indigenous ideas about kingship and divine authority which had been disseminated throughout Southeast Asia from the first century CE onwards.

---

6. Santoso, *Ramayana Kakawin,* p. 38. For the Majapahit precedent for this, see Clifford Geertz, "Centers, Kings, and Charisma: Reflections on the Symbolics of Power," in his *Local Knowledge: Further Essays in Interpretive Anthropology,* New York: Basic Books, 1983, pp. 121-46.

7. For further information on the World Ruler image and the literary tradition behind it, see P. J. Zoetmulder, *Kalangwan: A Survey of Old Javanese Literature,* The Hague: Nijhoff, 1974; and O. W. Wolters, *History, Culture and Region in Southeast Asia Perspectives,* Singapore: Institute for Southeast Asian Studies, 1982. The major study of precolonial Balinese states is Clifford Geertz, *Negara: The Theatre State in Nineteenth-Century Bali,* Princeton: Princeton University Press, 1980.

The major vehicles of the dissemination of Hindu and Buddhist ideas were Indian texts, such as the *Ramayana,* which had been locally adopted, or "localized."[8]

In the tenth century, when Javanese kingdoms were casting their own versions of the Indian epics, Bali was already mentioned in inscriptions as an emerging kingdom with all the accoutrements of Indian religion. Ancient sarcophagi in the shape of turtles and ancient bronze drums and tools testify to the development of Balinese social organization long before this time, but it was probably the pressure from the nearby kingdoms of Java which influenced early Balinese states to take on the Indian form of religion and statecraft which had swept over Southeast Asia in the preceding centuries. By the end of the tenth century Bali's social order had come strongly under the influence of Java. Javanese rulers started to assert their power, and inscriptions were put out in the ancient court language of Java. It was at this time that the adaptations of Hindu texts first started to spread to Bali, as part of Javanese cultural influence.

Javanese-Balinese relations fluctuated over the next few centuries, but the literary and artistic influences of Java, the larger island, remained strong. During the latter part of the eleventh century Bali again became more independent, only to be reconquered by a new Javanese kingdom, Kadiri, a few decades later. Kadiri is chiefly remembered as the dynasty that sponsored the composition of some of the greatest poetic works of Old Javanese literature. It was the Jaya dynasty, which ruled Bali as a branch of the Kadiri royal family, that fostered the development of this literature on Bali.[9]

After Kadiri came the greatest of Java's kingdoms, Majapahit, which conquered Bali in 1334.[10] Majapahit was the first kingdom to unite and actually rule over the whole of Java.[11] Although it was

---

8. On the concept of localisation, see Wolters, *History, Culture and Region.*

9. See Zoetmulder, *Kalangwan,* pp. 234-324.

10. For details of all these developments, see A. J. Bernet Kempers, *Monumental Bali: Introduction to Balinese Archaeology/Guide to the Monuments,* The Hague: van Goor Zonen, 1977, pp. 40-57. See further D. J. Stuart-Fox, Pura Besakih: A Study of Balinese Religion and Society, (diss.), Australian National University, 1987, pp. 307-9.

11. See Herman Kulke, "The Early and Imperial Kingdom," in D. G. Marr & A. C. Milner (eds.), *Southeast Asia in the 9th to 14th Centuries,* Singapore: Institute of Southeast Asian Studies/ Research School of Pacific Studies, Australian National University, 1986, pp. 1-22.

not an empire in the nineteenth-century colonial sense, its greatness was recognized over a wide area and it collected from as far
away as the Malay peninsula and from lesser rulers all over the
Indonesian archipelago. Majapahit put the seal on Javanese cultural
influence on Bali. After the 1520s, when Majapahit disappeared,
Balinese still maintained contact with other kingdoms in the archipelago (even Islamic kingdoms) based on the idea of a common
Majapahit heritage. Even today Balinese see their culture as essentially Majapahit culture. All the elements of the Golden Age of
Gèlgèl, the great palace, the state offices, and especially the ritual
life of the kingdom, were seen by the Balinese as coming from
Majapahit. When Majapahit installed its new rulers in Bali in the
fourteenth century they began a system with a single royal family at
the top. The ministers of this royal family, who also served as local
lords, were Javanese aristocrats, mostly descendants of the former
royal family of Kadiri.

Despite the sense of cultural continuity, sixteenth-century Bali
was very different from the Bali that had preceded Majapahit.
Dalem Baturènggong's rule was the end result of a massive transformation process. Balinese society of the tenth century was a society in which distant royal authority had a tenuous hold over the
loyalties of strongly organized villages. From this base it became
an expansionist kingdom in which royal authority was able to per-
meate daily peasant life to a far greater degree. Bali moved to being a far more king-centered society, organized into the four castes
of Hinduism. The constant element of Balinese society before and
after the transformation was that it was held together by personal
relationships.

The outlines of Balinese society prior to the age of Baturènggong are sketchy. What emerges from ancient inscriptions and texts
is the idea of a village-based society. In this society "core" groups
of villagers were most important. From them was elected a council
of "elders."

Other village residents included traders and craftsmen, for both
Bali and Java at that time had highly developed trading systems and
high standards in many arts and crafts. These traders and craftsmen
were included along with serfs, peons, and newcomers to the village

as a group outside the core, living in a separate part of the village.[12] Also living alongside this core in the territory of the village were officials answerable to royal authority, who acted as kinds of police and overseers of taxation, corvée and trade duties. The kings further placed themselves as supreme authority over the local lords who supervised and supported groups of temples and villages. Society was therefore organized into a hierarchy from villagers to king.

The coming of Majapahit rule to Bali started to change the importance of the village as an institution in the state. But it was not until the kingdom of Gèlgèl emerged, probably in the late fifteenth or early sixteenth century, that the changes took full effect. Majapahit and Gèlgèl are associated with the undermining of the unity of the village and the introduction of a new system of corvée labor. Formerly the villages of Bali were semi-autonomous, and their organization was similar to that of the *Bali Aga* or "original Balinese" villages that still exist in the east and in the mountains of the island.[13] What the Majapahit and Gèlgèl rulers may have done was break down the unity of the village by breaking it into smaller units called *bañjar* that grouped households according to corvée obligations.[14] Each *bañjar* carried out its obligations under a court appointed head or *klian*. This system displaced the councils of elders, and meant that there was no separation between core villagers and newcomers. Likewise the artisans and other outsiders ceased to reside outside the walls of the village, and the walls themselves disappeared, so that only individual house-yards were walled.[15] Such changes as

12. See J. G. de Casparis, "Pour une Histoire Sociale de l'Ancienne Java Principalement au Xème s.," *Archipel* 21 (1981):125-54, especially pp. 137-40.

13. On this point see also V. E. Korn, *De Dorpsrepubliek Tnganan Pagringsingan,* Santpoort: Mees, 1933; James Danandjaja, *Kebudayaan Petani Desa Trunyan di Bali,* Jakarta: Pustaka Jaya, 1980; and Danker Schaareman, *Tatulingga-. Tradition and Continuity,* Basel: Wepf, 1986. Thomas Reuter's extensive publications on highland villages represent the most advanced discussion of the "Bali Aga" question.

14. On the conceptual problem of how to define a *bañjar,* see J. & F. Guermonprez, "The Elusive Balinese Village," paper given at the KITLV Indonesia Workshop, *Balinese State and Society,* April, 1986. Guermonprez, however, does not take account of the close relationship between the *bañjar* and corvée made clear by V. E. Korn in his *Adatrecht van Bali,* The Hague: Naeff, 1932, pp. 94 & 129. Most of the papers from this workshop were edited by Hildred Geertz and published as *State and Society in Bali,* Leiden: KITLV, 1991.

15. Cf. B. J. Haga, "Bali Aga," in *Adatrechtbundels* XXIII, s'Gravenhage: M. Nijhoff, 1924, pp. 453-69.

this could only occur slowly, leaving relatively little evidence of their nature, and the system as a whole can only be retrospectively explained through the picture that emerges from nineteenth-century sources.

The new system divided the population into "outsiders" and "insiders." The peasantry, which constituted the majority of the population, were outsiders. Royalty and their priesthood were insiders—members of royal or priestly houses (called *puri* or palaces, and *geria* or priests' dwellings). Commoners who achieved high rank and office in the palace, or became elevated servants of kings and priests, received the title of *Jero,* meaning "inside," in recognition of their status. The same title was given to commoner wives of royalty or priests, but also to commoner temple priests and shadow play puppeteers. The female servants of the court were called the "insiders"—*pangjeroan,* just as male retainers were called "those who came near" the rulers—*parekan.*

Commoners occupied a vast range of ranks in state and religious offices and it was possible for a commoner to move from being an "outsider" to being an insider. Similarly slaves were not simply slaves. People dependent on the court could be the higher status *parekan* or retainers, on an intimate footing with the king, sharing in his cockfighting and, amongst other things, opium smoking. Others were soldiers, sharecroppers and palace workers who lived in the shadow of the court, called *roban,* which means they were "shaded" by the palace. The people who were slaves proper were called *sapangan.* These were people who could be bought or sold, and, in the case of women, who could be forced to go out as prostitutes to bring in money for the king.

Most commoners, however, wanted to be tied to the courts. The commoners who were soldiers, artists, artisans and performers for the courts shared in the beauty of court society. The hierarchy was spiritual as well. By rising in wealth, rank and status, people could elevate their whole family, ancestors and all. The rewards were entry to heaven in the afterworld, and a good reincarnation in later lives. All of this could be achieved through devotion to the king, and through the possibility of studying worthy literature under the guidance of the priests.

The World Ruler and His Priest

King Baturènggong's sixteenth-century state never really flourished until he gained a state priest of great power, one who could successfully produce the rituals that held the state together. This priest was Nirartha, the ancestor of most Balinese high priests, the initiator of the modern caste and ritual system of Bali, and the man who created a literary renaissance during the time of Baturènggong.

The *Ramayana* describes how priests were meant to serve kings through running rituals. They were also there to provide instruction in the "true duty of tribute and suffering" of kingship, while kings were meant to be the protectors of priests.[16] In the genealogies of royal and priestly dynasties it was the arrival of Nirartha that signaled the real inauguration of Bali's golden age—without him Dalem Baturènggong's realm was incomplete, under threat of chaos and pestilence.[17] Nirartha arrived some time before 1537,[18] and by that year had established himself at the center of literary activity on the island.

Literature and religious accomplishments go together; in order for a priest like Nirartha to be truly powerful, he had to control the power of words in their most subtle form, the complex sung poetry known as *kekawin* written in the Old Javanese language and using metrical systems originally from India. Nirartha's poetry was a blend of eroticism and mysticism presenting the same kinds of secret mystical knowledge that had to be harnessed in rituals. The chief poets of modern Bali have been his descendants and pupils.

---

16. Santoso, *Kakawin Ramayana*, p. 47.

17. Raechelle Rubinstein, "The Brahmana according to their Babad," paper given at the Balinese State and Society Workshop 1986.

18. This is the date of a manuscript of the *Sumanasantaka* poem copied by Nirartha and later recopied for the major palace of Lombok, Leiden University Library Oriental Manuscripts Collection (LOr) 5015; cf. LOr 5040, from the same Lombok collection, of the *Kresnayana*, dated 1544. There is a major problem with dating Nirartha using other of his texts, especially the *Nirartha Prakreta*, ed. and trans. by R. M. Ng. Poerbatjaraka, *BKI* 107 (1951): 201-25, which is dated to 1459, although it is unclear from the information in the colophon of this text whether Nirartha was really the author's name. Poerbatjaraka's idea that this manuscript was written in Surabaya was mistaken. See H. I. R. Hinzler, "The Usana Bali as a Source of History," in Taufik Abdullah (ed.), *Papers of the 4th Indonesian-Dutch Historical Conference*, vol. 2, Yogyakarta: Gajah Mada University Press, 1986, pp. 124-62, and H. I. R. Hinzler, "The Balinese Babad," in Sartono Kartodirdjo (ed.), *Profiles of Malay Culture*, Jakarta: Ministry of Education and Culture, 1976, pp. 39-52.

Building on the literature handed down from ancient Java, they contributed to the growth not just of a flourishing literary tradition in Bali, but to the theatrical, musical and artistic traditions that go with it. In that sense Nirartha's own literary achievements were symbolic of a strengthening and multiplying of the outward forms of culture during Bali's golden age.

Nirartha was responsible for the inauguration of caste as it is now known on Bali and for the elevation of the priests who perform worship to Siwa as the major priestly group. Prior to the arrival of Nirartha there were priestly groups who directed their worship mainly to Buddha and to the Hindu god Indra. Caste was known more as an academic term than a descriptor of social organization, and many of the priests of the pre-Nirartha period preserved their roles only by being relegated to the status of commoners. This is particularly so of the temple priests called *pamangku* and the exorcistic priests called *sengguhu*.[19]

Nirartha is the ancestor of a brahman or *brahmana* high priesthood that directed its worship to Siwa and carried out rituals for the court. Prior to his coming these brahmans probably did not form a continuing dynasty or descent group, and were just one of many amorphous groups of priests. After Nirartha the *brahmana* became a high priesthood added to the top of the existing priestly structure, a priesthood complemented by the smaller group of high priests who directed their worship to Buddha. In the retrospective accounts the ancestor of all the Buddhist high priests was Nirartha's nephew, so the structure was kept within the family.

The major tool by which the more amorphous groups of priests pre-dating Nirartha were displaced was the idea of an exclusive priestly caste, the *brahmana.* Only from Nirartha's descendants can come the Siwa-worshipping high priests or *padanda,* and only the descendants of Nirartha's nephew can be the Buddha-worshipping

---

19. P. A. Leupe, "Schriftelijk Rapport Gedaan door den Predicant Justus Hernius," *BKI* 3 (1859): 250-62, quoted in Korn, *Het Adatrecht,* p. 39n., refers to the *sengguhu* priests as the main priests of Bali. My thanks to Henk Schulte Nordholt for pointing out this reference to me. There may be some confirmation of the importance of the *sengguhu* in the fact that the surviving Hindu priests of the Tengger region in Java use ritual texts almost identical to those of the Balinese *sengguhu.* See Hefner, *Hindu Java-. Tengger Tradition and Islam,* Princeton: Princeton University Press, 1985.

priests. All the other categories of priest which have survived have been relegated to the lower castes.

Caste had "no validity in actual life" in ancient Java or Bali prior to the fifteenth century,[20] but it did exist in theory in the model of the World Ruler. In the model, the semi-divine or divine status of the ruler and the spiritual basis of kingship depended on his relationship with the priesthood. In the many stories about priests and kings the two groups were shown in a kind of uneasy partnership. Sometimes they were rivals for power, sometimes allies. Still today each group claims to be the highest caste.

Caste worked as an ideology to the advantage of the *brahmana* and the descendants of Dalem Baturènggong, who were the second caste of warrior-kings *(satria)*. The lords of other descent, those whose hereditary title is Gusti, formed the third caste *(wèsia)* which, in the Gèlgèl caste model,was the caste of court officials and knights. The rest, the other types of priests, lower court officials, peasants and traders, were all the lowest caste *(sudra)*. Caste was effectively an image of social order used to preserve a hierarchy thatexisted in much looser fashion before the sixteenth century.

From the sixteenth century until the present day caste has remained the ideal used to describe Balinese social order. It was always, however, an ideal which worked for the top two castes, but which was full of inconsistencies for everyone else. The descendants of Baturènggong's ministers, for example, who became the kings of separate states in the seventeenth century, were never from the second caste, but from the third. Likewise the other types of priests whose role was usurped by Nirartha, together with the various forms of state officials who had been relegated to the status of commoners of the fourth caste, claimed that the model did not apply to them. To make matters even more complex Balinese caste was linked to a principle of sinking status—if a man of high caste married a woman of low caste, and their male children continued to marry below them, then over three or four generations the family would lose their high caste status and become members of a lower

---

20. Th. Pigeaud, *Java in the 14th Century: A Study in Cultural History,* 5 vols, The Hague: Nijhoff, 1960-63, vol. IV, pp. 259-61.

caste. Through this principle the vast majority of Balinese who are today relegated to the fourth caste can claim descent from kings or priests of the highest castes.[21]

The fragile framework of caste was meaningless without some kind of everyday practice to support it. Nirartha brought Majapahit-style rituals that were meant, according to the legends of his coming, to be more efficacious than the rites of other Balinese priests. In essence, he introduced the present-day Balinese ritual order, particularly the making of holy water which is the key rite for the *brahmana* priesthood.[22] Even the appearance of the major exorcistic story used in the well-known dance-drama of the *Barong* dates from the era of Nirartha.[23] Magic and exorcism are important topics on an island like Bali, where tropical diseases and a high infant mortality rate have been part of the basic experiences of people on all levels of society.

With the new literature and rituals came a legal system to back up caste. Through the punishments of crimes such as murder, robbery and infringements of the rules of caste, the king and his priests kept the world in order, in accordance with ancient law books handed down from Java. They also demonstrated their power over their subjects, and ensured through violence that the royal and priestly order of things was not questioned.[24]

This Bali of the World Ruler and his priest was the Bali the Dutch first encountered at the end of the sixteenth century. The world ruler they met was not the long-deceased Baturènggong, but his son, Dalem Seganing. In later accounts Dalem Seganing is almost as

21. For further discussion of the complexities of caste in Bali, see James A. Boon, *The Anthropological Romance of Bali,* Cambridge: Cambridge University Press, 1977, pp. 146-64.

22. The scholar who has published most extensively on Balinese ritual was C. Hooykaas. See for example his *Agama Tirtha: Five Studies on Balinese Religion,* Amsterdam: North Holland Publishing Company, 1964, and *A Balinese Temple Festival,* The Hague: Nijhoff, 1977. See further David J. Stuart-Fox, *Once a Century: Pura Besakih and the Eka Dasa Rudra Festival,* Jakarta: Sinar Haraphan and Citra Indonesia, 1982; Ny I Gusti Agung Putra, *Upakara-Yadnya,* Dénpasar: Masa Baru, 1982.

23. R. M. Ng. Poerbatjaraka, "De Calon Arang," 82 (1926): 110-80. The role of disease and exorcism in shaping Balinese culture has been the subject of a number of studies by Barbara Lovric.

24. On Balinese law, see P. L. van Bloemen Waanders, "Aanteekening omtrent de Zeden en Gebruiken der Balinezen," *TBG* 8 (1859):105-279, especially pp. 201-66.

highly praised as his father, and perhaps some of the greatness of his rule has been retrospectively attributed to his father's time. The Dutch were looking for a single ruler with whom to deal, the main purpose of those dealings being to enter into a trading relationship by which they could have Bali at their economic convenience.[25] The Dutch only sought to find the major cities and trading ports, and to get information about political alliances, state organization, trade goods, agriculture, population and military might.

They found what they were looking for: a strong ruler with sufficient kingly splendor, principal cities at Gèlgèl and Kapal, with a busy port at Kuta in the south and a major harbor at what is now called Padang Bai. Through these harbors came spices from the islands of the east, Indian textiles from the west, Chinese porcelain from the north, and the other valuable items of international trade. Out of the ports came the rice of Bali and its subject island Lombok, as well as cotton and textiles.

The chief minister of Bali informed the Dutch that the king's subjects numbered 300,000, which made Bali one of the most densely populated islands in the world at that time, a reputation it was to maintain until the nineteenth century. Its density of over thirty-nine people per square kilometer exceeded that of China (thirty-seven) and South Asia (thirty-two), and was almost four times the population density of Europe at the same time.[26] At the end of the sixteenth century Bali's military might was considerable, and it was about to launch a major military expedition of 20,000 men to Java to challenge the major kingdom of Java, Mataram. The chief minister of Bali at that time, the man with whom the Dutch met, was Kiai Lér.

The Dutch image of the glory and power of the king of Bali was not, then, so far removed from the Balinese images of their World

---

25. See Boon, *The Anthropological Romance,* pp. 10-19.

26. Cf. Anthony Reid, "Low Population Growth and Its Causes in Pre-Colonial Southeast Asia," in Norman G. Owen (ed.), *Death and Disease in Southeast Asia: Explorations in Social, Medical and Demographic History, Singapore*: Oxford University Press, 1987, pp. 32-47. He uses the figure of 600,000 for the population of Bali, which does not make sense in the light of retrospective demographic evidence that puts the population at around 500,000 in 1800. Information from Kim Streatfield, quoted in L. Connor, In Darkness and Light: A Study of Peasant Intellectuals in Bali (diss.), University of Sydney, 1982, p. 87. The figures of 700,000 for the 1830s, rising to 720,000 in 1845, 892,500 in 1849, and 900,000 in 1874 seem to bear out this assessment.

Ruling King. The Dutch did not understand that the Bali they saw was the end product of a series of major historical changes, nor did they understand the subtleties of Balinese religion and social order, but they did share the Balinese sense of the king being at the center of this social order.

Although the idea of the World Ruler served to support the importance of kingship as the key element of society, it was a double-edged sword. The image of the World Ruler conveyed ideas of ethical behavior and the correct way for a kingdom to be run. Rulers who failed to live up to the image were likely to see their subjects desert them or their ministers rebel against them. Two such rebellions occurred in the 1500s; a third in the seventeenth century was to bring to an end Bali's golden age.

Romantic Princes: 1651-1815

In 1651 the great empire of Bali was shattered into smaller kingdoms, and for a century and a half new kingdoms regularly rose and fell. Not until 1800 did a stable set of nine kingdoms finally emerge. This age of political instability was also the age in which Bali was seen overseas as a savage and violent place, primarily because of its slave trading reputation. The new kings of Bali, however, did not see themselves as slave traders and despots. In their eyes this was a romantic time when handsome princes waged war and conquered princesses on the path to kingship. The Dutch "savage Bali" was not so far from the world of these war-mongering princes in its focus on violence, but the Dutch and the Balinese conceived of this violence in completely different terms.

In this time of new kingdoms everyone could be his own emperor, even if his empire consisted of only two or three villages. Between 1651 and 1800 the old image of kingship, the idea of the Hindu World Ruler, did not die out. Instead, one World Ruler was replaced by many, and the "world" of the kingdom shrank accordingly. To the idea of the World Ruler the courts added the romantic image of princes on the make, an image presented in narratives called Pañji stories—the one image simply complemented the other.

The various Pañji stories depict a prince who is unrecognized as such, but who gradually proves himself as a hero, taking on the name Pañji. The tales started in Java in the thirteenth- or fourteenth century, and spread from there as far as Thailand and Burma. Their major setting was the kingdoms of Java before Majapahit. These stories were known in Bali from the time when it was part of the empire of Majapahit, and from these origins the stories maintained a focus on Javanese culture and its continuation in Bali.

Pañji stories showed how the political changes going on in Bali worked. Although a few were known in Bali before the 1650s, after 1650 many more of these stories began to be written for different courts, and these stories became popular on all levels of society, particularly as they were presented in the grand theatrical form known as *gambuh,* which involved large casts and the bringing together of some of the most beautiful music and most intricate dance movements on Bali. The stories were particularly important to all the groups linked to the courts because they showed the courts in action, both in terms of the ideal lifestyle of princes and the workings of Balinese political culture.

The stories showed the courts as centers of luxury. Each court had many sets of orchestras playing the most beautiful music, and was adorned with paintings and carvings. The princes, princesses and courtiers went about in the most sumptuous of clothing—painted cloths from India or woven textiles from Java, shot with silver and painted with gold. Palaces were guarded day and night, and armies were always on the ready to charge out to battle playing their war orchestras—led by princes on horses and elephants.[27]

Wherever they went kings and princes were surrounded by thousands of followers, talking, laughing, jostling, carrying lances and umbrellas in an impressive show.[28] Art and life merged, as the same commoners who were involved in the court system performed,

27. There was only one Balinese king who actually claimed to have owned an elephant, but most others had small Timor ponies, of which black or red ones were regarded as the special horses of royalty. See P. J. Worsley, *Babad Bulèlèng: A Balinese Dynastic Genealogy,* The Hague: Nijhoff, 1972, p. 159 and H. de Graaf, "Goesti Pandji Sakti, Vorst van Boeleleng," *TGB* 83, 1 (1949):59-82, especially pp. 76-7. The archival materials cited by de Graaf are kept in the Western Manuscripts section of the KITLV, box 8, H 1005. Lintgensz, "Bali 1597" gives an equine population of 1000.

28. See the comment by H. van den Broek, "Verslag Nopens het Eiland Bali," *De Oosterling* 1 (1835): 158-236, especially pp. 200-2.

painted, sung or heard these stories of courtly romance. The emotions aroused by the beauty of the stories, which were especially rich in descriptions of sex and violence, were emotions which tied together commoners and their rulers.[29] The ties were explicitly sexual, since all the women of the kingdom were supposed to lust after the handsome princes, just as in one text it is said of the hero Pañji that women came to him, "unable to curb their passions any longer, and unashamedly offering their love to him."[30] Whether the women really saw princes that way is not recorded.

Suffused with passionate longing, these texts reflected aspects of courtly life and of personal development. Within the court context these stories helped to explain what was happening in the transition from one king to the next: they legitimized new kings by portraying them as having achieved their positions by merit as well as by birth. In this fashion the nature of kingship in Bali was seen to be in accordance with ancient patterns.

As the courts multiplied, as the number of kings, queens, princes and princesses increased, there was a need for more and more art, more paintings, jewelry, textiles, shadow-plays, dances, music, and so on. Cockfighting, martial displays, and opium smoking were all part of this. If commoners needed courts for prestige, courts needed commoners to maintain their identities.

Caught up in the romance of the courts, neither side would have seen themselves as being involved in a slave system. Slavery was simply the lowest form of service to the ruler—coerced service. The status of true slaves would have been doubly low because they were classed with those not willing to participate in the life of the courts.

The face-to-face aspect of the state put great emphasis on the character of a king. Where personality was so important, the transition from one king to the next was fraught with problems. Each king had many potential heirs, so it is a wonder that any kingdom survived more than one generation. If this sounds chaotic to us, then it was made to seem normal in the Southeast Asian context. The large body

---

29. On the Pañji stories, particularly the one known as the *Malat,* see A. Vickers, "The Desiring Prince: A Study of the Kidung Malat as Text" (diss.), University of Sydney, 1986.

30. S. O. Robson, *Wangbang Wideya: A Javanese Pañji Romance,* The Hague: Nijhoff, 1971, p. 113.

of Pañji stories grew up around the theme of competition between heirs to a throne, and these stories help to explain how Balinese saw what was going on after the empire of Gèlgèl was shattered.

Women had a say in the problem of succession, even if sometimes only indirectly. A chief wife usually achieved her position because she came from a powerful or rich family that could help shore up the king's power. So it was not simply the eldest son who inherited the throne, but the son of the chief wife. If the chief wife did not have a son, or if her son was weak, then the succession was not clear. In the king's "harem" one wife could displace another and even a chief wife could be replaced if she died early. The succession could then go either to the new or to the old chief wife's sons.

A familiar theme in the Pañji stories is that of a young prince emerging from out of nowhere to prove himself in battle, conquer beautiful women, capture booty in war, and have thousands who wanted to be his subjects. This theme was part of the political realities of succession; where a new king could not just step into his father's role, but had to build up his own personal networks; effectively he had to have his own power base or things could simply fall apart. Kingdoms were built up through alliances with other aristocrats, marriage, and the acquisition of followers who would become state officials and loyal subjects. All of these facets of kingdom building implied the accumulation of wealth. The worthy successor to kingship, or the founder of a new kingdom, was one who had proved himself in the tried and true fashion of killing other princes, establishing a treasury, and seducing or abducting princesses. He would wage war fearlessly, and "those of his opponents who survived would make their submission and offer young princesses."[31] The prince did all this in disguise, as he went in quest of his true queen, one of the many available princesses of the world. The ideal future queen was the prince's cousin, and finding her put a gloss of romantic love over the pragmatic nature of arranged marriages.[32]

It is easy to see this period of 150 years as an era of chaos after

---

31. ibid, p. 59.

32. See Boon, *Anthropological Romance,* pp. 197-202. My main disagreement with Boon's analysis here is the reductive character of his discussion of the romance theme in Pañji tales which is produced by his too-heavy reliance on the earlier work of Rassers.

the Golden Age of Gèlgèl. In that earlier era the kingdom looked very stable, and the idea of Bali as a major power in the Indonesian archipelago was easy to convey. However, throughout most of Southeast Asian history the big kingdoms have been the exception rather than the rule. The empire of Gèlgèl could only ever last briefly. Kings came to power without bureaucracies or direct networks of control over what was happening. Rule could only be carried out through lords or palace appointees, and therefore the character of the king and his personal relations with the various people of power in the kingdom were crucial to a smooth-running realm.

The Rebel and the New Kings: 1651-1700

The man who brought an end to the old kingdom of Gèlgèl in 1651 was Gusti Agung Maruti, the prime minister of the time. Very little is known about Gusti Agung—he told the Dutch little about himself, and practically all the retrospective Balinese accounts cast him as something of an ambitious villain. The letters he sent to the Dutch simply assert his status as ruler of Bali, discuss one or two details about slavery, and then express an interest in receiving gifts of the beautiful and expensive Indian chintz textiles which formed an important part of trade and royal display in the Indonesian archipelago. The Balinese accounts, written over two hundred years later, show Gusti Agung as having a lust for power and being motivated more by greed than by any sense of responsibility.

The man himself was probably partially motivated by desire for power, but his intervention in Balinese politics may have been more complex than that. He took over Gèlgèl at a point where the king, Déwa Pacekan, had died, and his two sons were fighting over the throne.[33] This was just another succession dispute, certainly, but Gusti Agung may have seen it as something that would have irrevocably destroyed Bali's power, and so may have been acting to save the kingdom.

---

33. The details of this have been obscured by the later Balinese accounts, which seem to leave out a number of the kings of Bali. A list of dates and names is provided by a text called *Babad Gumi* Gedong Kirtya MS 808. This text lists the deaths of I Déwa (Dalem) Seganing in 1623, of I Déwa Pambayun and I Déwa Ktut in 1632, and of I Déwa di Madé in 1638, whereas accounts using the later Balinese sources have it that Gusti Agung Maruti rebelled against I Déwa or Dalem di Madé: cf. Stuart-Fox, "Pura Besakih," p. 148.

Whatever his motives, his intervention opened the floodgates. With the fall of the dynasty of Baturènggong, those who had been lords or office-holders in the old kingdom of Gèlgèl now felt free to claim to be kings in their own areas.

In north Bali the hitherto loyal lord Gusti Pañji Sakti became king of a new kingdom of Bulèlèng around the 1660s. This was the same Gusti Pañji Sakti known to the Dutch, a truly heroic figure. He had been sent from Gèlgèl to rule the area north of the mountain range on its behalf, but gradually established power by maneuvering against the other major lords of the area, notably those of Sangsit to the east. To the west was the area of Bañjar, and there Pañji Sakti obtained his control by an alliance with a powerful priestly family who were immediate descendants of the eldest son of Nirartha.[34]

On Java there were other rebellions. The rise of Pañji Sakti coincided with a major revolt against the creeping Dutch interest in Java, a revolt started by Trunajaya, a prince of Madura with ambitions to create his own new world ruling kingdom. The resulting chaos for the Dutch provided an opportunity for militarily strong figures from all over the archipelago to stake a claim to what was going on in Java, and Gusti Pañji Sakti was not one to miss an opportunity.[35]

Pañji Sakti had competitors, the aspiring kings of south Bali, of which, from the late seventeenth century to the end of the eighteenth century, there were a confusing number. Two names that were to survive into nineteenth-century kingdoms were the neighboring south Balinese lords of Badung and Mengwi. Both of these kingdoms started off as relatively small areas, but both picked up on the slave trading boom through their shared access to the natural harbor of Kuta.

War became an institution in Bali. There were so many new kingdoms it was inevitable that they would be constantly clashing

---

34. For the late nineteenth-century version of this, see Worsley, *Babad Bulèlèng;* and de Graaf, "Gusti Pandji Sakti."

35. See Henk Schulte Nordholt, *Macht, Mensen en Middelen: Patronen van Dynamic in de-Balische Politiek* ± 1700-1840 (unpub. MA thesis), Vrije Universiteit, Amsterdam, 1980, pp. 32-54.

in order to assert their very right to exist as kingdoms. As soon as a kingdom emerged it had to fight to conquer and absorb all the neighboring lords, and then take on one of the bigger contenders in the kingdom stakes.

Gusti Agung Maruti had not wiped out the former royal family in his revolt; one of the main heirs to the throne had fled to the east, and in the 1680s was hiding out in the area controlled by the mountain lords of Sidemen, who, with the lords of Badung and Bulèlèng, were part of a coalition aiming to depose Gusti Agung. The religious sign that an attack on Gusti Agung should take place was apparently an eruption of Mount Agung, the mountain that dominates Bali's geographic profile. Gusti Agung was put to flight and a new royal house, which was a continuation of the Gèlgèl dynasty, was set up just three kilometers north of the old capital, at Klungkung, which the heir to the throne made the new capital of Bali. In 1686 one of the other lords, Ngurah Batulèpang of Batuan, was credited with defeating Gusti Agung Maruti in a battle in which 1200 of his followers died.[36]

By the beginning of the eighteenth century a new high kingdom was in place: Klungkung. The other kings acknowledged the new rulers and their title of Déwa Agung, but it was not enough to stop them being kings in their own right. The existence of one kingdom of higher status than the others was convenient for all, because it meant that there was still a "Bali"—that is to say that the principle of Bali as a world still existed, even though Bali now consisted of many kingdoms.[37]

The Birth of the Nine Kingdoms

At the beginning of the eighteenth century, Mengwi, in south central Bali, emerged beside Klungkung as a major kingdom. From obscure beginnings as descendants of a branch of Gusti Agung Maruti's

---

36. For the Dutch reports, based on a letter of 1687 claiming that Gusti Agung was killed, see de Graaf, "Gusti Pandji Sakti" and de Graaf archival notes. The Balinese *Babad Gumi* says that Gusti Agung was only defeated, not killed, in that year, and that in 1691 he was again fighting the king of Klungkung, with aid from Ngurah Jlantik.

37. For a Pañji story relating to the establishment of Klungkung, see C. C. Berg, "Kidung Harsa-Wijaya: Tekst, Inhoudsopgave en Aanteekeningen," *BKI* 88 (1931): 1-238.

family, Mengwi suddenly appeared on the site of the old west Balinese capital of Kapal and soon eclipsed Pañji Sakti's kingdom of Bulèlèng.[38] Like all the other new kingdoms, Mengwi waged war against its competitors, especially against Bulèlèng. The war was, however, followed by a marriage alliance when the king of Mengwi married Pañji Sakti's daughter.

The marriage came at around the time Mengwi eclipsed Bulèlèng on Java. After the wars and turmoil in the east of that island, Mengwi was able to send its own expedition to take command of the east Javanese kingdom of Blambangan, and in the process to gain control of the west Balinese minor kingdom of Jembrana, itself a territory disputed by all its neighbors.

As Mengwi and Klungkung emerged as the main players in central Bali, their relationship evolved into a kind of partnership. There were other competitors, of course: for example Sukawati, founded by one of the sons of the Déwa Agung. Sukawati expanded from an area of control asserted by the local ruler of Batuan, Maruti's conqueror, Batulèpang. Batulèpang lost control of the area soon afterwards, in Balinese legends cursed by a priest for debasing him when he asked for food, Batulèpang's house was destroyed and his descendants scattered. Sukawati only lasted a few generations and today is best known for the invention of the *lègong* dance, the dance of the little girls.[39]

Its competitors were Bulèlèng in the north, and the kingdom that was to become the most powerful in Bali, Karangasem in the east. Bulèlèng declined in its fortunes after the death of Gusti Pañji. In the 1760s it, along with Jembrana, was subsumed by Karangasem. By that stage Karangasem had grown until its dynasty ruled the island of Lombok and the whole of east Bali, including the former domain of Sidemen.

In the 1680s Karangasem had controlled only the small eastern

38. For the history of Mengwi, see Schulte Nordholt, Een Balische Dynastie: Hiërarchie en Conflict in de Negara Mengwi 1700-1940 (diss.), Vrije Universiteit, 1988, Haarlem: Multiprint Noord.

39. See R. van Eck, "Schetsen van het Eiland Bali," TNI 7 (1878):85-130,165-213, 325-56, 405-30; 8 (1879): 36-60, 104-34, 286-305, 365-87; 9 (1880): 1-39, 102-32, 195-221, 401-29; pt II: 1-18, 81-96, pt II, vol. 7, pp. 34-41; de Graaf notes.

tip of Bali, a valley between the eastern mountain of Bukit and the Turtle Hill. It successfully interfered in a succession dispute in Lombok, which allowed the first Karangasem kingdoms to be set up on Lombok. Decades of struggle followed, in which the rulers of the next island, Sumbawa, together with wandering aristocrats and pirates from South Sulawesi, fought to keep the Balinese out. By gaining control of Lombok, Karangasem gained what was then one of the major rice-bowls of Southeast Asia. In 1740 Gusti Wayahan Tegeh, one of the sons of the ruler of Karangasem, organized an expedition to take proper control of Lombok. He "civilized" the island by bringing over the priesthood, law books and other texts that embodied the essence of Balinese culture, and he set up Balinese kingdoms there along the lines of the ancient Javanese precedent of Majapahit. Some six Balinese kingdoms, all branches of the Karangasem dynasty, were then established on the island, all based closely together in western Lombok.[40]

The main king of Karangasem saw himself as a Pañji Prince in the process of kingdom building.[41] In the section of west Lombok where the new kingdoms were based, all the major centers were given names from the Pañji stories. The kings collected the greatest works of the Balinese and Javanese literary tradition and made their courts even greater centers of culture than those of their competitors in Bali. Paradoxically, by following what they saw as a Javanese model of culture, they were being ultra-Balinese. As often happens in colonies, the Karangasem kingdoms on Lombok tried so hard to be typically Balinese that they ended up being exceptional.

Karangasem conquered Lombok at the same time as it expanded to the west, and at one stage it actually succeeded in defeating Klungkung, although it allowed the latter state to retain its separate existence and rulers. The defeat of Klungkung was a prelude to the conquest of the district of Sidemen, which was carried out through

40. See W. Byvanck, "Onze Betrekkingen tot Lombok," *De Gids* 16 (1894): 134-57, 299-337; A. van der Kraan, *Lombok: Conquest, Colonization and Underdevelopment,* Singapore: Heinemann, 1980.

41. I Madé Kanta (pers. comm.).

the aid of the neighboring lords of Sibetan.[42] These same lords then assisted in the 1768 conquest of Bulèlèng.[43]

The other kingdoms that were to emerge towards the latter part of the century were, at the beginning of the century, either minor powers or non-existent. Badung remained a small domain under Mengwi's control for most of the period, while the kingdom of Tabanan, which bordered Mengwi and Badung to the west, was small and active only in waging the occasional war. At the end of the century the new kingdoms were Gianyar and Bangli; the former grew out of the power base of a distant relative of the Klungkung dynasty, the latter came out of a coalition of related lords who ruled in the north of Klungkung.[44]

Romantic Princes or Slave Traders?

The Dutch and the Balinese had very different perceptions about the role of slave trading in seventeenth- and eighteenth-century Bali.

The Dutch saw slavery as the basis of Bali's economy and felt that new lords like Pañji Sakti were able to become powerful because their ambitions could be supported by selling subjects.[45] The fact that all the powerful new kingdoms had their capitals close to harbors lent further support to this view. The Balinese saw that the growth of slavery supported the transformation of Bali from one kingdom to nine, but the nine kings perceived the new kingdoms in terms of the Pañji romances, which explained the kingdoms as a continuation of ancient Javanese politics.

Lords did not make themselves into kings simply because they saw that a new slave market had evolved in Batavia. What happened was more complicated: the new slave markets developed opportunities for lords. Theoretically there were always precedents for the establishment of new kingdoms, but while Gèlgèl was strong the

42. Stuart-Fox, Pura Besakih; Vickers, The Desiring Prince, app. 2.

43. On the date of the conquest, see the Balinese commemoration in S. O. Robson, *Wangbang Wideya,* p. 53; and J. Kats, "Een Balische Brief uit 1768 aan de Gouveneur van Java's Noordkust," *Feestbundel Koninklijk Bataviaasch Genootschap 150-jaarig Bestaan* 2 vols, Weltevreden: Kolff, 1929, vol. I, pp. 291-6.

44. Van Eck, "Schetsen," section III, p. 349 & XII, p. 212.

45. For more details see Nordholt, Macht, Mensen en Middelen, pp. 32-48.

lords did not have any basis for claiming to be kings. At a point of weakness in the first part of the seventeenth century, the lords seized on existing ideas of the right of rebellion and the path to kingship, and backed these ideas with the new economic possibility of selling subjects as slaves.

Where did they get the slaves from? Describing the mechanism by which slavery was run means describing what happened to the majority of Balinese while all these lords and princes were staking their claims for power. The history of Bali at this time was the history of "great men" involved in politics. But at the margins of this history is the story of Balinese peasants being shunted around the countryside, following their lords in battle, fleeing their homes before invading armies, or being sold into slavery.

Capture in war was the first means by which someone could be made into a slave. One Pañji story described how, as an army moved forward, it took prisoners: "all the villages were laid waste and razed to the ground, and their inhabitants were captured, both men and women."[46] Prior to the rebellion of Gusti Agung Maruti the majority of Balinese would have been called upon only occasionally to serve as soldiers against the king's enemies in Java or Lombok, but there were enough people to have meant that duties in war and of contributing labor and produce to royal rituals were not too onerous. After the seventeenth century every Balinese would have been more directly involved in warfare. As each local lord wanted to set himself up as a king, villagers found it harder to avoid being made into soldiers and subjects. Threats and promises kept them tied to lords. The proliferation of rulers and the increase in warfare meant that if a group of peasants did not have a lord, they would be immediately taken over. Villagers had a vested interest in ensuring that their lord won his battles. If he lost and the enemy captured their village, they, their wives and children could be sold to foreigners as booty.

There were also more subtle means of enslaving villagers. Increasingly the revamped version of ancient Javanese law administered by the kings and priests came to be used as a mechanism for turning out slaves. The ancient law books set down the death penalty

---

46. Robson, *Wangbang Wideya*, p. 117.

for such serious crimes as murder and black magic and heavy fines for other crimes, such as theft. The power of life or death that these courts wielded meant that the death sentence could be converted to a sentence of slavery at the discretion of the judges. If poorer peasants could not pay their fines, then they too could become the property either of the court or of the individual to whom they owed money, and likewise could be sold.[47]

The kings even helped put people into debt by staging large cockfights in their capitals. The passion and extravagance encouraged by this exciting sport led many peasants to bet more than they could afford. As with any gambling, the hope of great wealth and the drama of a contest fuelled ambitions that few could afford and at the end of the day, when the last spur had sunk into the chest of the last rooster, many peasants had no home and family to return to. They, their wives and children would be sold in Java. The kings also profited from a tax on this staging of cockfights.

Women were inevitably losers. Although they never took part in cockfights, they were sold with their husbands. Widows who were left without male heirs became state property, and with their goods and any daughters could be disposed of as the rajas saw fit. Some females who were thus given slave status were incorporated into the court as concubines or servants; the unlucky ones became roving prostitutes.

As kingdoms proliferated, so did the state courts, the numbers of cockfights, the royal rituals, and all of the other activities associated with being part of a kingdom. All this depended on having large numbers of followers. The new kings needed to insinuate themselves into the village sphere, and they did this through the system of service.

Kings and States

The Pañji model stressed the positive side of slavery and royal protection. Peasants did have something to gain from the state after all, and their participation in the courts was part of royal patronage of

---

47. See also the discussion of slavery in Alfons van der Kraan, "Bali: Slavery and Slave Trade," in A. Reid (ed.), *Slavery, Bondage and Dependency in Southeast Asia,* pp. 315-40, St Lucia: University of Queensland Press, 1983.

culture. Service or tribute to the king was a means by which subjects could share in the romance of princes.

Because the tribute system differentiated between those who were outsiders and those who were insiders to the courts, royal patronage provided the possibility for commoners to become "insiders." Commoners were appointed to state office, but in itself this did not automatically allow them to become insiders, since each royal family also had extended networks of family members and itinerant aristocrats it could also use in state offices. The most important feature of becoming an insider was participation in the culture of the courts, and by this means the courts maintained the identity between their cultural activities and Balinese culture as a whole. For the artists and others there was the direct reward of special rice field grants, relief from various forms of taxation and work duties to the king,[48] and royal bestowal of signs of status that showed these people were indeed insiders, elevated above their neighbors. As major figures in the state, commoners who were part of the court would also have been entitled to a share in the redistribution of wealth that accompanied state rituals.[49]

The Pañji model explained to all those who were linked to courts the many different facets of the political culture of Bali from the late seventeenth century onwards: the luxurious lifestyle of the courts and the prestige that went with it; the "Javaneseness" of Balinese culture; the simultaneous existence of many kingdoms; and conflicts within royal families, which went hand in hand with ties that bordered on the incestuous.

In the Pañji stories many kingdoms existed, but they were interrelated. The kings of each were brothers, brothers-in-law or cousins, and one kingdom had higher status or greater importance than the others. To the Balinese the comparison with the many kingdoms and Klungkung was obvious: it was the kingdom of higher status, to which the others should defer.

---

48. See P. de Kat Angelino, "Over de Smeden en Eenige Andere Ambachtslieden op Bali," *TBG* 61 & 62 (1921-2): 207-65 & 370-424.

49. For a discussion of the material dimension of royal rituals, something overlooked by Geertz in his *Negara,* see A. Vickers, "Writing Ritual: The *Kidung Karya Ligya/Geguritan Padem Warak"* paper given at the Balinese State and Society Workshop 1986.

The Pañji stories were about cousins and brothers either fighting with each other or becoming close allies. In these kingdoms where everyone was so closely related sibling rivalry and incest were always strong possibilities. As a defined set of Balinese kingdoms emerged towards the end of the eighteenth century dynasties began turning in on themselves, and the life of the courts became closer and closer to the life depicted in the Pañji stories.

The story of the birth of the kingdom of Bangli was a case in point. In the eighteenth century the main ruler of the area was a lord of the king of Klungkung, Déwa Rai of Taman Bali, a ruthless schemer and an oppressor of his people. He married his cousin, Déwa Ayu Dénbañcingah, daughter of the former head of Bangli district, and became involved in a plot to overthrow his uncle, the ruler of Nyalian. The plot involved a takeover of the area by Klungkung and Gianyar, and the adoption of Déwa Gedé Tangkeban, son of the ruler of Nyalian, by Déwa Rai. Déwa Rai's reputation for cruelty, and the hatred that his subjects felt towards him, were used by his adopted son, who had an affair with his adoptive father's wife. Together they induced disaffected followers to murder Déwa Rai. Déwa Gedé became king of Taman Bali, then married Déwa Ayu Dénbañcingah, his adopted stepmother and cousin, to become king of Bangli, her family district, which gave its name to the new kingdom.[50]

Similar examples come from other kingdoms. The royal house of Badung split into factions that were descended from three brothers, and within each faction cousins married cousins and fought with brothers at a confusing rate. Throughout the nineteenth century the fortunes of each branch waxed and waned, with the Kesiman branch of the family holding most of the power up until the 1860s.[51]

Cannibalism was added to the charge of incest leveled against the ruling branch of the Karangasem dynasty, the most contorted of dynasties from the 1790s until the 1840s. The kingdoms of Bulèlèng, Karangasem and Singasari on Lombok passed from hand to hand

---

50. P. L. van Bloemen Waanders (with P. J. Veth), "Bijdragen tot de Kennis van het Eiland Bali," *TNI* 2 (1868): 370-410.

51. See Schulte Nordholt, Macht, Mensen en Middelen, pp. 63-106.

between a set of brothers and their sons. The relationships became even more convoluted than in Badung as cousin married cousin, and brother killed brother, until in 1823 one of the kings of Bulèlèng, Gusti Pahang, threw out his cousin, the king of Karangasem, and married his own sister. This was too much for most of his followers and priests. They deserted him and let him be killed, cut up and the pieces thrown away as punishment for his crimes. The cousin who came back to kill him was rumored to have practiced human sacrifice and cannibalism to regain power.[52] If the defamatory victor's rumor had any truth in it, it may be related to rituals found elsewhere in Southeast Asia where headhunting and devouring the liver of enemies bestowed great might upon a winner in battle.

With the proliferation of kings during the period 1650 to around 1800 the Balinese needed layers of image and meaning on their society. The idea of the World Ruler was enough to sustain a king and a king-centered society, but now there were many World Rulers, each of who was keen to fight the others. The Pañji tales of courtly romance added the necessary new layer of meaning to the idea of the World Ruling King.

Bali was, as the Dutch had thought, a warlike society. Warfare was one aspect of what princes did to prove themselves, how they ran their politics, how they acquired wealth, wives, subjects and slaves. The courtly stories romanticized warfare by making it a normal part of existence on Bali, but they did nothing to disguise the bloody and deadly effects of war. If anything they exaggerated the casualties and the gore to make the princes sound even more heroic. In one description of a battle, enemy corpses were described as "piling up like mountains, and their blood was like the sea."[53] Victorious princes were supposed to follow Indonesia-wide practices of taking enemy heads in battle, and drinking the blood of foes in victory.[54]

At the beginning of the nineteenth century Bali was locked into a situation where cultural activity had to increase as the competing courts and princes multiplied. Although the number of kingdoms

---

52. Vickers, "The Desiring Prince," app. 2.

53. Robson, *Wangbang Wideya*, p. 137.

54. ibid.

became fixed, there was still a great deal of movement within kingdoms, and still a number of wars between kingdoms. The models of the World Ruler and the romantic princes were not adequate to explain all aspects of the social and religious forces at work, so during the nineteenth century new layers of images were developed.

Ancestors and Dynasties: 1815-1908

The nineteenth century started with a bang for Bali: the largest natural explosion ever recorded, the eruption of Mount Tambora on Sumbawa, to the east of Lombok in 1815. In the period between this eruption and the smaller 1883 explosion of Krakatau, to the west of Java, the Balinese rulers had consolidated their kingdoms and strengthened their images of ancestors. These rulers, drawing on the expertise of the *brahmana* priests, sponsored the writing of extensive genealogies that linked them to the ancient kingdoms of Java. While they were doing this, dynasties were splitting and warring internally, and increasingly power had to be shared between aristocrats and commoners. At a time when royal power was divided, charters of ancestry helped to bolster kingly authority.

Families traced their ancestry back to great moments when gods and angels procreated or ancient kings swept all before them. These families needed to keep in touch with their ancestors and to channel the magical powers of the past into the present. Knowledge of origins was necessary in order to puzzle out the complexities of status and power that had been created, thus triggering a fashion for genealogy writing. Combined with the diffusion of the aristocracy was an increase in the power of commoner families, meaning that the aristocracy had to share power. As a reaction to this the aristocracy needed to assert its separateness and nobility and in order to do so it laid greater stress on its origins in Java's Majapahit empire. At the same time a new genre of literature, and theater developed which focused on the role and identity of commoners.

Klungkung tended to set the lead for the other kingdoms, and much of the story of the nineteenth century occurred in and around Klungkung. It was Klungkung that was responsible for the writing of the first major modern dynastic genealogy in 1819, and Klungkung that is credited with a key role in developing a new art form related to the rise of commoners in the state: the *arja* dance drama and its complementary poetic form called *geguritan*. The kingdom also held some of the most spectacular state rituals of the era, asserting its high status through the symbols used in the rituals and demonstrating the political importance of religious ceremonies. Klungkung could not dictate to or control, the other kingdoms, but it was still the central kingdom of Bali, a kind of passive center around which the other states were organized.[55]

At the end of the eighteenth century Déwa Agung Putra I, direct descendant of Baturènggong, put Klungkung back on the map of Balinese politics. He did so with help from Karangasem, because his wife was the leading princess of that eastern kingdom.

Déwa Agung Putra was a strong ruler, a manipulator, who not only fought his own wars, but started wars for other people, and it was his ability to initiate warfare that led to his own death. Déwa Agung Putra had fought to keep the throne of Klungkung from his uncle, Déwa Agung Pañji. Putra's father, Déwa Agung Sakti, was the mad king of Klungkung, who outlived most of his children. He was left to himself in the main palace of the capital, while Putra set up a new palace at the port of Kusamba, close to his Karangasem supporters, and Pañji fell back on Gianyar's support. When Putra won control of Klungkung, he ensured that relationships with Gianyar would be uneasy for decades. Both Gianyar and Klungkung became embroiled in the family feuding that created the new state of Bangli by taking sides with opposing branches of that family. At the end of the series of wars that inaugurated Bangli's existence, in 1809, Déwa Agung Putra had what is a bad death in any culture—he had a bamboo bridge over a ravine cut out from underneath him.[56]

In Bali such a death is particularly inauspicious, for it means that special rituals for the dead need to be held. Dispensations had to be received from the priesthood to allow the rituals to go ahead. Despite this disadvantage, his children spent the next four decades commemorating his name and holding the rituals for his immortal remains.

---

55. Cf. James J. Fox, "The Great Lord Rests at the Center: The Paradox of Powerlessness in European-Timorese Relations," *Canberra Anthropology* 5,2 (1982): 22-33.

56. For this date see van Eck, "Schetsen," pt III, p. 346.

Klungkung was in a mess in 1809. When Déwa Agung Putra was killed the old palace in Klungkung proper was completely run down, and could not be used again until Déwa Agung Sakti, the mad king, had died. The running of the state was in the hands of Gusti Ayu Karang, the Karangasem queen. She was not the first of Bali's ruling queens—already Badung and Mengwi had had widows in the role—but she created new conditions for her daughter, Déwa Agung Isteri Kanya, to become the "Virgin Queen" of Klungkung in later decades.

The Karangasem queen is not well remembered. Decades after her death stories were still circulating about her ferocity, how, for example, she had a princess of Badung, one of her co-wives, poisoned in an act of jealousy.[57] After the death of Déwa Agung Putra I only one son, not one of very high birth at that, was left alive. For fear of the wicked stepmother, this son had to be hidden in the house of a loyal commoner family at Lebah, near the main river that flows by the capital of Klungkung.

A queen was not acceptable to all the factions in Klungkung politics. The Virgin Queen had the support of her mother's family and from the newly arrived priestly house of Geria Pidada, which had come to Klungkung from Karangasem during the period of the dispute over succession. Many other powerful families felt that only a male could be ruler, and so Klungkung was left with two rulers in an uneasy coalition: the Virgin Queen and her stepbrother, Déwa Agung Putra II. When he came to the throne he brought with him the commoner family of Lebah which had sheltered him as a child. Their leader now became one of the powerful *patih* or chief ministers of the state. From the circumstances of his rule it appears that Putra II was not a particularly strong character, whereas the Virgin Queen's reputation tended to reflect her mother's ferocity. To the Dutch she was an Amazon, but to her ruling clique she was the epitome of wisdom and cultured spirituality.

Déwa Agung Putra II's ascent occurred at the worst possible time, at the eruption of Mount Tambora. This eruption was terrible

---

57. See R. Friederich, *The Civilisation and Culture of Bali* (trans. R. Rost), New Dehli: Susil-Gupta, 1959, p. 117.

in its scale, sending out an estimated 150 to 180 cubic kilometers of ejecta (as opposed to the 20 cubic kilometers from Krakatau) and causing as many as 96,000 deaths overall (Krakatau only caused 36,000 deaths).[58] The explosion itself sent shock-waves that were being felt on Bali long afterwards. The death toll was probably much higher than the 25,000 or 3% of the population estimated by some Dutch observers. Corpses littered the roads and beaches of Bali. On nearby Lombok, for example, one-sixth of the population was estimated to have been wiped out. Late in 1815 there was a mudslide in Bulèlèng that killed 10,000.[59] The layer of ash which the eruption left on top of everything was over 30 centimeters thick. This may have eventually been good for soil fertility, but initially it wiped out Bali's rice crop. Bali's rice production was usually supplemented by the rich rice-bowl of Lombok, but since that island was even more heavily affected, famine followed, with rat plagues and epidemics.

The famine and disease resulting from the eruption continued for a decade. An epidemic of 1817 claimed thousands of lives, including the king of Badung.[60] In 1818 the Dutch emissary, van den Broek, reported as many as thirty-five corpses lying in the streets, by the side of the road between Badung and Gianyar. In 1821 a seaman reported corpses littering the beach in north Bali, and people begging to sell their children to him to buy food.[61] In 1828 a smallpox epidemic in south Bali again struck rulers and subjects alike, leaving the workforce so depleted that the rice crop could not be planted, and causing all rituals and cockfights to be suspended. Corpses littered the seashore again.[62]

---

58. These figures come from a review by T. Simkin of R. S. Fiske's *Krakatau 1883, RIMA* 19,1 (1985): 215-17.

59. For the mudslide, see Worsley, *Babad Bulèlèng,* pp. 237-8. For the other figures see M. Le baron P. Melvill de Carnbee, "Essai d'une Description des Îles de Bali et de Lombok," *Le Moniteur des Indes Orientales et Occidentales,* La Haye, Belinfante Frères, 1846-7, pp. 87-92, 160-80, 252-62, 280-94, 331-8, 380; van den Broek, "Verslag," p. 183; and Schulte Nordholt, Macht, Mensen en Middelen, p. 147.

60. Dubois letters, 12 August 1828, no. 73, Arsip Nasional Republik Indonesia, Bali 4/11.

61. Van den Broek, "Verslag," p. 176; J. Olivier, *Land- en Zeetochten in Nederland's Indië, 1817-1826,* Amsterdam: Sulpke, 1827, vol. I, p. 450 n.

62. Dubois letters, 12 August 1928, no. 73, 30 September 1828, no. 88 & 9 November 1928, unnumbered.

The response amongst the rulers was to use up the state reserves of wealth to try and keep their kingdoms going. Once the initial crisis was over and the subsequent mouse plagues and crop destruction were spreading, they held exorcistic and other rituals to stem the pestilence and disease. Some kingdoms called off all warfare in order to concentrate their spiritual energies on this time of crisis; others used the period to take over weaker kingdoms. This strategy was employed in a particularly successful manner by the rulers of the kingdom of Mataram on Lombok, who in the first part of the nineteenth century absorbed all neighbors.

After this devastation came a period of reconstruction and the emergence of a new Bali. In Klungkung the Virgin Queen and her brother began this reconstruction on many levels. Déwa Agung Isteri Kanya herself was famous for her religious and literary activities. She and her brother sponsored the restoration of the old palace of Klungkung, to which they returned. They were also strong supporters of the many state temples, and the Virgin Queen spent much of her reign meditating in the Flower Garden Temple to the north of the capital. She wrote Old Javanese poetry, and sponsored a number of priests in her circle to do the same.[63] During their joint reign the school of traditional painting in the village of Kamasan, two kilometers south of Klungkung, was rejuvenated.[64]

Bali as a whole began to revive by the late 1820s, increasing its rice output dramatically, and developing new export crops such as indigo and coffee to compensate for the disappearing market in slaves. It now looked to the new English entrepot of Singapore, founded in 1819, which was a major provider of opium to Bali.[65] One of the roles of opium was as a luxury item in the courts. Royalty led the fashion in its use, and all those who aspired to the glories of the courts followed suit. At the height of opium usage the

63. See A. Vickers, "The Writing of Kakawin and Kidung on Bali," *BKI* 138 (1982): 493-5. The text has been edited by C. C. Berg, *Kidung Pamañcangah: De Geschiedenis van het Rijk van Gèlgèl,* Santpoort: Mees, 1929.

64. A. Vickers, "A Balinese Illustrated Manuscript of the Siwaratrikalpa," *BKI* 138 (1982): 443-69.

65. See Schulte Nordholt, Macht, Mensen en Middelen, p. 99. On Bali's trade with Singapore, see Wong Lin Ken, "The Trade of Singapore 1819-68," *Journal of the Malayan Branch of the Royal Asiatic Society* 33 (1960).

island was importing 200 chests a year, each kingdom consuming between 20 and 40 of those chests.[66] The aristocratic Pañji vision of the sumptuous palace life took on greater meaning in the drug-induced haze of the courtly world.

Writing Family Histories

Klungkung took the initiative in history writing while Bali was still in crisis. In 1819, while the effects of Tambora's eruption were still being felt, Déwa Agung Putra II sponsored one of the major works of literature about the origins of the nineteenth-century kingdoms, the *Kidung Pamancangah*. The text itself tells how Majapahit created the Gèlgèl dynasty in Bali, and how Gusti Agung's revolt eventually led to the establishment of Klungkung. Readers were asked to draw a comparison with the present day: the founding of Klungkung out of the ashes of defeat was meant to be compared with the return of the ruler to the main palace of Klungkung, after chaos and exile under the influence of Karangasem. This text showed the main features dynastic genealogies were to follow in the following decades.

The establishment of Gèlgèl and the subsequent shattering of that glorious kingdom by Gusti Agung became the key events around which other dynasties could hang their genealogies. Over the nineteenth century genealogies for each royal house were written, usually by the *brahmana* attached to those houses. Each of the houses was related in these genealogies either to the main Gèlgèl dynasty (this was the case for Klungkung, Bangli, and Gianyar) or to the knights of Majapahit who came over during the Majapahit conquest (as was the case for Karangasem, Mengwi, Badung, and Tabanan), although it is typical of these genealogies that family origins could change in the light of new events.[67]

Because the genealogies were written with an eye to the branch of the family that would refer to them most often, they tend to be unreliable as sources of Balinese history. They might mention every

66. On the figures for opium consumption, see P. L. van Bloemen Waanders, "Aanteekeningen omtrent het Zeden en Gebruiken op Bali," *TBG* 8 (1859): 105-279, especially p. 187; and "T," "Bali en Lombok," *TNI* 2 (1874): 439-55.

67. See for example the changing origins of Mengwi, Friederich, *Civilisation and Culture,* p. 113; Schulte Nordholt, Macht, Mensen en Middelen, pp. 17-72.

Topèng dancer, 1930s.

sister of every grandfather of one recent branch of a family, and completely omit other branches. It was only important to state the original ancestors and the ancestors of specific branches, in the format of "X begat Y begat Z." Colorful historical details came in when they were important for the fortunes of a dynasty. Descriptions of the dissolute nature of some of the more hopeless kings of Sukawati, for example, were important because they explained how the kingdom fell apart and was taken over by Gianyar. We may be amazed at the eccentricities, decrepitude and plain incompetence of some of the ancestors mentioned in these texts, but it was as important for people to know about these as about the more noble and charismatic achievers.

The eighteenth century is often a blur in these texts. It was important to locate where families were at the time of the Maruti rebellion, and some of the accounts stopped there. The more important elements were character depictions of the key ancestors, the winners and losers. Winners, men who elevated the dynasty dramatically, were usually designated with the title of *Sakti,* which means supernatural power, moral energy, and charisma.

Not everyone had a genealogy written, but those who did not had the benefits of Balinese theater. Ancestors were displayed to society at large through dance-drama called *topèng,* which means "masked." In this theatrical form the masked form of each of the key ancestral figures was presented. The oldest surviving set of such masks, kept in a temple in the village of Blahbatuh and probably dating back to the eighteenth century, shows the key figures in the genealogies and their characteristics.[68]

In this set the noble kings like the rulers of Gèlgèl are all finely featured, with simple, light complexions. The lower-ranking characters have rough features, bordering on the comical, while many of the other lords have broad, strong features which represent their dynamic nature. These kinds of conventional ways of depicting the major characters are important in Balinese thinking about ancestors. They can be fitted into character types, so that the present-day descendants may know what their ancestors were like as people.[69]

This is not just an antiquarian interest. Balinese believe in reincarnation, and it is the character of an ancestor who is reborn in his or her descendants. Genealogies and the theatrical display of ancestors tell people about themselves and their immediate families. These same ancestors achieve the status of deities and are commemorated in ancestral temples, which are active entities seen

68. H. H. Noosten with W. F. Stutterheim & I Gusti Gedé Lanang, "De Historische Maskers van Poera Panataran Topèng, te Blahbatoe (Bali)," *Djåwå* 21 (1941): 1-26. These masks have a distinctly Javanese appearance, in line with the legend that they were taken from Java by the ancestor of the Blahbatuh royal house.

69. See Deborah Dunn, Topèng Pajegan: The Mask Dance of Bali (unpub. diss.), Union Graduate School, 1983; Elizabeth Young, Topèng in Bali: Continuity and Change in a Traditional Dance Genre (unpub. diss.), University of California at San Diego, 1980.

as determining the fortunes of families in the present. This means that the texts about families are also part of the system of ancestor worship in Bali.

Genealogies were and still are important for telling families of noble birth where they stand in relation to other families. With so many royal families and branches of royal families it became difficult in the nineteenth century to know whether marriages were being made among equals or not. An important characteristic of Balinese hierarchy is the idea that a woman should not marry beneath her, that is, that she should not marry someone of lower family or caste. To do so would lower the status of the whole family. Written genealogies were needed to keep track of all the details of marriage and the status of family—"Oh yes, it's all right for our daughter to marry Gusti A, because his ancestor was the elder brother of ours... we just needed reminding of the fact."[70]

Commoners and the Sense of Status

The craze for genealogy writing that began in the nineteenth century was part of a battle for status among and within kingdoms. Status and hierarchy are at the heart of most of Balinese culture. Texts like the *Ramayana* described kingdoms and Pañji texts detailed the process of becoming a king, but the genealogies were necessary in a new context where families had to situate themselves in relation to other families. The World Ruler concept and its attendant notion of caste were one way of ordering the hierarchy, and the Pañji stories kept the courts as the focus of social stratification, but these were not enough. Descriptions of commoner life were needed to maintain the overall sense of status difference within each of the states. Such stories highlighted the ordinary man as fat, pockmarked, wayward, but with an innate quality which could be put to the use of his family or the state. He quarreled with his wife, but loved his children dearly and strove to bring them up with a full sense of duty to religion. Folk-tales in which women are the protagonists reveal complex wrestling with fate, in which integrity has its own rewards.

---

70. For discussions of Balinese dynastic genealogies in general, see Worsley, *Babad Bulèlèng,* and H. I. R. Hinzler, The Balinese Babad."

Two state priests of Bulèlèng, Padanda Ida Gedé Madé Gunung and
Padanda Ida Gedé Wayan Buruan, 1865.

Only two groups tried to set themselves above the struggle for
status: the Klungkung royal family maintained that it was the major
and original family against which the others had to compare themselves for status, while the *brahmana* families held that caste set
them irreproachably above the aristocrats. Even these two groups
were challenged: when the upwardly mobile kingdom of Mataram on Lombok was expanding to take over east Bali it challenged
Klungkung's authority as the original dynasty; and when the *brahmana* set forward their claims to caste they were challenged both by
commoner priestly families such as the Blacksmith clan (*Pandé*), as
well as by other commoners who argued that the *brahmana* did not
live up to the ideal purity on which their theory of caste was based.

The Pandé, as with a number of other groups, held that their ancestors were equal in status to *brahmana*.

The status struggle became important not only because dynasties were becoming increasingly complicated and dividing up, but also because non-aristocratic families with high functions in the state were emerging.[71] Slavery had virtually ceased to be an export industry, so it was much harder for kings to get rid of troublesome commoners by selling them abroad. Most of the states had influential commoner families, whose leading members were heads of the taxation system and chief judges for the kingdoms.[72] In Klungkung the Lebah family supplied chief ministers for what we might now call "foreign affairs." Alternative descriptions (to those from the standard Dutch sources) of Balinese states describe how power depended on the major state offices of the royal courts and the headship of the local rulers. In most kingdoms holders of these positions were commoners.[73] An example is Bulèlèng at the beginning of Dutch rule. There sixteen out of the twenty-six district heads or *pambekel gede* were commoners, while in Gianyar, a new state run along more "feudal" lines, twenty-seven out of the fifty-four village heads or *pambekel* who stayed loyal to the king in 1884 were commoners.[74] The emergence of such commoner houses made it all the more imperative for aristocrats to assert that they were aristocrats, that they had a right to be given more respect than the powerful commoners.

At more or less the same time as dynastic genealogies became important in the nineteenth century, a new genre of sung poems appeared to define the difference between commoners and aristocrats.

---

71. Schulte Nordholt, "Een Baiische Dynastie," p. 114.

72. Korn, *Het Adatrecht,* p. 288, for the Sawunggaling family of Dénpasar and their Pamecutan equivalent, I Madé Kemoning.

73. Raden Sasrowijoyo, *Serat Purwacarita Bali,* Batavia: Landsdrukkerij, 1868.

74. Van Bloemen Waanders, "Aanteekeningen," p. 140. He also notes that the *triwangsa* or three upper castes numbered 750 out of the 6434 households in the state, and that the officials of village, state, and irrigation works numbered 1400 households, while the *pangayah* or commoners who did service to the king were 3300 households, and slaves 700 households. The Gianyar figures come from the *Geguritan Rereg Gianyar,* Hooykaas-Ktut Sangka manuscript copying project no. 3844 from Blahkiuh, pp. 3, 37-44. This text also names the important member of the Lebah family of Klungkung at that time as I Pageh (2,29). Ktut Krutuk seems to have been one of I Pageh's immediate descendants.

These poems told stories of commoner heroes and heroines and were called simply *geguritan* or "poems." The best of them were about love, black magic, spirituality and life in the state, describing in remarkable detail how people lived on a day-to-day basis, their spiritual lives, and their relationships to the political system.[75] With the *geguritan* poems a new dance-drama form, *arja,* developed as a kind of operetta telling the same stories as the poems.

While most *geguritan* were actually written by commoners, some were written by priests or aristocrats who took on commoner personae in order to make a statement about where people fitted in society. This commoner viewpoint helped to give the texts a feeling of realism in describing the actual life of everyday people. The poems both confirm the picture of an ordered hierarchy and disturb that picture. They disturb it by raising such ideas as the possibility of a commoner being granted the status of a king as a boon from the god Siwa. Although we might presume such things did not really happen, the mere existence of the idea reflected the fluidity of status in nineteenth-century Balinese society. Similarly the attributions to commoner authors, whether true or not, said something about social adjustment to the increasing importance of commoners in society. It was not enough to have one or two commoner extras or stagehands in the dramas of romantic princes. Now it became imperative to show all the aspects of commoner life—how peasants lived from day to day, the threats of black magic which confronted them, domestic disputes, or participation in the rituals of kings. Commoners like Father Brayut in the poem of the same name *(Pan Brayut)* were portrayed as having their own spiritual lives by which they could attain a kind of fulfillment independent of the rituals sponsored by courts. These texts all showed commoners as being innately coarse, lacking in the refinement of princes and princesses. But for all this,

---

75. C. J. Grader, "Brajoet: De Geschiedenis van een Balisch Gezin," *Djåwå* 19 (1939); J. Hooy-kaas-van Leeuwen Boomkamp, *De "Goddelijk Gast" op Bali: I Bagoes Diarsa, Balisch Gedicht en Volksverhaal,* Bandoeng: Nix, 1949; C. Hooykaas, *The Lay of Jayaprana: The Balinese Uriah,* London: Luzac, 1958; C. Hooykaas, *The Balinese Poem Basur: An Introduction to Magic,* The Hague: Nijhoff, 1978; A. Vickers, "Writing Ritual"; P. J. Worsley, "Een Blik in het Balische Volksleven," paper given at the Balinese State and Society Workshop 1986; and Putu (Barbara) Davies, Bali as if Seen Through a Key Hole: The Gaguritan Japatuan (unpub. B. A. Hons thesis), University of Sydney, 1988.

commoners were the living pulse of the kingdom, the force which kept corrupt kings in line. The political message in the texts was that commoners were there to stay, but should remain in their proper place, in villages.

The descriptions of the coarseness of commoner life in these poems reveal an element of satire; commoners may not have been as refined as kings, but their rituals and art bordered on a parody of the noble activities of the Pañji-like princes in their palaces. This was good for the princes in that it relegated commoners to the borders of courtliness, but it also shows a profoundly ironic view of the order of things. Balinese commoners may not have been too ready to take princely posturing all that seriously.[76]

The Kingdoms Crumble: 1884-1908

It was not so much the Dutch who ended the kingdoms of Bali as the Balinese rulers themselves. All the nineteenth-century Balinese kingdoms suffered internal pressures from upwardly mobile commoners, and external threats from other kingdoms. Intense and constant competition from the middle till the end of the nineteenth century saw the end of a number of kingdoms. In the face of continuous warfare, the Balinese rulers' inability to present a united front acted as an open invitation to the Dutch. The wars of 1846-9 had also weakened Bali's trade severely, making it difficult for the states to maintain a steady basis for their existence. Despite experiments by various rulers in organizing state authority, none seemed able to both hold the state together internally and maintain the sovereignty the Dutch required.

The Balinese carried on as if the Dutch were not there. The kings signed treaties if they thought there was some advantage from trader from access to gifts such as the rhinoceros received by the rulers of Klungkung, or even from recognition of status by an outside power. However when the Dutch took over Bulèlèng and Jembrana in 1856, the Balinese kings refused to treat them as brother rulers. The Dutch could not be given the same status as Balinese aristocrats,

---

76. See Vickers, "A Balinese Illustrated Manuscript," for an example of depictions of commoner mobility.

and therefore could not be seen as participants in the same struggles for status—struggles which were oriented around divine ancestry and ritual life, two things the Dutch did not seem to have.[77] The division of the mountains created the illusion that the Dutch were not there. Bali north of the mountains could be forgotten or traded with much in the way Java was, while the interconnected kingdoms of south Bali, with their closely tied rice-growing systems, continued as before.

While the Balinese rulers thought they could cut themselves off from the Dutch, the Dutch had effectively cut the Balinese off from the rest of the archipelago. Bali had always had a wide network of trading and cultural contacts with the various kingdoms of Java, Kalimantan, Eastern Indonesia, and even Sumatra, but as all these areas fell under Dutch control, the Balinese kingdoms found that they could only turn in upon themselves, their outside sources of economic, literary and artistic stimulation lost.

The period from 1850 to 1888 was a time in which Bali's political existence was frozen by the increasing pressure of Dutch colonial expansion. During this time the Dutch recorded no less than seven outbreaks of smallpox, five of cholera, four mouse plagues which devastated the rice crops, and a final earthquake in 1888, with a known total of 15,000 to 18,000 dead in one of the worst of the plague years, 1871.[78] Such misfortunes were a constant feature of Balinese life, but their abundance brought instability and a feeling of imminent political disaster.

The process of disintegration began at the beginning of the nineteenth century, when the king of Mataram on Lombok, one of the Karangasem kings, took over all the other kingdoms of the island. His sons continued the process of takeover on Bali in 1849, by allying themselves with the Dutch and thereby getting rid of their enemies, the rulers of Bulèlèng and Karangasem. In managing to regain control of their ancestral kingdom of Karangasem the kings of Lombok made a clear challenge to the status of Klungkung. Klungkung's success in 1849 in establishing a treaty that held the Dutch

77. See Vickers, "Ritual and Representation in Nineteenth-Century Bali," *RIMA* 18 (1984):1-35.

78. Schulte Nordholt, "Een Balishe Dynastie," p. 126.

at bay gave the other kingdoms a sense of false security. They felt that they could defeat the Dutch or the other new enemy Karangasem-Lombok, but the latter kept up the pressure from Klungkung's borders through the next decades of the century and many of the kingdoms around Klungkung were in a permanent state of war.

During the later part of the nineteenth century the Balinese kingdoms resembled a house of cards. In 1884 one of the lords in the kingdom of Gianyar initiated a rebellion against his king, and virtually the whole of south Bali collapsed into a series of mini-states.

Klungkung stepped in, and, according to the different versions, either made Gianyar's lords throw the king out, or saved him. The first possibility is the more likely, because Klungkung gained a large slice of Gianyar out of the rebellion. For nearly ten years the king of Gianyar and his sons were virtual prisoners in Satria, east Klungkung. In the meantime Karangasem stepped up hostilities, and various of the Gianyar houses staked their claims to supremacy. Other Gianyar districts played the game of politics and put themselves under the protection of Karangasem-Lombok.[79] Ubud was small district in the foothills of Gianyar at the time, a side-branch of a side-branch of the Sukawati dynasty which had ruled central Bali in the early eighteenth century, but it took revenge for the replacement of Sukawati by Gianyar by overthrowing Gianyar's enemies and making the new king's son dependent on Ubud's power. Ubud looked poised to take over the whole of the kingdom at the end of the nineteenth century, but the new king of Gianyar saved himself by agreeing to become a subject of the Dutch.

The instability of the Gianyar wars led, in 1891, to Tabanan and Badung crushing Mengwi with Klungkung's help, so that various of the smaller hill districts went over to Klungkung. Badung had invaded Mengwi before, in the 1820s, but now the two kingdoms actually divided Mengwi up between them, and it ceased to exist as a kingdom. The elderly king of Mengwi did not seek refugee status, as had the king of Gianyar. Instead, seeing the end, he was carried out to face the enemy, his ancestral kris in his hand, in the act of

---

79. Van der Kraan, *Lombok,* p. 37.

puputan or putting an end to the kingdom.[80]

Further instability was provided by the Dutch conquest of Lombok in 1894. Gusti Gedé Jlantik of Karangasem may have thought that instead of taking over Lombok the Dutch would give it to him, and rid him of the burden of being a vassal of his uncle. Instead he virtually had to surrender to the Dutch to survive.

The demise of the Balinese kingdoms was as much their own faults it was the triumph of the Dutch. The status struggle was always more important than a united political front against imperialism. By underestimating the Dutch, the south Balinese kings turned the toe-hold of Bulèlèng into the first steps in the relentless march of colonial power. In 1906 and 1908 the Dutch finished their march in Badung and Klungkung, and the rulers there only had the choice between marching out to be cut down by the Dutch guns, and thus to receive the reward of entry into the heaven of Wisnu, or abject surrender, in which their royal authority would be completely devalued in their own terms. The gesture of the bloody and suicidal *puputan* was for them the most appropriate way of marking the end of their whole way of life and social order.

The pre-colonial period of modern Bali saw a build-up of Balinese self-images: Bali the empire, Bali the island of warring kingdoms, Bali the locale of family competitions, and Bali the island of commoners. As the Dutch formed their images of Bali they drew on what was already there, although the Balinese rulers seemed less receptive to influences from the European ways of thinking about Bali than the Europeans were open to Balinese perceptions.

The rich artistic and ritual life which developed over this period as a part of the multiplication and competition of kingdoms became the key element of the way Bali developed in the twentieth century. Once the Dutch had transformed the social structure that allowed these outward manifestations of culture to exist, then the Balinese had to find new ways to express that culture. They did this by both coming up with new cultural forms and by seeming to maintain the old forms unchanged, a happy blending of tradition and modernity in unhappy circumstances.

---

80. Described in Geertz, *Negara*, p.11.

By the end of the nineteenth century two aspects of the Balinese self-image had been exposed as a kind of self-deception. The ideas of the World Ruler and of romantic princes had not prepared Balinese rulers for the realities of late-nineteenth-century imperialism. The Balinese self-images all fitted Bali into the world of traditional kingship in the Indonesian archipelago. This was all right as long as the Balinese were dealing with Javanese, Sasaks, or Malays, but the status struggles and images of internal order in Bali were unsuited to colonial politics. In the decades after the colonial takeover a readjustment of Balinese self-image and images of Bali was required.

CHAPTER THREE

The Birth of Bali the Paradise

With colonial control of Bali came the beginnings of the idea of Bali as a paradise. Expatriate Europeans constructed for themselves the idea of Bali as a place of cultural and natural fertility, and lived according to this image. In their wake the first generations of colonial civil servants —people born in the Indonesian archipelago, with less commitment to the Netherlands than to the East Indies—found in Bali the perfect cultural expression of their love for their first home.

After the colonials came broad-minded travelers from all over the world, members of an international upper class looking for artistic thrills from exotic native life, or seeking an alternative to the stale European culture of the early decades of the twentieth century. These people lived in elegant simplicity in a country where even moderate wealth could buy servants, cars, art collections and picturesque Balinese-style houses in little native villages.

Although the travelers, bureaucrats and scholars ranged in their attitudes to Balinese culture and society from stuffy disapproval to wide-eyed excitement, they formed a common set of ideas about Bali, ideas in which the images of lithe bare-breasted maidens, young dancing girls, and malevolent witches came to represent the essence of Balinese culture.

The Dutch began to appreciate Balinese culture as they began to acquire parts of Bali. The negative image of warlike Bali faded at the end of the nineteenth century, yielding, by the 1930s, a positively glowing ideal of Bali as a paradise. The seeds of the new image were sown by nineteenth-century European scholars with a deep appreciation of the island's culture and a taste for literature, as well as titillation of a less elevated kind. Almost as soon as the Dutch were in complete control of Bali they made this paradise into a tourist destination, and then the image really flowered.

From savage Bali, the Dutch and then the other European visitors to the island turned to female Bali (the island of bare-breasted smiling women) then to cultured Bali (the island where everyone is an artist). The Dutch scholarly tradition provided the images of cultural and artistic richness that were later taken up by anthropologists. These images acted as a counterpoint to the more stereotypical images of Bali provided by tourist promotion.

Along the way the views of the various visitors met to produce the image of Bali which persists today, forming and elaborating this view of the balmy ocean fantasy resort through an outpouring of books, films, and photographs. The weight of popular opinion ensured that this image of Bali from the European "Golden Age" of the 1930s survived into the post-war period, where films such as *The Road to Bali* maintained the purely fantastic and exotic idea of Bali.

The Orientalists

In the early history of European images of Bali only two positive images emerged: the first is the sixteenth-century view of Bali as civilized yet exotic, and the second is the nineteenth-century enthusiasm of Sir Thomas Stamford Raffles. With these precedents in mind, one man, a mid-nineteenth century Dutch aristocrat and intellectual, paved the way for greater respect of Balinese culture.

Preacher, parliamentarian, humanitarian and scientist, Wolter Robert Baron van Hoëvell (1812-79), almost single-handedly transformed Dutch colonial thinking about the natives of the Indies, and about the Balinese in particular. Van Hoëvell was vitally interested in all the peoples of the Indies. He combined the freedom of expression of an aristocratic background with the energy of a man of action, someone who would convert the knowledge gained in his field trips to the islands of the Indies into action in the parliamentary arena. Like Raffles's belief in political economy, van Hoëvell's humanitarianism was fired by the thirst for knowledge of the world, which was the outcome of the Enlightenment and the boom in scientific developments occurring in Europe at that time.

In the mid-nineteenth century, when the disciplines of the natural and social sciences as we know them today were taking shape, van Hoëvell rode the crest of the new wave. Like Raffles he was inspired by the drive for spiritual and intellectual progress, which was part of the enthusiasm of colonial expansion. He was the "learned and indefatigable President"[1] of the major organization dedicated to scientific knowledge of the Indies, the Royal Batavian Society for the Arts and Sciences. This body had been founded in the last quarter of the eighteenth century, and pre-dated similar English colonial institutions. Through this organization he sponsored scientific expeditions to Bali and published a number of important articles by himself and other scholars in the Batavia-based journal he edited, the *Journal of the Netherlands Indies*.

Like that of other scientists of the day, his scientific knowledge was broadly based. For him science took in not only the natural sciences, but what we call philology, history and anthropology. He wanted to know all about the religion of Bali, to investigate its many texts, to discover the Indian origins of Balinese culture, and to see how both functioned within Balinese society. From Raffles and other early nineteenth-century scholars van Hoëvell knew some of the details of Balinese Hinduism, and had come to read some of the very first translations of Balinese texts in the literary language of Old Javanese. He considered this literary lead quite useful, for Bali was to him "the place where The Hindu religion subsists undisturbed alone in the whole archipelago... the key that will enable us to penetrate the knowledge [of the literary and poetical life of India] as it once animated the Javanese."[2] His scientific interest was

---

1. Introduction to W. van Hoëvell, "Scientific Researches on the Islands of Bali and Lombok," *Journal of the Indian Archipelago and Eastern Asia* 2 (1848):151-9; for more information on van Hoëvell see Rob Nieuwenhuys, *Oost-Indische Spiegel*, Amsterdam: Querido, 1978, pp. 98-107.

2. Van Hoëvell, "Scientific Researches," pp. 152 & 159. His main writings on Bali were "Eenige Mededeelingen omtrent het eiland Bali van Abdullah bin Mohamad el Mazrie," TNI 7 (1845): 140-201; *Nederland en Bali, eene stem uit Indiëtot der Nederlandsche Volk*, Groningen: Oomkens, 1846; *Reis over Java, Madura en Bali in het Midden van 1847*, 3 vols, Amsterdam: van Kampen, 1849-54.

humanitarian in emphasis, and he did more than any other to show that the peoples of the Indies had their own cultures, which were worthy of being valued on equal (or perhaps almost equal) terms as European culture.

Van Hoëvell's writings were the basis of political action. His argument about the value of the cultures of the Indies was important to his political campaigns against the inequities and sufferings caused by the infamous "Culture [or Cultivation] System" by which the Netherlands Government exploited the peasantry of Java. Van Hoëvell had earlier, in 1848, the year of revolutions, been forced to leave the Indies after he was implicated in a protest for the rights of Eurasians. After that he fought in the Netherlands Parliament for the rights of the Javanese peasantry. He worked in association with other prominent Dutch, promoting the famous author, Multatuli, whose novel *Max Havelaar* did more than any academic or economic work to create public awareness of the suffering of the Javanese peasantry under the Culture System. Eventually they succeeded in having the Culture System abolished, only to have it replaced in 1870 by a kind of laissez-faire capitalism that allowed the Javanese peasantry to be exploited by private companies instead of the Dutch Government.

Van Hoëvell's legacy was to be the fostering of a group of scholars and administrators known as the Ethici, because they were the creators of the Ethical Policy that acknowledged Dutch responsibility for the exploitation of the peoples of the Indies. They tried to repay that exploitation through enlightened welfare policies.

But all that was not to come until the turn of the century. During the 1840s, at a time when the Dutch were bringing military attention to bear on the island, van Hoëvell's fostering of scientific knowledge of Bali had the effect of making Bali known to the Dutch as it had never been before.

On Bali he found a ready contact who could help launch scientific investigation into the island, Mads Lange, the hero of the ocean-going trade of the nineteenth century. Lange provided the resources for van Hoëvell and his associates to go to Bali and meet with Balinese kings, priests and aristocrats on better terms than any of their predecessors. His trade center was a base from which they could operate in their quest.

Van Hoëvell's chief agent on Bali was a German called Friederich, an itinerant alcoholic scholar who seemed to wander around
southern Bali in a daze and yet went on to write one of the first
really informative accounts of the relationship between Hindu religion, literature and society on the island. Friederich was steeped
in the German Romantic tradition with its interest in ancient Sanskrit and Indian literature, which made him the perfect person to
deepen Bali's reputation as the museum of the "classical" culture of
the Indies, ancient Javanese culture.[3] Behind this interest in ancient
Sanskrit writings lay an appreciation of their literary worth, as well
as a belief that Sanskrit was one of the oldest descendants of an
original ancient Indo-European culture from which all languages
and cultures had been derived.

Friederich was a high-minded, perhaps arrogant, European
scholar cast into a fieldwork environment which neither the Romantic poets and philosophers of Germany nor the brahman Sanskrit
experts of India, whom they idolized, could prepare him for. Friederich arrived on Bali on one of the ships of the expedition against
Bulèlèng in 1846, hardly the place for an objective scientist to be.
He found little in north Bali to interest him, and was even beaten to
the manuscripts of the sacked palace of Bulèlèng by another member of the Batavian Society, Zollinger, who later published accounts
of Bali and Lombok in van Hoëvell's journal. The most notable
thing about Zollinger's reports of Bali was that he was the first to
mention the existence of what he called a kind of "tiger" mask used
in Balinese rituals. This was the *Barong,* later famous in descriptions of Balinese kris dances. The earliest photograph of a Barong
was taken in Batavia in the same year.[4]

Both Friederich and Zollinger published detailed descriptions of
the cremations and the accompanying widow sacrifices of Balinese
royalty, accounts filled with horrified fascination at the barbarity of

---

3. For this German Romantic tradition and its elevation of brahmans, see James A. Boon, *Other
Tribes, Other Scribes,* Cambridge: Cambridge University Press, 1982, pp. 217-25.

4. "Een Uitstapje naar het Eiland Bali," *TNI* 7 (1846): 1-56. For the photograph, which is probably of a mask in the Batavian Society's collection (now the National Museum in Jakarta), see
Jane Levy Reed, *Towards Independence: A Century of Indonesia Photographed,* San Fran-
cisco: Friends of Photography, 1991.

the people.[5] After the expedition against Bulèlèng, Friederich decided to head south, where he stayed with Mads Lange. He used Lange's networks in order to obtain Balinese palm-leaf manuscripts and learn how to read them, as well as to find out about Balinese history and social organization.

The main reason van Hoëvell's Batavian Society sent Friederich to Bali was that he knew Sanskrit, which they thought would enable him to understand the *Kawi* language of the ancient literature (sometimes referred to as "Old Javanese"). The theory that Balinese religion was a branch of Indian Hinduism led the society to believe that the literature of ancient Bali should be in the classical language of India, but in fact the *Kawi* language has absolutely no grammatical connection to Sanskrit. Friederich went to Bali looking for the Sanskrit texts praised by Goethe and Schiller, and although he could not find them, found a vast body of other literature.

With his knowledge of Indian Hinduism, where the Brahman *pandits* (priestly experts) had long been the major sources of information for westerners, it was logical for Friederich to elevate the Balinese version of brahman priests as the true bearers of culture. The rest of the people were of little interest to him. He saw the priests, of course, in the anti-Islamic terms of Raffles, saying that, "The priests bring before our eye the stage at which the Javanese stood before the introduction of Muhammedanism." For van Hoëvell they were "the only remaining preservers of the old literature and religion." He elaborated on this by saying that they were, "the expounders of all laws and institutions; and of the knowledge of antiquity they have scarcely lost or forgotten anything from their faithful adherence to traditions."[6]

Lange was not all that impressed with Friederich, especially his alcoholism (a common problem of Europeans in the Indies) and his disdain for Balinese other than the high priests knowledgeable in Sanskrit. In his letters, Lange wrote of Friederich, "He drinks like the Devil...." Practically every morning Lange had to trip over empty

---

5. See A. van der Kraan, "Human Sacrifice in Bali: Sources, Notes and Commentary," *Indonesia* 40 (1985): 89-121, especially pp. 107-11 and 116-17.

6. R. Friederich, *The Civilisation and Culture of Bali* (trans. E. R. Rost), Calcutta: Susil Gupta, 1959, p. 2.

bottles to get to Friederich's tent. Lange, however, promised that, "I shall look udt for him, also assist him to gett sem manuscripts, but what I see he coleckts, I did not place any value in befoer [sic]," that is that he would help Friederich collect the texts although he felt they were not of the highest quality and were easily available. He added, indulgently, "However late him goe alange."

Some months later van Hoëvell came to see how things were going, and this made Friederich worse: "Mr Frederick has turned *raven mad* seen Mr van Hovell has been her," Lange reported. This time it was not Friederich's drinking which was the problem, but his violence towards Balinese: "he have flogged an Ida at Suny [Sanur?]—and the other day at Deva Mate Reis feast he floked hes Brother—Deva Mate Kareng—in hes Hoarse wip [sic]. He quarrels with every one."[7]

Hardly the picture of a dedicated scholar, but Friederich did manage to produce a number of articles explaining the debt of Bali to ancient Indian learning. He was no doubt aided by his glorification of the brahmans, which meant that he could limit his research to one source, and by his interest in written sources, which would have allowed him to pursue his work during bouts of sobriety.

The net result of all these articles and books on Bali by van Hoëvell and his associates was a new image of Bali as an island of culture and learning, at least amongst its priestly and aristocratic classes. The new positive image was still tempered with tales of incestuous and cannibalistic kings, and of interminable warfare and intrigue—all the features of the degenerate Orient. In the particular version of this degeneracy applied to Bali, only the Balinese versions of Indian brahmans, the high priests of the *brahmana* caste, were considered to be worthy and important informants about Balinese culture. Only they were responsible for the preservation of ancient Java.

The view of Balinese culture produced in the mid-nineteenth century was to have important implications for over a hundred years. Bali began to be taken more seriously, and began to be the locus for

---

7. Letters to Resident Mayor, 5 Aug. 1846 & 18 Aug. 1847, Lange-Mayor correspondence, Koninklijk Instituut voor Taal-, Land- en Volkenkunde Western Manuscripts archive H 1081.

scholarly activity, but only in a derivative sense. The classical literature so prized by these European orientalists, as students of theist
came to be known, was not seen as intrinsically Balinese, but something Hindu which fate had preserved for posterity on this island.
Generations of scholars engaged in the study of this literature did not
realize that a great deal of what they saw as Javanese or Indian was,
and still is, written by Balinese.

The Next Generation: 1870s-1900s

The civil servants and missionaries who became the first European
colonial residents of north Bali refined Raffles's picture of the noble,
hard-working peasantry as the base of society on the one hand, and
on the other elaborated on the vision of Hindu literature and religion
produced by van Hoëvell's circle. Of the new generation of scholars
two in particular were of major importance for their enlightened
view of Bali: the cantankerous Eurasian linguist, Herman N. van der
Tuuk, and the ethically-minded future resident of Bali and Lombok,
F. A. Liefrinck. Both arrived in Bali in the 1870s, when the administrative program of Bali's first bureaucrat, P. van Bloemen Waanders,
was just starting to work, and north Bali was being reorganized to
conform with Dutch ideas of Balinese tradition.

Both Liefrinck and van der Tuuk were the inheritors of a trend
towards increased knowledge of Balinese life and culture set in motion by Baron van Hoëvell in the 1840s and Raffles at the beginning
of the century. This trend involved greater penetration of the societies of the Netherlands East Indies by scientific knowledge, under
the idealistic umbrella of helping the peoples of the Indies through
benevolent colonial welfare policies. Van der Tuuk and Liefrinck
provided a new vision of Bali that classified it as one of the most
important cultures of the Indies.

The opinionated and deeply learned Herman Neubronner van
der Tuuk was born in Malacca (now in Malaysia) in 1824, just as it
was about to be handed over to the British by the Dutch. He spent
his childhood in Surabaya in East Java and lived on Bali from 1870
until his death in a Surabaya hospital in 1894. Scholarly and acer-
bic, he had no time for many of the conventions of his day, and was
regarded by most of his Dutch associates as a total eccentric. He

adopted Balinese dress and lifestyle and could be found wandering the beach every afternoon in pajama trousers and native shirt, bareheaded and barefooted, carrying his "inseparable rough-hewn cudgel which weighed several kilos."[8] He only visited the Netherlands for study and, since he was of mixed descent, he probably found it hard to find acceptance in the mainstream of Dutch society.

It is difficult, in the light of van der Tuuk's background, to see him as a European. This background had an important impact on his work, for he was one of the first of his generation of scholars to emphasize what anthropologists and linguists nowadays call fieldwork—making the effort to study living languages by living amongst native speakers. In his writings he railed against "armchair" scholars who wrote their dictionaries from the comfort of the Netherlands or Batavia and in his commitment to working amongst the people he studied, he was fifty years ahead of his time.

Van der Tuuk came to Bali with its reputation for ferocity high in his mind. In fact he put off going to the island in 1868 because of wars between Bangli and Mengwi, and the Dutch expedition of that year, and went to Lampung in south Sumatra instead. In 1870 he found it difficult to find servants in Batavia to go with him to Bali, because the Javanese and Malays were also scared of Bali's reputation. Some of his first letters from Bali complained about the despotic nature of the Balinese kings, and the fear under which traders must live.[9]

Van der Tuuk had an immense knowledge not only of the classic European literature of his day, but also of Indian literature, which he tempered with a taste for mystery novels. Like Raffles and Friederich, he saw the brahmans as the best sources of information and the true bearers of culture. He compared the Balinese with the Bataks of Sumatra, with whom he had previously lived, and decided that, "So far the Balinese please me more than the Bataks." It was not all Balinese, however, who so pleased him, only the members of the priestly caste whom he considered as scholarly soul mates:

8. J. Jacobs, *Eenigen Tijd onder der Baliers: Een Reisbeschrijving,* Batavia: Kolff. 1883, pp. 10-11.

9. Letter to the Netherlands Bible Society, 3 Jan. 1870, quoted in R. Nieuwenhuys (ed.), *H. der Tuuk: De Pen in Gal Gedoopt,* Amsterdam: S. A. van Oorschot, 1962, p. 130.

A Balinese high priest in the midst of his holy-water ritual,
as depicted by Danish artist Tyra de Kleen.

"The Brahmans here are highly cultivated and gentle of character. It is a pity that the government does not take more notice of them, since [our] civil servant ignores the unconscionable savagery of the king."

Just to qualify this he added another anti-aristocratic story, one which implicitly showed the Netherlands East Indies Government in a bad light for allowing such things: "The other day a grey-beard was scourged here with thorned leaves, because he had purchased a load of goods in the king's name. When his body was covered with welts, he was bound and left in the sun from eleven to twelve o'clock."[10]

Van der Tuuk chose to stay and devote himself to compiling a dictionary of Balinese and the poetic *Kawi* language, living away from the main European settlement of Bulèlèng. His later letters were not so full of these stories of royal cruelty, even though, in 1886, he was seriously wounded with a grass-cutter in an attempt on his life. The assassin was a "coolie" from Karangasem, who, the

---

10. Letter to the Netherlands Bible Society, 23 Sept. 1870 quoted in ibid., p. 134.

Dutch Resident was relieved to know, was not politically motivated. He had been put up to it by a Déwa Ktut Kramas of Karangasem, probably out of revenge for some unspecified slight.[11]

Van der Tuuk was a deeply anti-Christian Bible translator. His lexicographic project did not suit his initial sponsors, the Netherlands Bible Society, who were hoping for more immediate results than van der Tuuk was offering. Van der Tuuk was probably not all that happy with their sponsorship anyway, since he, like many of the Ethici and devotees of the writer Multatuli, was basically opposed to missionary activity in the Indies.

Throughout his period on Bali, van der Tuuk was particularly scathing on the subject of the first missionary to come to Bali, Rutger van Eck, and wrote critically of van Eck's publications about Bali and the work of his successors from the Utrecht Missionary Society. When one of these was murdered by the only convert van Eck had made, van der Tuuk was less than sympathetic, and glad to see the Netherlands Indies Government ban missionary activity on Bali: "Christianity, especially the Calvinism of the Utrecht missionaries, is spiteful, and here it is spread by boors who are made into fanatics in Holland."[12] When van der Tuuk visited Lombok in 1874 he took with him a brahman so that he and his fellow travelers could carry out their devotions.[13]

Fortunately the Netherlands Indies Government agreed to take van der Tuuk on, and in 1873 he became a civil servant assigned to pursue his linguistic activities on Bali. In this role he was very influential, advising other scholars and visitors who came through the island, and eventually, after his dictionary was posthumously published, becoming the main source of knowledge of Bali.

One legacy of van der Tuuk's activities was to live on in modern Indonesia. In his work he employed Balinese and Javanese scribes to copy manuscripts. One was a young Javanese schoolteacher who married a Balinese girl. This teacher, no doubt partly influenced by the world opened up to him through his association with van der

11. ibid., pp. 74-5.

12. Letter to R. C. D'Ablaing, 20 October 1881, p. 158.

13. ibid., p. 145.

Tuuk, became interested in Theosophy, an interest he was to pass on to his son, Sukarno, later the first President of the Republic of Indonesia.

Eroticism and Ethnography

One of the first of van der Tuuk's visitors to write extensively about south Bali was a medical doctor, Julius Jacobs, the man who discovered the Balinese female breast. Jacobs, like van der Tuuk, spent his life in the Indies, more often than not living amongst"natives" in preference to his colonial compatriots. His fascination with native life went far beyond his calling as a medical man; he was really an ethnographer, describing natives in terms not only of their health practices, but also in the way that their health and sexuality related to the organization of daily life and to artistic activities.

Jacobs went to Bali in 1881 to further a campaign of smallpox vaccination begun by the civil servant van Bloemen Waanders. There he met van der Tuuk and was very impressed with the profound knowledge and Balinese lifestyle of this "true bookworm" whose thatch-roofed house was scattered with piles of manuscripts. Van der Tuuk told Jacob he lived a celibate life because he did not want his lifestyle disturbed by "a woman trying to bring regulation and order into his household."[14]

Despite his acceptance of all the unfavorable aspects of Bali's image produced by his predecessors, Jacobs's curiosity brought him to a new appreciation of Balinese culture. His travel book was one of the first major works to show Bali as exotically cultured, adding to the allure of Bali through its graphic depictions of the excesses of Balinese eroticism.

Jacobs was a man with vast experience of the Indies, but he did not have much prior knowledge of Bali. On arrival he was pleased to play the all-observing guest, first in the company of van der Tuuk, then in the courts of the various Balinese rajas. When interpreting what he saw, he returned to van der Tuuk for further enlightenment. It is to van der Tuuk's explanations and insights into Balinese life

---

14. Jacobs, *Eenigen Tijd,* pp. 10-11. Van der Tuuk seems to have modified this view later, since he did have a woman "housekeeper" in later years.

that we should look when reading Jacobs's detailed descriptions of the lifestyles of the courts, cultural activities and medical problems of south Bali.[15]

Jacobs's book of his journey was an important milestone in the transformation of Bali's image in the European imagination. He managed to incorporate information from contemporary publications with descriptions of Bali as a center of vital artistic activities: the villages ringing with beautiful music from the gamelan orchestras, the courts full of sex-mad despots able to stage spectacular performances of all kinds of dances for their guests. Mixed with these observations came detailed descriptions of the medical problems of what we would now call a Third World nation, a country bereft of the advances of European technology.

It was not only the cultural descriptions in Jacobs's book that were important. For the Dutch version of the Victorian era he offered images of the island as a place of sexual license. He was the first European writer to discover what would fascinate the authors and tourists of a later era: the bare breasts of Balinese women. Being a man of science, however, he offered his observations only in the interests of ascertaining where the Balinese fitted into the racial hierarchy. Illustrating his observations, he noted the raised area of the "typical" Balinese breast beneath the aureole, deducing that this, and hip width, indicated racial similarities between Balinese, Javanese and other "Malays."

As with many medical men of his day, Jacobs's prurient interests coincided with ideas of how human actions and character were linked to physiognomy. Race was important in the scheme of things because each race was held to have particular basic traits that, in turn, determined character.

Jacobs's discussions of Balinese women placed great emphasis on the idea of them living in "harems," thus creating a link between Balinese court life and the sensual perceptions of Middle Eastern potentates, perceptions that are still strong in western thinking about Asia. He recalled with horror (real or perhaps mock) how one of the rajas offered him a dancing girl as company for the night, and

---

15. See for example his comments on the missionary question, ibid., pp. 210-16.

recounted how some of the court dancers were in fact prostitutes, whose livings supported the rajas, and, even worse, some were male prostitutes in drag.

Given the detailed information Jacobs provided on Balinese sexual practices complete with the relevant Balinese terms, no doubt supplied by van der Tuuk, we cannot but wonder whether Jacobs in fact did take up these offers in the line of fieldwork. Jacobs did make the disclaimer that such descriptions were only put in "for the sake of colleagues and orientalists," but clearly he was offering, and implied that Bali was offering, the kind of titillation not publicly admitted in Europe. To make them more "scientific," Jacobs laced his descriptions with Latin, French and German as well as Balinese. An example is his description of what he called *"Lesbische liefde"* for which he gave the following definition which was meant to explain lesbian sexual activities as the clashing of clitorises: *"(metjèngtjèng djoeoek),* literally "to hit cymbals against each other without making a sound"; in Malay *"bertampoeh laboe"*; tampoeh = the crown of a fruit, perhaps a play on the *clitoris)."* He explained that lesbianism "prevails amongst the women with its *digitale* and *linguale* variations."

Although he provided much information on the sexuality of men, women clearly fascinated him more. Evidence of strong heterosexuality this may be, but it is also in line with the direction taken by medical science in Europe at the time. In this research the physiognomy of races was not simply a matter of skin color or bone-structure, but of the development of all parts of the body, particularly the breasts, sexual organs and buttocks.[16] In relation to lesbianism, Jacobs commented that, "The strongly developed clitoris, with which experts say many Balinese beauties are blessed, greatly promotes this abuse." Europeans thought that Malays, especially Malay women (like other, particularly black, races), had excessively large sexual organs, which meant they were more promiscuous than European women. Thus he went on to tell how, "In spite of the

---

16. Sander L. Gilman, "Black Bodies, White Bodies: Towards an Iconography of Female Sexuality in Late Nineteenth-Century Art, Medicine and Literature," pp. 223-61 in Henry Louis Gates Jr. (ed.), *"Race," Writing, and Difference,* Chicago: The University of Chicago Press, 1986.

'entrée libre' that most of these daughters of Ham display, *onanie* and *masturbatie* are widespread, especially amongst the younger generations. They call this *'njoktjok'."* Just in case we should have doubted any of his evidence, he went on to add that Balinese harem women all had a wax *"plaisir des dames,"* and that for others nature provided items to satisfy their lusts: "Yams and bananas are much used by the Balinese girls as delicacies, but not *only* for eating."[17]

For Balinese men, he said, impotence was a major worry, affecting even the highest king of Bali, the raja of Klungkung. According to Jacobs, the high incidence of impotence was not a product of the sexual voraciousness of Balinese women, but was linked to male overindulgence, and the various natural products and practices used to heighten sexual pleasure. Too many wives and too much opium was Jacobs's prognosis.

The work of van der Tuuk and Jacobs represent a stage of European knowledge in which Europeans delved further and further into the details of Balinese life. This knowledge was not disinterested, and the processes of its acquisition show how much it went hand-in-hand with increasing colonial control over the island. Linguistically and physically Balinese were fitted into a hierarchy of the world's races. The racial disposition to sexual overindulgence they shared with other "Asiatics" made them inferior to Europeans, but their cultural wealth put them above many of the other "primitive" peoples Europeans encountered in their colonies.

The Village Republic

As scholarship opened up more intimate details of Balinese life to outside gaze, Europeans also started to take an increasing interest in knowing about all levels of Balinese society. Most European commentators of the day, when they did get their information from Balinese sources, spoke only to members of the ruling class, either the brahmans so respected by van der Tuuk, or the rajas who introduced Jacobs to various aspects of Balinese society. Just as van der Tuuk's life was drawing to an end European scholars focused attention on

---

17. Jacobs, *Eenigen Tijd,* pp. 129, 135 & 146. For other European commentaries on Asian dispositions to lustful behaviour, see Rana Kabbani, *Europe's Myths of Orient,* London: Pandora, 1986, especially pp. 50-66.

peasants and the village as the basis of Balinese society. The chief exponent of this idea was Frederick Albert Liefrinck, who after he had coped with famine and rebellion on Lombok in his position as Resident of Bali and Lombok from 1896 to 1901, went on to become a member of the supreme advisory body in colonial government, the Council of the Indies.

Unlike van der Tuuk and the others who worked on Bali Liefrinck was temperamentally the antithesis of the eccentric scholar. He was very much a "straight" civil servant, an organizer with a view to advancing up the ladder of the colonial service. Van der Tuuk expressed his interest in Liefrinck's writings in his own letters, adding, however, that he thought Liefrinck made too much use of van Eck's writings, "I can't understand how Liefrinck never twigged about van Eck. Van Eck always spoke of Liefrinck with a kind of disdain."[18] Liefrinck later dedicated one of his books to van der Tuuk.

There was no inconsistency in the fact that Liefrinck was a member of that group of idealists known as the Ethici, who were concerned with promoting the welfare of the peoples of the Indies, but yet was, with his brother, instrumental in the Dutch conquest of Lombok. Liefrinck's views of Lombok were formed by earlier visits to the island with van der Tuuk, and in his report on these trips he presented a view which van der Tuuk had already made clear in his first letters from Bali, that the Balinese rulers of Lombok were Hindu despots who oppressed the predominantly Muslim Sasak people. Enlightened European rule would relieve their plight.[19]

In line with this sympathy for the Sasak people, Liefrinck was to give full expression to his ideas of the "village republic" in Bali. The idea of the village republic was in part a response to what van Bloemen Waanders and others of Liefrinck's predecessors had perceived as the anarchic state of Balinese government. They saw that villagers had a say in choosing to which lord they paid homage (and tax) and often exercised this right by fleeing from unpopular lords.

---

18. Letter to J. L. A. Brandes, quoted in Nieuwenhuys, *H. N. van der Tuuk*, p. 180.

19. For Liefrinck's report and the subsequent war, see A. van der Kraan, *Lombok: Conquest, Colonization and Underdevelopment, 1870-1940*, Singapore: Heinemann, 1980, pp. 31-2.

Village life in Bali by Loiuse Koke, 1930s, from *Our Hotel in Bali.*

This information on villagers' rights to choose, and studies of the autonomous nature of the irrigation systems and village councils, led Liefrinck to conclude that villages functioned as egalitarian and autonomous units, that they were the real basis of Balinese society, and that the aristocracy was primarily an oppressive imposition. A Balinese kingdom, especially one not under Dutch control, was seen as "nothing more than an agglomeration of villages"[20]

According to Liefrinck and his successors, the original or *Bali Aga* villages in the mountains reflected the true, republican, if not democratic, nature of Balinese society, over which the fourteenth-century Javanese kingdom of Majapahit had imposed a despotic aristocracy. Later scholars found validation of the original or autochthonous status of the older villages in resemblances between organizations and practices in these and villages in other parts of Indonesia, particularly areas where Hinduism never took hold.

---

20. F. A. Liefrinck, *Bali en Lombok: Gescriften,* Amsterdam: de Bussy, 1927, p. 312 (from an article orig. pub. 1886-7.)

Liefrinck's idea was not entirely new. It had come into Dutch thinking and colonial administration via Raffles, and from there even influenced the thinking of Karl Marx.[21] The dispersion of the idea through both Dutch colonial practice and European writing about the Orient shaped Liefrinck's thinking about the value of peasants, even if they were seen as a group, not as individuals. This background was combined with the practical expedient of producing a theory of Balinese society which would make sense out of, and could be applied to, the perceived anarchy facing the first Dutch rulers of Bali.[22] From Liefrinck came the mission, taken up by other civil servants such as Schwartz, "to simplify the village administration and return it to its original state."[23]

From Massacres to Marketing

In the wake of the death march of the Balinese rajas in the *puputans* of 1906-8, when the Dutch invaded Bali and killed off or exiled thousands of aristocrats and their followers, the Dutch drew upon the scholarly appreciation of Balinese culture to ease their consciences. The work of Liefrinck and van der Tuuk, in particular, provided the Dutch with strong scholarly traditions which could be put into action in their administration of the island. The scar on the liberal imagination of the Netherlands produced by these massacres had to be healed, and preservation of Balinese culture, in combination with tourism, were the most effective balms for the healing process.

Only six years after the Klungkung *puputan* came the first tourists and the first tourist inducements to visit Bali. The Dutch steamship line, the KPM, had been running to north Bali since the late nineteenth century, but it was pigs, not human passengers, which had formed its main cargo. These boats primarily went to Bulèlèng to pick up copra, coffee, and the pigs which were Bali's prime export

21. See A. D. A. de Kat Angelino, *Staatkundig Belied en Bestuurszorg in Nederlandsch-Indië*, 2 vols, The Hague: Martinus Nijhoff, 1920-30, vol. II, p. 30.

22. See further Henk Schulte Nordholt, *Bali: Colonial Conceptions and Political Change*, Rotterdam: Comparative Asian Studies Programme, 1986, p. 3. Liefrinck explicitly refer to Raffles, in Liefrinck, *Bali en Lombok*, p. 9, and the whole of this article on rice cultivation in Bali is aimed at bringing Balinese practices into line with what the Dutch had already established on Java.

23. Quoted in Schulte, Nordholt, *Bali: Colonial Conceptions*, p. 32.

to places like Singapore. The boat-trip became known as the "pig express" *(Babi Expres)* until well into the 1920s.[24]

In 1914 the KPM issued the first tourist brochures to feature images of Bali. Realizing the advantages of this island, the line followed this with a series of advertisements and books in English, all along the lines of:

Bali
You leave this
island with a
sigh of regret
and as long
as you live
you can never
forget this
Garden of Eden.[25]

This and the enticing photographs of jungle scenery, palm trees and rice fields were enough to start luring tourists into making side trips from Java.

The lures are clearly shown in one of the first tourist pamphlets, written by an Englishwoman, Helen Eva Yates, for the KPM. She called Bali the "enchanted isle." She promised the traveler simplicity and artistry, a native people, "still intent to live their own simple way as in the Middle Ages," but who were also, "highly artistic, with an inherited devotion for an old faith that is charming in its sincerity." The island itself was "as yet unspool by modernism," but most of all it was "a land of Women."[26] This last aphorism heralded

24. See Willard A. Hanna, *Bali Profile: People, Events, Circumstances, 1001-1976,* New York: American Universities Field Staff, 1976. See further M. Picard, "Tourisme Culturel" et "Culture Touristique." Rite et Divertissement dans les Arts du Spectacle à Bali (These de doctorat de 3ème cycle, EHESS), Paris, 1984, pp. 56-8. Revised English version: *Bali: Cultural Tourism and Touristic Culture*, Singapore: Archipelago Press, 1996, Indonesian version: *Bali: Pariwisata Budaya dan Budaya Pariwisata*, Jakarta: KPG, Forum Jakarta-Paris École française d'Extrême-Orient, 2006.

25. Tourist advertisement, from Wim Bakker, *Bali Verbeeld,* Delft: Volkenkundige Museum Nusantara, 1985, p. 30.

26. Quoted in Picard, "Tourisme Culturel" et "Culture Touristique," pp. 71-2. This pamphlet is undated, but Yates later wrote a book on Bali with the same title. Picard, p. 56, dates the first tourist pamphlets, put out by the Dutch Toeristen Vereeniging, to 1914 and then the early 1920s.

the many images of half-naked women which were to follow.

The civil servants who followed up the lead of van der Tuuk and Liefrinck were ambivalent about this tourism. As part of the Ethical movement in the Dutch civil service they felt that the Netherlands owed a "debt of honor" to its colony. This group of scholarly civil servants, who lived more closely to the Balinese than their more pragmatic colleagues, were horrified by the earlier *puputans,* and wanted to atone by preserving Balinese culture. Of course, preservation presented its own dilemmas. On the one hand this preserved culture would be the great attraction of the island for tourists, but on the other too much western influence through tourism was felt to be bad for that same culture.

"Traditional" Bali which they wanted so much to preserve was the Bali systematically described by Liefrinck and the other earlier scholars. Following their guide, successive Residents of Bali and Lombok conducted surveys on land ownership, slavery, and the other major legal issues of the day. They banned slavery and widow sacrifice, disapproved of activities such as cockfighting, phased out the use of opium, and altered the structure of state organization. They could do this and still "preserve" Bali because Liefrinck had shown them that the real Bali lay in his village republics. The Dutch Government was eager for the world to think about Bali in terms of positive images, and tourism was the best way to present those images—that is, the best way to wipe away the bloody stain of imperialism.

The Scholarly Tradition

The consummate cultural foundation of Dutch Bali was set up soon after Liefrinck left Bali to become a major councilor in the colonial administration. The Kirtya Liefrinck-van der Tuuk, named after the two men who did most to bring Bali into the modern imagination, was dedicated to furthering their study of Balinese law books, administration, religion, and literature, by serving as a major library of Balinese manuscripts and western books on Bali. The foundation symbolized the unity of purpose amongst the civil servants, even though they tended to divide into two different interest groups, each following the tradition of one of these great men.

Liefrinck's disciples were those civil servants dedicated to studying traditional law, which the Dutch called *adatrecht*. They concentrated on land ownership, inheritance, and other issues directly related to the social reorganization that Dutch rule was bringing to the island. For them, colonial policy was a matter of aligning traditional law with the rules of the civil service, which was dedicated to the idea of "peace and order," *rust en orde*.

The policy they followed, one of so-called "indirect rule," was a tried-and-true method developed in Java over the previous three centuries. In the early twentieth century the ethical administrators more fully codified the policy. It became a kind of dualistic or pluralistic administrative system with one set of administrators for native affairs and one for the higher Dutch policies. At the same time the scholars of traditional law formalized a similar legal system: one set of "traditional" laws for local contingencies, and an overarching Dutch law for higher issues. Likewise in the economic field, Dutch theorists came up with the idea of a dualistic economy—one native, agrarian economy and a separate international, capitalist economy. The view underlying all these policies was that the natives were caught in some kind of primitive or less advanced stage of development, and so had to be "protected" and preserved from the destructive effects of the twentieth century.[27] This Dutch idea of "preservation" and "protection" by separating the different groups in society in a hierarchical manner has the same roots as the *apartheid* of modern South Africa.

Not all scholars toed the official line. Those who had to institute these policies tended to be divided in their views of the inhabitants of the Indies. Some were far more sympathetic to the native point of view, or at least what they thought might be the native point of view. Probably the most outstanding scholar of Balinese traditional law, Victor Emannuel Korn, was one such dissenter from the strict interpretation of colonial policy. Korn (1892-1969) was apprenticed at an early age to the colonial bureaucracy, but used his experience

---

27. On "dualism" and "pluralism," see de Kat Angelino, *Staatkundig Belied;* and J. S. Furnivall, *Netherlands India: A Study of Plural Economy,* Cambridge: Cambridge University Press, 1939.

there as the basis for a detailed study of traditional law which gained him his PhD at Leiden University, the heart of colonial scholarship, in 1922. He played the role of a solid bureaucrat but underneath this he had a more sardonic view of the negative effects of colonial policy, and a much more empathetic view of Bali than his colleagues.

Although he was posted to different parts of the Indies, his major contribution was to the study of Bali, where he devoted himself to an appreciation of the minute details and infinite variations of Balinese life and custom. His crowning work was a monumental study of Balinese traditional law, based on his doctoral dissertation, in which he revealed to the scholarly world that their complicity with colonial administration was not a neutral activity, but in fact involved fundamental interference with the social structure the Dutch claimed they were preserving.

Like the sad characters in Maugham's short stories of Malaya, Korn took a Balinese *defacto* wife whose existence could never be officially acknowledged, and who had to be left behind when he moved on from Bali. She is rumored to have left him with syphilis, which towards the end of his life forced him to live alone and eventually claimed his sanity. Korn wrote as a professional administrator but, as with his personal life, rankled under the formalistic rules of colonialism, and ended up a critic of those rules.

Korn sought to come to terms with the infinite variations of traditional practices over the island by listing every different term or practice he could discover. In doing this he exposed his predecessors' work, because he showed that in their administrations they were constantly rationalizing things for bureaucratic convenience. As they rationalized, they dropped the majority of Balinese practices and utterly changed the practices they retained. By the very act of preserving Balinese culture, the colonial administrators of Bali were in fact changing it. In particular, by making caste into a rigid set of rules these administrators ossified a more fluid set of social conventions.[28]

---

28. V. E. Korn, *Het Adatrecht van Bali,* The Hague: Kolff, 1932. For a commentary, see James A. Boon, *The Anthropological Romance of Bali,* Cambridge: Cambridge University Press, 1977, pp. 52-4. For other aspects of Dutch administrative attitudes, see Schulte Nordholt, *Bali: Colonial Conceptions.*

The philological scholar-administrators were van der Tuuk's heirs. These were linguists and archeologists dedicated to discovering ancient Bali through its texts and material remains. Chief amongst the philologists were the archeologists Pieter van Stein Callenfels, an enormous man who carried a skull called Ahmad with him wherever he went; Willem Stutterheim, who shocked the Dutch establishment by living with his archeological assistant, a talented young American dance researcher and later professor at Cornell University in the United States, called Claire Holt; Roelof Goris; and Christian Hooykaas, the aloof and conscientious linguist appointed as a language-scholar to work in the Kirtya Liefrinck-van der Tuuk after Goris.

Goris was one of the enigmas of the Bali set. Short, dressed usually in baggy bombay bloomers, he was a shy, odd-looking scholar whose pedophilia separated him from the other civil servants. In many ways alienated from his peers, he sought refuge in ancient texts, which he pursued as part of an abiding interest in the Hindu roots of Balinese religion, an interest that went back to the nineteenth-century scholar of Bali, Friederich. The other feature Goris shared with Friederich, alcoholism, was probably due, in part, to his alienation from the mentality of the Dutch civil service. During the Indonesian Revolution he chose to express that alienation by turning his back on the Netherlands and becoming a citizen of the new Indonesian republic, so living out the last years of his life a sad and forlorn figure maintained by the goodwill of Balinese academics.

All of these scholars added depth to the impression of Bali as an island of culture. They were already arguing that Bali was "a thing apart... more finely tuned than any other part of the Indies"[29] In their work and their role as administrators they created an image of orderliness, which was both good for tourism and good for colonialism. The colonial scholars' knowledge of Bali, however, was neither pro-Balinese nor anti-colonial. For many scholarly knowledge

---

29. The title of an article against the reintroduction of missionary work to Bali by V. E. Korn, "Bali is apart... is fijner bezenuwd den eenig ander deel van Indie," *Koloniaal Tijdscrift* 14 (1932): 44-53.

reinforced imperial superiority, and even the more sensitive claimed to know more about Bali than the Balinese, so they could tell the Balinese what to do with their culture.

First Tourists

The swift transition from war to tourism came via art. One of the first print-makers and painters to romanticize Bali was W.O.J. Nieu-wenkamp, who had visited Bali in 1904. Nieuwenkamp came back in 1906 as an artist travelling with the Dutch military forces, when he sketched the landing invasion force at Sanur, and then the razed palace of the king of Dénpasar. He made a series of subsequent travels all over the island, where he had a chance to work together with Balinese artists. Nieuwenkamp studied their art initially through copying some of the drawings collected by van der Tuuk, but when he arrived in the field, he had the chance to go directly to the source. He sought out the innovative I Ketut Gedé in north Bali, van der Tuuk's favorite artist, but also went to the painters' village of Ka-masan in the south.[30]

The languid and sensuous artworks that resulted were one of the best advertisements for Bali that Dutch culture had produced. The linear style of Balinese painters fitted very well with Nieu-wenkamp's own Art Nouveau style, and their interaction was very much in accordance with the ideals of the Arts and Crafts Movement that dominated in northern Europe at this time. Nieuwenkamp's approach to collaboration with Balinese showed the positive side of Dutch colonialism. While Nieuwenkamp's books were restricted to the Dutch-language market, the visual appeal of his prints guaranteed wider interest, and helped set the style for new kinds of tourist advertisements that were appearing.

The early decades of the twentieth century saw the halcyon days of tourism, days of genteel travel and languid sojourns. It took six leisurely weeks to get to Bali from America. Ships went to Batavia from the United States, or Europe or Australia. This was of course tourism for the upper classes. In 1916 it cost £62 in Australian currency

---

30. Bruce W. Carpenter, *W.O.J. Nieuwenkamp: First European Artist in Bali*, Singapore: Didier Millet/Periplus, 1997.

W.O.J. Nieuwenkamp's romantic prints of Bali, such as this one,
helped to create a new view of Bali in the early twentieth century

to go there from the West Coast of America, via Japan, Hong Kong
and Singapore, and £103 from the East Coast of America via Europe
(Genoa or Marseilles). From Batavia it cost £6 8s. for a side-trip to
Bali and Lombok lasting five days. The fare from Sydney to Batavia
was £36 15s. return (second class), at a time when the bare minimum
weekly wage needed to support a family was around £2 2s., and some
employers were paying well below that.[31]

Within a few years other companies had entered the market. The

---

31. *Come to Java,* Batavia: Official Tourist Bureau, and *To Java by the Royal Packet,* n.p.,
    Koninklijk Paketvaart Maatschappij. Information on Australian minimum wages from Anne
    O'Brien (pers. comm.), citing the 1907 Harvester Judgement for the figure of £2 2s. Accord-
    ing to the Commonwealth Statistician the average Australian income for 1910-11 was £4 3s
    1d. From the available statistics, wages seem to have changed little over the next decade.

route had changed by the time Miguel and Rose Covarrubias went to Bali on the *Cingalese Princess* in 1930, travelling from New York via the Suez Canal, the Pacific, the China Sea and eventually Surabaya, then Bulèlèng. Others, such as the newly married Gregory Bateson and Margaret Mead, came from London and Paris via the Suez Canal, stopping at Singapore to join the KPM's tour of Makassar and the outer islands before heading south to Bali.[32]

For some, such as the beachcombers, Bali was the last stopping place on an indirect ramble through the Pacific and Asia. Although the beachcombers were romanticized in their day, they were usually young men with more money than sense. Hickman Powell, an American dilettante, was very much in this mould. He had "wandered in far places," which he luridly described in terms of "the human scum of Soochow Creek... the naked Igrarote" of the Philippines, living in poverty, and "the fierce Moru of Zamboanga, gallant in green and purple." Powell made Bali all the more inviting as journey's end, describing it as "the last paradise," in contrast to virtually the rest of the world: "I had glimpsed the beauty of the earth's end. She was a slattern, soiled wench..."[33]

The leisurely way of reaching Bali gave all these travelers the feeling that they knew much about the Pacific and Asia before they even got to Bali, which meant they tended to see Bali in terms of the other stopping-off points on their way. Bali was either the last of many islands of the South Pacific, or the last part of Asia, in turn tropical paradise and mysterious East.

The journey by boat gave people time to do a bit of reading, to gossip with others who had already been to Bali, perhaps to learn some basic Malay for the sake of communication, or merely to lie about in the sun. This meant, though, that people already arrived with expectations. Usually these were fulfilled, although after the build-up of Bali as paradise it became something of a convention for writers to express initial disappointment about the first view of Bali, the harbor of Bulèlèng. In these same accounts, the disappointment

32. Miguel Covarrubias, *The Island of Bali,* New York: Alfred A. Knopf, 1937, repr. Kuala Lumpur: Oxford University Press, 1972, and Singapore: Periplus; Jane Howard, *Margaret Mead: A Life,* London: Harwill, 1984, p. 187.

33. Hickman Powell, *The Last Paradise,* London: Jonathan Cape, 1930, p. 3.

quickly turned to relief as south Bali fulfilled all the travelers' expectations and more.[34]

Everybody disembarked at Bulèlèng to be met by one or two local entrepreneurs hiring out the big American cars which took visitors to the south and to the first real hotel, the KPM's Bali Hotel, built in 1925. This was the kind of luxury hotel where the rich and famous, such as Charlie Chaplin, could stay in style at $US7.50 a double per night, to be entertained by Balinese dancers and to dine on the feasts of rice and a multiplicity of side-dishes, which the Dutch called *rijstafel,* at a cost of around $3.50.[35] Cheap private accommodation, usually with a few servants, was provided by Balinese princes and later by European entrepreneurs. By the 1930s some of those entrepreneurs were building new hotels to compete with the Bali Hotel. Robert Koke, for example, established a hotel at Kuta Beach, for which he and his business partner would poach guests from the Hotel Bali.[36]

By 1930 there were about 100 tourists per month visiting the island, hardly a great number by today's standards, but still quite significant for the time. By 1940 the number was up to 250 per month.[37] The only thing approaching mass tourism was the intermittent visits by the tourists on five-day package tours. The ships would unload their passengers so that they could be taken into the city of Dénpasar to watch dance performances at the Bali Hotel. Balinese might come down to the beach at Sanur to the east of Dénpasar to watch the arrival, but few had much contact with the visitors, except when they were coopted to carry the foreigners on sedan-chairs through the surf. Even the sale of tourist objects, carved wooden heads of dancers and so on, was run discretely through a few small shops mainly owned by Europeans. One of the most famous of those was run by two German brothers, Hans and Rolf Neuhaus, who had left Germany at the end of the 1920s to travel the world, and began their enterprise as an aquarium on the beach at Sanur in 1935. They

---

34. For examples of this see Powell, *The Last Paradise,* Covarrubias, *Island of Bali,* and A. S.Wadia, *The Belle of Bali,* London: Dent, 1936, p. 16.

35. Hanna, *Bali Profile,* p. 105.

36. For information on this hotel, see Louise Koke, *Our Hotel in Bali,* Wellington: January 1987.

37. Hanna, *Bali Profile,* p. 104.

made arrangements with the KPM for groups of tourists to visit the aquarium, and ended up as major marketers of Balinese paintings and carvings. Their prices, for example f3 (Aust. 5s.) for the standard tourist souvenir of a carved wooden dancer's head, drastically undercut any of their competitors in Dénpasar.[38]

There were, of course, tourists and tourists. Those who stayed longer than the day or so set aside by the steamship lines wrote disdainfully of their more transitory brethren. A number stayed for months, visiting the European and American expatriates who had decided to make Bali their home, or finding their own corner of Bali in a prince's courtyard not too far away from the beach or the town.

Stories Home

Europeans at the time were obsessed with the idea of going abroad. The world was Europe's oyster, not only because imperialism had reached its apogee, extending further than ever before, but also because Europeans were longing to get away from the familiar world made stale by the slaughters of the First World War. The exotic world outside Europe was more inspiring than the familiarity of home, although these travelers always returned refreshed and with a stronger vision of the virtues of home.[39] During the first stage of development of Bali's tourist image, up until the early 1930s, Bali became only one small part of the tourist map, a mere appendage to the better-known Java. In this first stage the images were fairly roughly put together, and the stage itself could be summarized as the era of bare breasts, the most obvious of Bali's attractions.

Bali gradually evolved into one of the most romantic stops on the tourist itinerary, and what fed the romantic image was the host of new books and articles on the island. Thrilled by the barrage of new sights, sounds, and smells in Bali, the longer-staying travelers and more permanent residents rushed into print to tell the rest of the world about Bali's magic spell. They found a ready outlet for their prose in a host of new tourist magazines, such as the Dutch-sponsored *Inter-Ocean,* as well as the widely-known magazines which

---

38. Bakker, *Bali Verbeeld,* pp. 28-31.

39. Paul Fussell, *Abroad: British Literary Travelling Between the Wars,* Oxford: Oxford University Press, 1980.

Image from "The island of bare breasts," 1930s tourist postcard.

were designed to inform America and Europe about the exotic side of the world, foremost amongst them *National Geographic.* The titles of these books and articles say as much about propensities to purple prose in the 1920s and 1930s as they do about Bali: "the tropical wonderland," "the natural paradise," "the blessed isle," "the lotus isle," and "the island of the gods." Beyond the luxurious tropical greenery and climate, many were struck by the abundance of art, dance, and ritual, calling it, "the land of rhythm," "the land of art and religion," and "the island of temples and dances." Others enjoyed "cheerful days with brown men," "bliss in Bali," or fell under the influence of the "belle of Bali." Some, like the Dutch officials, were worried about the growth of tourism and the effects of westernization, particularly Christianity, and called "the last paradise" a "disappearing paradise."[40]

Authors struggled to find words to match the beauty of the island. They said it excelled the best the Pacific had to offer, and was at the same time more accessible than some of the other "darker" parts of the East. Above all they were seemingly dumbfounded by the sight of women going topless without any social stigma and most of the books are filled with comments on this, as well as endless photographs of these women. From the perspective of grey, post-Victorian London, or a Europe ravaged by the First World War, or an America still bound by its Puritan past and entering the Great Depression, sensual and exotic Bali promised unheard-of delights.

With the prose came visual images—photographs, paintings, and etchings showing palm trees and lush rice paddies; the inevitable bare-breasted women, and handsome, lithe young men; and, exotic arts, strange trance dances, and brahman high priests performing esoteric rites.

The most memorable images for many tourists came from the prose and pictures of a German book first published in 1920, and later to be reprinted in many languages, *Bali,* by Gregor Krause.[41]

---

40. For a bibliography of these and other tourist and travel works about Bali, see David J. Stuart-Fox, *Bibliography of Bali: Publications from 1920 to 1990*, Leiden: KITLV Press, 1992.

41. Krause, *Bali: Volk, Land, Tanze, Feste, Temple*, Hagen: Folkwang Verlag, 1920 (2 vols), 2nd edn 1921-22 (1 vol.); Dutch trans. 1926, French trans. 1930. Published with the Dutch writer Karl With.

Krause (1883-1960) was a kind of free-thinker, who inherited the role of a medical doctor writing about Balinese culture from Julius Jacobs. He was one of those dislocated souls born in a city that was alternately German, then Polish. After training as a medical doctor he left Germany in about 1910 in search of adventure in Asia. By 1912 he had gained employ with the Netherlands Indies army, with which he served on Bali, where he lived in the central Balinese kingdom of Bangli and become enchanted with Bali's art. Interned in South Africa and London during the First World War for his nationality, he returned to the Netherlands Indies, working again for the government service and later for private enterprise in Kalimantan and Java. He and his wife settled down in Sumatra, adopting two local girls, and stayed there until the 1950s, when the family retired to the Netherlands.[42]

It should be remembered that the kinds of upper-class tourists who went to Bali in those days were educated in the major European languages, and would have been able to read Krause's book even if their first language was English. Even if they could not read it, they could always look at the pictures. Krause's book had everything needed to entice those dreaming of an Eden outside the despoiled and decadent Europe which they knew. The book began on a high philosophical level invoking the unity of man and nature and arguing that the community of this Hindu island had attained such a unity through their religion and society. Krause described how this unity was put into practice in daily life, quoting Balinese sayings such as "the villagers cultivate and manage the Land, it is however the possession of the Gods." A photograph of a religiously devout peasant seems to sum up Krause's contention. The peasant is shown plowing his rice fields, worshipping the rice goddess as he goes. The Balinese were truly in tune with the rhythm of the seasons, and thus with the cycles of the divine.

Krause explained how the Hinduism of Bali reached its present form when Bali was what he called a "colony" of the great Hindu-

---

42. For information on Krause, see the recently published edition and translation of his book by H. W. Mabbett, which includes many hitherto unpublished photographs of Bali by Krause, *Bali 1912*, Wellington: January 1988.

Javanese empire of Majapahit. The kings of Bali were the descendants of the colonizers, a kind of imposition that depended on the goodwill and acceptance of the devout villagers. With these kings, Krause wrote, came the four-caste system, of which the three upper castes formed only five percent of the population.

Like many converts, Krause was unquestioning in his dedication to his cause, colonialism. Interspersed with the book's descriptions of daily life in the rice fields and the markets, Krause described a Balinese king and his palace. Krause used a passage on the despotic nature of kingship to introduce the account of the last stand of the kings of south Bali against the Dutch. This was the first of many such accounts in tourist literature, and the versions of the story became more and more florid and romanticized as time went on. Krause favored the view that this event was a sign of the catastrophic end of an old order, regrettable but inevitable. The passage on Balinese kingship ends with the words of the Balinese peasant farmers tilling the fields while their lords were being killed: "The Gods have so willed it." For Krause, and for most writers after him, the aristocracy was simply a veneer on the "real" Bali and consequently its devastation was not seen as having a fundamental effect on Balinese society. In the book the bloody *puputan* was "normalized" by being reduced to the level of timeless tourist exotica. In its treatment of the massacre as an unreal event with no meaning for the majority of Balinese, Krause's book was a blatant apology for colonialism.

After this description of Balinese kingship there was a startling shift to a discussion of how Balinese art had an organic relationship to the community and religion, Krause's favorite theme. He also managed to throw in a few lines which showed his reading of Jacobs on the subject of physiognomy. He admired the way that "the always powerful chest muscles [of Balinese women] provide the most favorable foundation for beautifully formed breasts."[43] He followed this with details of Balinese temple feasts, dances, and, that ultimate of rituals, cremation. After this book, it became almost *de rigeur* for all writers to end their Bali books with a cremation, to symbolically mark the end of their writing and the end of a spiritual

---

43. Translation Mabbett from *Bali 1912*, p. 10.

journey. The finishing touches in the Krause book were a discussion of the influence of Sanskrit and of words from Malay and Balinese as they related to original primitive society or ancient Greece and Egypt, to rice worship, and to animism.

If all the elements sound odd in juxtaposition, they make sense as an enquiry into the spirit of Bali. The book was an attempt to show how the true "folk" of Bali, the peasantry, harmonized with the universe through art and rice farming. For Krause this harmony and sense of community represented humanity as it should be, a state of grace to be regained by fallen Europe.

The photographs in this book say more than the text. So strong are these images that they take the reader beyond the metaphysical musings of the text, acting as a magnet for future generations of tourists and travelers. They were intended as a supplement to the main argument, but somehow they drift away from the text, making Bali seem a strange and wonderful island as they take on a life of their own. They show the beautiful forests and fields which provide settings for thatched-roofed and mud-walled villages, feudal displays of obeisance to decadent-looking kings, wild and fantastic dances, carving, and rituals, and most of all bare bodies—young men and women who exude vitality and abandon themselves to the joy of nature.

Balinese women move though the photographs, sometimes in ordered, sleepwalker like roles, carrying offerings nearly twice their own size on their heads. At other times the women are shown swaying and writhing in trance. Balinese men move lithely through the rice fields, or stand outside temples and houses, posing nobly for the camera. Balinese children are seen huddling together warily before this metal and glass eye of European consciousness, or are captured in ceremonial dress kneeling before the shrines of their ancestors. Every image of Bali shows an unmatched restraint and a charm broken only by outbursts of self-stabbing in the ritual dances, or by demons lurking at the gates of temples and amongst the elaborate and astounding offerings to the gods.

The Krause photographs were the first of many outstanding images published of Bali. From the 1920s onwards there were a number of photographic studios based on Java and Bali that produced the first postcards and photographs for the official government tourist bureau promotions. The most beautiful of these photographs came from a young woman, Thilly Weissenborn, who was one of a large number of Dutch men and women born and raised in Indies society. Like many of her counterparts she favored the cooler mountain air of Java to the steamy coastal towns and after training in the Armenian-owned Kurkdjian studio in the hot, dirty port of Surabaya she moved to the hill-station of Garut, in west Java. When she moved to the gracious hill-station she set up her own Lux Photo Studio. Both Surabaya and Garut were major stops on the standard tourist routes through the Indies, and so her only competitors for the trade in tourist images were a small number of Japanese and Chinese studios on Bali, in Singaraja and Dénpasar. The outstanding quality of her photographs meant the tourist authorities chose them above others for use in tourist magazines such as *Tropical Netherlands, Sluyter's Monthly,* and *Inter-Ocean,* which had all been established in the Indies in the early 1920s to reach international audiences.[44] By the quality of her work she single-handedly spread the message of Bali through the official Dutch tourist networks.

Her most memorable Bali photographs all have a kind of shimmering light. They show young men in near-deserted temples; palmtrees framing incredibly elaborate and bizarre temple carvings; the very handsome young king of Karangasem sitting on gaudy antique European furniture, dressed in rich brocades, his wife and daughter beside him; the inevitable bare-breasted women gazing into the half-distance or standing, smiling against intricately carved stonework; or, most exquisite of all, a beautiful young dancer richly arrayed in her costume, holding a flower, and framed by a gong.

If earlier images of bare-breasted women reflect the way Bali was seen as a South Seas paradise, then the dancing girl images show Bali as part of the mysterious East. Thilly Weissenborn's photograph of the dancing girl captures all the lure of Bali. It has the quality of an invitation, the girl's hand raised as if she is beckoning us to come to Bali, but at the same time she does not look directly into the camera. Her eyes turn mysteriously, as if she has the inscrutability of

44. Ernst Drissen, *Vastgelegd voor Later: Indische Foto's (1917-1942) van Thilly Weissenborn,* Amsterdam: Sijthoff, 1983.

The dancing girl by Thilly Weissenborn

the whole of Asia under her gorgeously carved and elaborate head-dress. Her costume and appearance do not show the kind of fresh and natural sexuality evinced by the women photographed topless in the street. Instead, her charm comes partly from the sexual distance implied by her youth, as if she not only held the promise of hidden pleasures and fecundity, but maintained the remoteness of an ancient yet young civilization. The flower she holds, like the gold flowers in her headdress, speak of the natural lushness of the island, and the decoration of her dress implies that this natural lushness is closely linked to cultural riches. Of course her pose is not the usual one of a Balinese dancer—Balinese girls do not sit cross-legged making mystical looking gestures like this one—but her stilted pose is reminiscent of other features of mystical Asia, of Buddha figures or ancient Hindu statues. The look evoked is one of "deep brooding eyes that seem to be seeing things in time far distant."[45] It was no accident that this photograph was so frequently chosen by the tourist authority for reproduction in their tourist pamphlets. After publication of Weissenborn's book, other less beautiful photographs of dancing girls proliferated, making the dancing girl a recurrent image of Bali.

First Films

The posed nature of the photograph of the dancing girl draws attention to the fact that in the 1920s and 1930s an image of Bali was being created. People were not simply recording what they saw, but, consciously or not, were selecting and highlighting, even staging, what they thought Bali meant. The first films of Bali, made at a time when the expatriate lifestyle was just establishing itself, were part of this process.

In 1926 the first moving pictures of Bali were made available to the world by a German film maker: they were brief and eerie scenes of a royal cremation and sacred trance dances, simply titled, *Cremation* and *Sang Hyang and Kecak Dances*.[46] The royal crema-

---

45. Dan Davies-Moore, "The Girls of Bali," *Inter-Ocean* 9 (1928): 485-9, especially p. 485.

46. Reference to these films comes from the Utrecht film foundation catalogue, but no information is available on the maker of the films, W. Mullens.

tion featured the corpse of a queen of Bangli being carried on to a cremation tower before being taken to the graveyard and burnt in a sarcophagus shaped like a lion. The trance dancers were young girls performing the *Sanghyang* or "angel" dance in which the spirits of divine women enter their bodies. To Europeans the sight of little girls swaying in an incense-filled atmosphere, surrounded by seated men with arms akimbo, would have looked particularly weird. The German makers of the film may have worked with Krause, who was based largely in Bangli, especially since these images fit into the scheme of his book. They add depth to the idea of Bali's culture, but present probably the most extreme and exotic visual aspects of that culture.

In 1927 the image of the witch was brought to the screen in the first fiction film set on Bali, *Calon Arang.* Little is known of this film, and no copies survive, but the makers probably had links with the Italians who owned the moving picture theater at Dénpasar, where Charlie Chaplin played on the screen for enthusiastic Balinese audiences. The only article about it described *Calon Arang* as "a commendable departure from the stereotyped Hollywood pattern of tropical romance," which the writer defined as palm trees, beachcombers, "and the inevitable bevy of dusky beauties such as never were on land or sea."[47] This comment tells little about the film, but it does show how conscious the image-makers of Bali were of trying to add depth and respectability to the idea of Bali.

Calon Arang is the story of an old hag who threatens pestilence and destruction on a kingdom. Her threat is unsuccessfully challenged by a knight sent to assassinate her. Although she eventually survives she is held at bay by the power of a great priest. In dance-drama performances of this story the witch is presented as the horrible figure of *Rangda,* a giant demon with a meter-long tongue, pendulous breasts, wild straw for hair, curling fangs, claw-like nails, and round staring eyes. The priest takes on the benevolent form of *Barong,* a kind of terrible beast not unlike the lion of Chinese lion dances. As the *Barong* and *Rangda* fight, followers of the *Barong* rush with drawn krisses to stab the *Rangda,* but she turns her magic

The expatirate hero of the 1930s, Walter Spies, artist, musician, ethnographer, dreamer, at home with his parrot and monkey in Campuan, Ubud.

on them and they try to stab themselves. Such is the *Barong's* power that the sharp blades do not penetrate the skin of these entranced performers.

The *Rangda* and the kris dance became one of the most potent of all the elements of Bali's image, an element which could be counterpoised to the superficial image of the tropical paradise. The gentle figure of the little girl was balanced by the horrible figure of the witch, and the idea of trance and self-stabbing frenzy. If Dr. Krause tried to emphasize harmony and the organic community in his description of Bali, then the *Rangda* represented the other side of this image, the feeling that lurking under the harmony there were wild forces ready to run amuk. "The Island of the Gods" has also been called "The Island of the Demons," most notably in a German film of 1931, and later in a Dutch novel of 1948.[48]

Walter Spies and the Balinese Idyll

The images of Bali began to crystallize in the late 1920s around

---

48. Johan Fabricus, *Eiland der Demonen,* Amsterdam: De Muiderkring, 1948.

one man, or at least around one man's social set. The year of the screening of the first feature film on Bali, 1927, was the one when Walter Spies (1895-1942) came to live permanently on the island. In his fifteen years contact with Bali he was a primary catalyst in the image-making process. Like van der Tuuk, Spies was a man of great influence, as much through the impact of his personality as his wisdom. Spies and his associates challenged the "Bally Hoo" of the more vulgar aspects of Bali's tourist images,[49] presenting instead their own version of the real Bali as a rich culture based on an authentic folk tradition.

Spies, the dazzling, aristocratic-looking esthete, arrived on Bali as a painter fresh from a stint as court musician for the Sultan of Yogyakarta, in central Java. Walter Spies was the son of a Moscow-based businessman, and had his first taste of the Orient in Russia. As the artistic and musical child of a prosperous cosmopolitan man, Spies knew some of the leading artists and composers of the 1920s, including Friedrich Murnau, Germany's leading experimental film-maker, whom he befriended. Murnau's version of the *Dracula* story, *Nosferatu* (1922), influenced Spies's technical interest in light and shadow. More importantly, Spies brought its sense of menace and dark brooding forces to bear on Bali, in the form of an interest in the *Rangda* and *Barong* dance-drama performances of the *Calon Arang* story.[50]

Spies was a sensitive and somewhat reclusive man, particularly when he was painting. But his deep feeling for matters cultural made him well liked amongst the expatriate community of Bali, and amongst the Balinese with whom he lived. As a homosexual he joined other young men looking for a paradise away from the strict mores of Europe, and he believed that he had found it in Bali. When Spies was tried for having sex with under-aged boys in 1939 his friend, the anthropologist Margaret Mead, wrote in his defense,

49. G. Gorer, *Bali and Angkor: Looking at Life and Death,* London: Michael Joseph, 1936, quoted in Howard, *Margaret Mead,* p. 181.

50. On Spies, see Hans Rhodius, *Schönheit und Reichtum des Lebens: Walter Spies (Maler und Musiker auf Bali 1895-1942),* The Hague: Boucher, 1964; Hans Rhodius and John Darling, *Walter Spies and Balinese Art,* Zutphen: Terra, 1980. John Stowell has written a definitive biography of Spies, and I am indebted to him for many insights into Spies's life and influences, as well as some disagreement with my characterization of Spies!

explaining Spies's life in Bali and his "continuing light involvement with Balinese male youth." She argued that Spies was seeking a "repudiation of the kind of dominance and submission, authority and dependence, which he associated with European culture."[51] On Bali homosexuality was, she said, not a matter for moral condemnation, simply a pastime for young unmarried men. Spies's homosexuality may not necessarily have added to his own sensitivity and cultural awareness, but it did contribute to the positive openness in his relations with Balinese, particularly Balinese men. Mead added to her defence by pointing out how difficult it was to accurately document ages on Bali, questioning whether the young men really were under the official age of consent for men, of twenty-one. Unfortunately Mead's eloquent defense of Spies fell on deaf Dutch Calvinist ears, and Spies was jailed for his "crime," although the representations made on his behalf meant he got a lighter sentence than some of his co-accused.

Bali's image as a homosexual paradise was perhaps one unintended consequence of the image of Bali as a woman. After the heavy praises heaped on Balinese women by Dr. Julius Jacobs and his successors, Balinese men were viewed by western visitors as equally beautiful and, to some degree, passive. Many of Spies's friends, including Mead, saw Spies and Bali as temperamentally linked, and felt there was something in his character that drew him to innocent and cultured Bali. Conversely, there was something in what they saw as the spirit of Bali that was perfect for Spies. There was always the element in this link between Spies and Bali that many of his friends were so impressed by him that they tended to read his personality into Balinese culture.[52]

Although the pattern of perceiving Bali had already been established before Spies's arrival in Bali in 1927, he and those associated

---

51. Quoted out of context in Rhodius, *Schönheit und Reichtum,* p. 359, but originally part of a lengthy letter in defence of Spies (from the Margaret Mead-Gregory Bateson fieldnotes, Manuscripts Division, Library of Congress) which involved an explanation of the inability to measure Balinese ages, an important factor in the trial, since the charge was one of sex with a minor.

52. See the analysis of comments in Rhodius's book by James A. Boon, "Between-the-Wars Bali: Rereading the Relics," in George Stocking (ed.), *The History of Anthropology* IV, Madison: University of Wisconsin Press, 1986, pp. 218-46.

with him were to enshrine that pattern in both tourist literature and more profound research on Balinese society. Spies only direct contribution to the tourist industry was his work on a guide book with the learned government archeologist and philologist, Roelof Goris. Spies his own photographs and advice to Goris for this work, *Bali: Religion and Customs.*[53]

Like Krause, Spies was vitally interested in the peasant farmers who were seen as embodying the real spirit of Bali. During his time on Bali, he enquired into all aspects of this spirit through collecting proverbial wisdom, folktales, and all kinds of tunes. He took photographs of everything he found expressive or exceptional, and peopled his painted landscapes with peasants and legendary figures set on shimmering, multi-layered terrain. In this interest, however, the German Romantic tradition once again converged with other European images of Bali. The romanticized folk were the same Balinese peasantry who were held up in the nineteenth-century Dutch idea of the village republic as noble egalitarian figures.

Spies probed the darker side of this image, particularly in his work on the film *Island of the Demons,* made by Victor Baron von Plessen, a German rural aristocrat and Dr. Friedrich Dahlseim, and Jewish expert on documenting "primitive" societies. Because these two knew little about Bali and relied on the artist's expertise, the film gave Spies the chance to express his own vision of Bali.

The film was a love story about two peasants whose harmonious village life was destroyed by a *Rangda*-like witch, who created an epidemic that devastated the happy village community. Only exorcistic rituals could stop her, and return the village to its normal state. The film ran the full gamut of the images that interested Spies. First came the beautifully filmed scenes of rice-terraces reflecting the sky, and of hard-working and happy peasants in the fields. Then came the ideal community, disrupted by a bitter woman whose shifty looks betrayed her evil nature, who was eventually revealed in the form of *Rangda.* Throughout the scenes of witchcraft and exorcism Spies wove documentation of Balinese dances and rituals. This

53. R. Goris & Walter Spies, *The Island of Bali: Its Religion and Ceremonies,* Batavia: Koninklijk Paketvaart Maatschapij, 1931.

documentation guaranteed the authenticity of the scenes, showing that they were giving an insight into the "real" Bali behind the superficial tourist images.

There were times that Spies had to stretch this authenticity for the sake of the film, very revealing moments which show just how relative ideas of Bali's reality can be. One of these moments was the deployment of the modern version of the *kecak,* what is now known as the "monkey dance" in which men sit in a circle and chant. Spies had seen this recent adaptation of the *Sanghyang* or "angel" trance dance, which used this kind of *a cappella* male chorus. The Balinese dancer Limbak of Bedulu had provided a narrative form—a new *Ramayana* story element—and increased the number of men performing in order to add to the drama, and Spies grafted this adaptation into the film.

Spies had worked on another film before *Island of the Demons.* In the 1920s the son of a famous American family, André Roosevelt, had called on Spies's knowledge of dance and Balinese narrative to provide material for his film, *Goona-Goona,* also called *The Kris.* Roosevelt had lived on Bali in the 1920s as an agent for American Express and Thomas Cook, in partnership with M. J. Minas, an Armenian who owned a travelling film-house.[54] Spies ended up doing a lot more work for the film than just scripting, and it went on to become quite well known and fashionable in America, where in New York high society it made *guna-guna,* a Malay and Javanese term for love magic, into a popular phrase. In fact it can be credited with linking sex and magic in the popular image of Bali.[55]

At the same time these films were making an impact, a colonial contribution to broadening the image of Bali was gaining attention. In 1931 the great modern colonial exhibition was held in Paris, and all the imperial powers vied to display the cultural riches of their colonies. The Dutch contribution was truly spectacular—ancient Javanese statues, beautiful textiles and many other types of Primitive and Hindu art shown in two buildings that recreated the

54. Hanna, *Bali Profile,* p. 105.

55. See the comments by Covarrubias, *Island of Bali,* p. 391; and John Darling, in his filmography in Leonard Leuras & R. Ian Lloyd, *Bali: The Ultimate Island,* Ringwood: Viking, 1987, pp. 238-41.

Dutch idea of traditional Indonesian architecture. Unfortunately one of these buildings was burnt to the ground during the exhibition, destroying some of Indonesia's great treasures, and undermining colonial arguments that Europeans could look after native culture better than the natives. Bali had pride of place in the Colonial Exhibition. Balinese arts and crafts were on show, and the Netherlands Indies Government organized a Balinese dance troupe, mainly from Paliatan, near Ubud.

In the history of western theater the Paris Colonial Exhibition is chiefly remembered as the place where Antonin Artaud, this century's most influential theorist of drama, first saw Balinese dance. So struck was this Surrealist playwright that he used the experience as the basis of his liberating theory of the "theater of cruelty," an idea of total theater in which the expressive force of the body elevates dance and drama into a mystical act of communication. Before he was committed to an insane asylum, Artaud formulated his views of the importance of Balinese theater in a text that has had a major impact on the most important performers and directors of modern times.[56] In many ways Artaud's reactions typify the way Bali suddenly took center stage in world thinking about the East.

Love and Death on Bali

The famous from Clemenceau to H. G. Wells all visited Bali in their time. Barbara Hutton, Charlie Chaplin, Noël Coward, and numerous others, rich, titled, or simply curious, all came to the home of Spies in the hills of Ubud. These visitors were sent by mutual friends, or learned of Spies through his growing reputation in the salons of New York, Paris and Berlin.

Spies had found the archetypical lifestyle around which the social set built its images. He found cooler climes in the foothills of Ubud, which made it preferable to Dénpasar, and eventually built one of his houses there. Waited on by handsome boys, with his pet monkey and cockatoo, this tall, thin-featured expert came to represent Bali and all its pleasures.

The key tourist spots of Bali up to the present-day all became

---

56. See his *Le Theatre et son Double,* Paris: Gallimard, 1964.

famous in this era. Single-handedly Spies made Ubud the alternative area for genteel tourism, the center of an artistic lifestyle. His good friends Katharane and Jack Mershon, an American dancer and her photographer husband, made the beach area of Sanur famous, helped by the German Neuhaus brothers with their aquarium and art shop. Sanur too had its artist, the Belgian aristocrat Adrien Le Mayeur de Merpres, who fulfilled the dream of Bali by marrying a spectacularly beautiful young dancing girl, Ni Pollok. Le Mayeur was in his fifties, Pollok only a teenager, but that did not seem to trouble the authorities at the time. Also living partly in Sanur and then in the mountains in Iseh, where he took over Spies's second house, was the Swiss artist Theo Meier. Even amongst the expatriates, Meier's lifestyle was decidedly decadant, and although he cultivated a group of interesting Balinese artists, he was generally disdained by the other Europeans.

In 1936 the first hotel on Kuta Beach, west of Sanur, was built by an American, Robert Koke, and his English-American partner, Vanneen Walker, also known as Miss Manx, Muriel Pearson, Ktut Tantri, and later, when she became a radio propaganda broadcaster during the Indonesian Revolution, Surabaya Sue. The two fell out, but the hotel remained in the hands of Koke and his wife until the Second World War.[57]

One of Spies's most famous guests was the very popular novelist, Vicki Baum, who came to Bali via Hawaii to write a novel "in the style of Melville or Conrad."[58] A prolific writer with some experience of the East, Baum had already lived in Malaya, China, and Japan. Her works were already well known in a number of languages, particularly English, and her sense of writing for a large audience was furthered by a move to Hollywood, where she became a screenwriter. In her novel, originally called *Love and Death on Bali*, but translated as *A Tale from Bali*,[59] Baum described an old Dutchman who had been living on Bali from the end of the nineteenth century

57. Koke, *Our Hotel.*

58. Walter Dreesen, "Albumblatt für Vicki Baum," *Merian,* special Bali issue 10/31, Hamburg: Hoffmann und Campe, 1978.

59. Originally called, in German, *Love and Death on Bali,* English publication, London: Bles, 1937, repr., London: Michael Joseph, 1973, Kuala Lumpur: Oxford University Press, 1978.

as the source of her notes on Balinese culture and history. The aim of these alleged notes was to lend authenticity to her story of the sufferings and experiences of Balinese villagers at the time of the Dutch conquest of south Bali. The Dutchman was in fact fictitious: her sources were Walter Spies and his associate, the scholarly civil servant C.J. Grader. One part of her novel deals with an outbreak of leprosy and the performance of exorcistic rituals against it, and could almost be a prose version of the film *Island of the Demons*.

Following Spies, Baum helped to spread the idea of the noble peasantry of Bali, at the same time acting as an apologist for Dutch imperialism. At the beginning of the novel she paid tribute not just to Spies himself and Katharane Mershon, the American dancer from Sanur, but to the earlier scholars of the village republic, Liefrinck and *controleur* (district officer) Schwartz, "renowned for their knowledge of Bali and they love the island dearly."[60]

She continued in this vein with high praise for the Dutch as colonists, something she related to the appreciation of Liefrinck for the peasantry. In her novel the embodiment of the noble peasant is Pak whose "pacifist existence... was perhaps of more importance than the collisions in Bali between the vigorous *Realpolitik* of Holland and a heroic and medieval pride of arms." She went on, "Since then the Dutch have carried out an achievement in colonization that reflects the highest credit on them."[61]

These introductory comments were borne out by the passage of the narrative, which intertwined descriptions of the humble peasant life of Pak with a love story and the events of the *puputan* in Badung in 1906. She added to the text lines from the Indian *Bhagavad-Gita,* the Sanskrit poem made famous as the greatest work of Indian philosophy by the Theosophists (westerners seeking the wisdom of the East). The Balinese were ignorant of the *Bhagavad-Gita* itself, but that did not stop Baum from putting its lines into the mouths of Balinese priests and princes. As with other books about the Orient, there was substantial blurring of the difference between the various Asian cultures. Like Krause, Baum showed the Balinese organic

---

60. ibid., p. 9.

61. ibid.

peasant life as essentially fatalist, in line with the Theosophists' idea of the way Asian philosophy was practiced in everyday life. Her exemplary peasant says, "what the gods will must come to pass."[62] In the end the book advanced an argument that peasants like Pak had more to gain from benevolent European rule than from the arbitrary government of traditional despots.

In telling her story Baum provided considerable detail about many aspects of Balinese life and culture, detail which could only have been gained through her association with Spies. There were long descriptions of day-to-day life in villages, priestly houses and palaces, which gave the book an immediacy heightened by the fluency of Baum's prose. Descriptions of cockfights and the inevitable kris dance performance were not given gratuitously, however, for they had a role in the explanatory thrust of the novel.

Baum wanted to explain how good the Dutch were, but she had to reconcile this with the bloody *puputan,* hardly a shining example of beneficence towards the natives. She did this by describing the *puputan* itself as something inevitable, something in which the Dutch were virtually unwilling participants, forced there by the venality of a Chinese merchant whose ship had been wrecked on the coast, and through the pride of the Balinese ruler who refused to surrender to European rule.

As the Dutch mowed down the Balinese, they did so unwillingly in Baum's tale. A humanitarian officer, Dekker, represented the Dutch response as they opened fire on the Balinese: "Some of the officers turned their heads aside or put their hands over their eyes. Dekker, for one, was unable to endure the sight of men killing their wives and then themselves, of mothers driving a kris into their infants' breasts. He turned away and vomited."[63] She did not portray the accompanying native troops as sharing the noble sentiments of the Dutch, who had to restrain them from looting the jewels of the dead.

In conversation later the Dutch explained the Balinese motivation not as any anti-colonial stand, but as "the holy madness," the

---

62. ibid., p. 19.
63. ibid., p. 502.

trance possession shown in the *Calon Arang* performances. "Do you remember taking me to that kris dance, Visser?" van Tilema asked. "I believe they were in trance to-day, too, to behave as they did. I even believe they were glad to die." In case we missed the point, Baum puts this comment in the mouth of one of the Dutch speaking to the Resident: "It's a lesson to us all, Resident, how we ought to treat the Balinese. Hats off to such a death as theirs."[64] And so, Baum seems to say, the Balinese aristocracy contributed to the praiseworthy Dutch policy of preserving Balinese culture by getting killed.

This book bears the imprimatur of Spies's ideas. It is unclear whether he would have agreed so whole-heartedly with Baum's support of imperialism, but on the other hand he was never against imperialism, only opposed to the stuffiness and formality of petty bureaucrats. What Baum was displaying was a typical European attitude to colonialism, which, at the time, was only questioned by a few such as E. M. Forster and George Orwell. All those in the Bali set agreed on the importance of preserving Balinese culture, and saw enlightened colonialism as the way to do it. They thought some of the less sensitive and aware civil servants were an impediment to Bali, but worked closely with the more enlightened ones, such as Roelof Goris, who with a number of others raised a strong defense of Bali against the influence of missionaries in the 1930s.

Clarifying the Picture of Bali

Spies devoted great energy to filling in the details of the broader picture of Balinese life and culture. He researched the arts, and was co-author of a definitive book on Balinese theater, *Dance and Drama in Bali,* published in 1938.[65] His partner was Beryl de Zoete, a gifted English writer from the fringe of the Bloomsbury set. De Zoete was the lover of Arthur Waley, one of the most famous translators of Japanese and Chinese literature of his day, and she travelled throughout Asia, documenting theater, and added her lucid prose to the expert

---

64. ibid., p. 503.

65. Originally published London: Faber & Faber, 1938, repr. Kuala Lumpur and Jakarta: Bhratara, 1973. The foreword is by the famous Orientalist Arthur Waley (see Alison Waley, *A Half of Two Lives,* London: Weidenfeld & Nicolson, 1982). Some of Spies's other articles on Balinese culture are republished as appendices in Rhodius, *Schönheit und Reichtum.*

information provided by Spies. They had assistance from Christian Grader, a tall young civil servant who devoted his spare time to the study of Balinese social systems, and was happy to work with Spies, whom he saw as providing a great many insights into Bali.

Spies shared his musical interests with the American McPhee, a composer, musicologist and friend of Aaron Copland. After the war it was McPhee who single-handedly spread the fame of Balinese music, and who in his compositions and writings on Balinese music influenced modern masters such as Philip Glass and Peter Sculthorpe.

Spies worked very closely with the archeologist Stutterheim, and it was Stutterheim and his companion, Claire Holt, who elevated Spies's name by giving him credit for the creation of modern Balinese art. In this account traditional Balinese painting was becoming stagnant, a spent force, until the arrival of Spies. Balinese artists who saw Spies's work or were supervised by Spies's friend, Rudolf Bonnet, suddenly developed a new school of painting.[66] Bonnet, who arrived in Bali a few years after Spies, was a fatherly, if not paternalistic Dutch artist, most of whose work consisted of fairly conventional portraiture, and who would probably have gone unremarked through history were it not for his friendship with Spies and his active promotion of Balinese artists. He advanced the claim of Spies's influence through a number of articles on Balinese art that presented their adopted home of Ubud as the real center of new art.[67]

Through their work in two new institutions, Bonnet claimed, he and Spies helped to shape the proper development of Balinese art and to protect it from the destructive influence of tourism. The institutions were the new Bali Museum, destined to be the ultimate instrument of cultural preservation on Bali, and the Ubud-based artists' association of Pita Maha, the spiritual home of modern art. The Museum, beside preserving Balinese art, acted as a "clearing

---

66. W. F. Stutterheim, "Een Nieuwe Loot aan een Oude Stem," *Elsevier's Geillusteerde Maandschrift* (1934): 391-400.

67. R. Bonnet, "Beeidende Kunst in Gianjar," *Djåwå* 16 (1936): 60-71; and an article in R. Goris and P. L. Dronkers, *Bali: Atlas Kebudayaan/ Cults and Customs/ Cultuurgeschiedenis in Beeld,* Jakarta: Government of the Republic of Indonesia, 1953?, p. 159.

A French fantasy on the *puputan* (from Le Petit Journal 1849).

Poster advertising the Bali Hotel by Dutch Painter Willem Gerald Hofker
(copyright holder unknown).

1930s travel poster issued by the Travellers Official Information Bureau of the Netherlands (copyright holder unknown).

1930s travel poster from KPM (copyright holder unknown).

Balinese Girls by Rudolf Bonnet, 1955.

Balinese depiction of westerners, c.1880s, from North Bali, possibly the work of I Ketut Gedé. Pignments on panel, 34.7x21.2, c.1900, originally collected by W.O.J. Nieuwenkamp, Nusantara Museum Delft, photo Anthony Forge, courtesy Nusantara Museum and Forge estate.

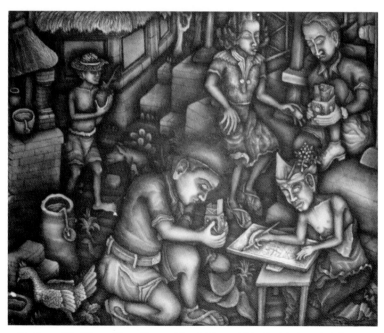

Ida Bagus Ktut Togog Warta, Batuan, Theo Meier and friends visit the artist's house, c.1938, ink on paper, former collection Theo Meier, courtesy Museum Pasifika.

The Bali Nirwana Resort versus tradition, cartoon by Jango Pramartha, early 1990s, courtesy the artist and Linda Connor.

Aerial view over Bali (Nusa Dua) © Øystein Lund Andersen (iStockphoto.com).

Dewa Putu Mokoh, Bom Bali (the Bali Bombings), 2006, ink and acrylic on canvas,
60x80, Collection Chris and Mary Hill, photo Bo Wong.

Possibly I Nyoman Ngendon, Batuan, scenes of daily life on Bali, c.1940, 55x55cm,
watercolour and ink on paper, originally collected by Theo Meier, former Haks collection,
courtesy Singapore Batuan Collection.

Bali Burger by Ida Bagus Surya Dharma, 1995, ink and watercolor on paper,
17x24.5cm, courtesy the artist and Linda Connor.

Balinese version of daily life, as shown in the story of the *Brayut* family. Details of painting possibly by Kumpi Mesira, Kamasan village, pigments on traditional cloth,

23x380cm, c.1900, Forge Collection, Australian Museum, E74195, courtesy Australian Museum, photo Emma Furno.

Walter Spies, *Road on Bali*, 1928, courtesy Walter Spies Foundation
and Horst Jordt.

I Made Budi, Batuan, Razia Narkotika (Drug Raid), 2000, 40x25cm, acrylic on paper, courtesy Singapore Batuan Collection, photo Ken Cheong.

I Ketut Manggi, Batuan, Serangan Island, 2007, 50x70cm, acrylic on paper, courtesy Singapore Batuan Collection, photo Ken Cheong.

An example of late 60s and early 70s travel marketing (*Papineau's Guide to Bali: Island Paradise*, Denpasar, Bali: BAP Bali, c.1970).

Mangu Putra, Denpasar I, oil on canvas, 2005, 140x200cm, courtesy Thomas Freitag, photo Koes Karnadi.

house" for work which they selected as the best of Balinese art.[68] The artists' association, which began in 1936, had a similar intent of nurturing painting and keeping the influence of commercialism at bay. Through both organizations exhibitions of Balinese painting were sent to other parts of the Netherlands East Indies, and to the Netherlands. Up until his death in 1978, Bonnet was well remembered and respected by Balinese artists and cultural authorities for his role in the promotion of Balinese art.

Bonnet, after initial hesitation, steered Balinese artists in the direction of his own aesthetic interests.[69] He wrote an article in one journal in the most schoolmasterly of tones attacking modern Balinese innovations in architecture, with illustrations of these innovations labeled "bad," next to pictures of traditional style buildings which he labeled "good."[70] Quite clearly he promoted those artists who fitted his criteria, at the expense of others of equal or greater talent. For example Pan Seken of Kamasan village, Klungkung (c. 1893-1984) was one of the best traditional artists of his generation and a member of Pita Maha, but his work did not feature in Bonnet's critical writing on Balinese art.

Traditional art was static, the new art dynamic, according to Bonnet, Bali's foremost archeologist, Willem Stutterheim and the other writers on Balinese painting. The content of Balinese art, they argued, had changed from Hindu mythology to scenes of everyday life, which allowed for originality and self-expression.[71] This was not really true, as traditional paintings have always included scenes of daily life, either as the subject matter in legends such as *Pan Brayut,* the story of a raucous commoner family, or as little border

---

68. On the Bali Museum, see Th. Resink, "Het Bali Museum" *Djåwå* 18 (1938): 73-82. The committee of the Museum included Resink himself, an artist and engineer, Grader, the KPM tourist agent G.H. Hendrikse, Spies, Bonnet, Goris, and the Regent of Badung, Cokorda Alit Ngurah from Satria, as well as I Gusti Bagus Nagara from Jembrana. My thanks to John Stowell for updating this list, and also to information from Garrett and Bronwyn Solyom from their unpublished study of the Museum.

69. I am indebted to Hildred Geertz for detailed information from her research on the interactions of western patrons and Balinese artists in the 1930s. See further Bakker, *Bali Verbeeld.*

70. Philokalos, "De Keerzijde," *Djåwå* 16 (1936): 139.

71. Bonnet in Goris & Dronkers, *Bali,* p. 159. See also Claire Holt, *Art in Indonesia: Continuities and Change,* Ithaca: Cornell University Press, 1967, pp. 173-4,180,185 & 187.

scenes on the bottom of mythological images.[72] Experimentation with new media and styles had also been going on in Balinese art since the nineteenth century.[73]

Bonnet and his associates never let the facts get in the way of a good story. They saw themselves as helping Balinese painting take off from its medieval limitations to a Renaissance-like height. The historical parallels were very clearly drawn by a number of writers.[74] The assumptions were always paternalistic: the West was already developed and artistically mature; Balinese culture was being helped by benevolent westerners to go through the proper stages of development and maturity. So the ethical ideas of protecting and preserving Bali did not, in practice, prevent change. Instead, they meant that change should occur according to the tastes of the western preservers. Spies probably did not share Bonnet's sense of paternalistic mission so enthusiastically, but he went along with it, and no doubt would have enjoyed the later romanticizing of himself as the "father" of modern Balinese art. No matter that some of the Balinese artists being patronized were far more talented than either Bonnet or Spies.

Covarrubias and "Island of Bali"

In terms of Bali's image, Spies's greatest influence was on the author of the definitive book on Bali, Miguel Covarrubias. Originally published in 1937, Covarrubias's *Island of Bali* has outlasted all other travel books to become the key descriptive work on Bali, known practically to all visitors to the island.

Miguel Covarrubias's (1904-57) background shows just how cosmopolitan the Bali set had become. This plump, urbane and highly cultivated man was born of a wealthy and politically influential Mexican family; he mixed in American and French circles,

72. See for example A. Forge, *Balinese Traditional Paintings,* Sydney: Australian Museum, 1978.

73. H. I. R. Hinzler, *Catalogue of Balinese Manuscripts... The Balinese Drawings from the van der Tuuk Collection,* 2 vols, Leiden: Brill, 1986-7.

74. Bonnet, "Beeldende Kunst"; cf. Bakker, *Bali Verbeeld,* p. 26; H. Paulides, "Oude en Nieuw Kunst op Bali, Tegen den Achtergrond van het Westen," *Cultureel Indie* 2 (1940): 169-85; see also J. Kats, "Moderne Beeidende Kunst op Bali," *Maandblad voor Beeldende Kunsten* 14, 3 (1937):67-73; and H. F. E. Visser, "Tentoonstelling van Hedendaagsche Balische Schilder- en Beeldhouwkunst," *Maandblad voor Beeidende Kunsten* 14, ll (1937):321-30.

Mario, the innovative genius of dance in 1930s Bali, as depicted by Miguel Covarrubias.

and made his fame principally as a cartoonist. By the time of his death he had been elevated to the status of a national hero in his home country, even though he spent much of his life outside it.[75] Like others of his set he roamed the world, following the cultured and famous to Paris and living mainly in the United States. Beside *Island of Bali* he wrote a travel book about his native Mexico, but did not achieve great things in other fields. His chief talent was his ability to synthesize and popularize other people's ideas.

The introduction to *Island of Bali* is like a summary of all the elements of the Bali experience as it had evolved by the 1930s. Covarrubias and his wife, Rose, read Krause's book and so "developed an irresistible desire to see the island."[76] After travelling by steamer from the United States, and learning Malay on the way, they arrived in north Bali. They stayed there only long enough to meet the indefatigable entrepreneur Patimah, a hard-headed but charming middle-aged woman who had experienced the old and new aspects of Bali. She was said to have narrowly escaped widow suicide after the death of the last raja of Klungkung, who died in the *puputan* of

---

75. See Maurice Horn, *The World Encyclopedia of Cartoons,* New York: Chelsea House, 1980, p. 173. A good study is Adriana Williams and Yu-Chee Chong, *Covarrubias in Bali,* Singapore: Editions Didier Millet, 2005.

76. *Island of Bali,* p. xvii.

1908. From her they obtained a car and her life story, and headed through the inhospitable mountains to the glories of south Bali.

First stop was the Dutch steamship line's Bali Hotel, but the pair quickly escaped from proto-urban Dénpasar to the "real Bali" of mud walls and thatched roofs a block away from the hotel.[77] Not long after they had acquired a prince as a landlord there, they met Spies, whom Covarrubias described with great respect as "Bali's most famous resident," and "an authentic friend of the Balinese and loved by them."[78]

In fact the couple had a letter of introduction to Spies from André Roosevelt, maker of *Goona-Goona,* and were introduced via the KPM's tourist agent, Bob Mörzer Bruyns.[79] By omitting these factual details, Covarrubias gave the impression that he had arrived on Bali without preconceptions. As he saw it, his views were not shaped by tourism, but by Spies himself.

According to Covarrubias's book, he and his wife left Bali to be in time for the Colonial Exhibition in Paris in 1931, but returned to be confronted by tourists, missionaries, Balinese with a developing taste for western ways, and growing (but allegedly hitherto unknown) poverty. All these were threatening to wreck the "real" Bali, but enough of their Bali survived for Miguel to finish his book, which was supplemented by an album of photographs by Rose, and cultural illumination from Spies.

If the introduction has all the elements of the classic experience of Bali in the 1930s, then the text itself, over four hundred pages, gives depth and importance to the various elements of Bali's image. The book abounds with colorful prose, clear descriptions, diagrams, drawings, and lively retellings of ancient legends. Most of the eminently quotable generalizations do not stand up to rigorous scrutiny, but then Covarrubias's aim was to present a "bird's-eye-view" of Bali.[80]

The main text of the book began with a description of Bali's

---

77. ibid., p. xx.

78. ibid., p. xxi.

79. Letter of Rose Covarrubias in Rhodius, *Schönheit und Reichtum,* p. 278.

80. *Island of Bali,* p. xxv.

geographical role as "the last Asiatic outpost to the east."[81] This refers to the famous Wallace Line, named after the nineteenth-century colleague of Darwin who described a sharp division between the flora and fauna of Asia and that of Australia. The line marking the division coincides with the strait that separates Bali from its neighbor, Lombok. To underline the point, Covarrubias exaggerated his description of Lombok's aridity, making it sound dramatically different from Bali.

When Covarrubias described the people he was really in full flight: "Like a continual under-sea ballet, the pulse of life in Bali moves with a measured rhythm..."[82] Taking up the Krause approach, he went on to tell us that, "no other race gives the impression of living in such close touch with nature, creates such a complete feeling of harmony between the people and their surroundings." In this Covarrubias repeated conventional ideas of "race" as a term loosely used to denote what we now call "culture," but which then still bore overtones of common blood and distinctive physical traits.

In the second chapter Covarrubias took up the idea of the original Balinese as the basis of the village republics. He described the villages in the mountains that preserved the original culture, known as *Bali Aga*. This, according to the theory inherited from Liefrinck and the colonial theorists, was the culture displaced when Bali was conquered by the Javanese empire of Majapahit. To enliven the material Covarrubias added rumors of cannibalism to the reputation of these original Balinese. In this and the ideas of race he brought together all the features of Bali's image found in earlier writings.

From the original Balinese, Covarrubias moved on to a description of the community. Again, in line with the writings of his predecessors, he portrayed harmonious Balinese laboring in the fields, dedicating themselves to the rice goddess. Rice farming was presented as the basis of the community, just as rice fields were the "soul" of the Balinese landscape. This point was reinforced by dwelling on the image of the rice goddess, the figure known as *cili,* which was copiously illustrated with drawings by Spies after

---

81.   ibid., p. 7.
82.   ibid., p. 11.

Balinese offerings.[83] The Majapahit conquest of Bali, according to Covarrubias, brought "feudal domination by an aristocracy" over the innately autonomous villagers, an overlay of caste on top of egalitarianism.[84] Here was the idea of the village republic repeated in its purest form.

The soul of the Balinese community was art, for "everybody in Bali seems to be an artist."[85] This was an idea almost directly taken from Spies. Spies saw the Balinese as universally artistic, enabling them to make painting, dance or music part of the rhythm of daily life, along with working in the fields, feeding pigs, bearing children or cooking. For Spies this art was a prayer to the "holiness of life," a deep spirituality in the community.[86] This again was a potted version of the romantic image of Bali.

Further interest was added to the book through detailed descriptions of Balinese sexual life, taken mainly from Jacobs's nineteenth-century account, and stories of sorcery, reinforced by drawings of bizarre magical figures. The finishing touches, as with Krause's book, were informative descriptions of cremation rituals, the glorious final moments of Balinese life.

The barrage of *bons mots,* legends and explanations fill in what all the other writers only outlined. Covarrubias's passionate curiosity and gift for illustrative example enabled him to capture the essence of Bali, and in *Island of Bali* the genre of travel and descriptive works on Bali found its highest pinnacle. The book was a summary of all the images of Bali from the 1930s, and was so popular that Spies wrote to the author, "I see every tourist with it... And to everyone who asks me something, I say: look in Covarrubias."[87] The contradictions in the image disappeared quite magically in the fluid style of Covarrubias's writing—there was no apparent problem with Bali being both a caste society and an egalitarian one, no problems with modern art developing and yet traditional Bali being

---

83. ibid., pp. 172-81.

84. ibid., p. 46.

85. ibid., p. 160.

86. Letter quoted in Rhodius & Darling, *Walter Spies and Balinese Art,* p. 71.

87. Quoted in Rhodius, *Schönheit und Reichtum,* p. 359

preserved, no clash between the beautiful young dancing girl and the witch.

Margaret Mead, Gregory Bateson and Anthropology on Bali

On to the Bali scene of the 1930s strode the forthright Margaret Mead, one of the most important anthropologists of her time. Diminutive in size but not in force of personality, Mead, with her lanky third husband, Gregory Bateson, arrived to sort out the culture of Bali. While they set the record straight on some aspects of Bali's image, they were equally seduced by the Spies circle into seeing Balinese culture in terms of the most important elements of the image: harmony, artistic wealth, and the meeting of the dancing girl and the witch.

In the 1930s Mead and Bateson were at the forefront of modern anthropology, developing it as a profession and making the study of the cultures of the world truly scientific. Mead (1901-78), in particular, is one of the few academics whose work has reached a broad audience, which has given currency to her ideas about culture and the way that it forms personality. Through her work, to which she was devoted, she challenged puritanism and racism then dominant in American society. Mead's devotion and strong will were essential for survival in the male-dominated academic arena, and she proved her strength by tirelessly moving from one fieldwork site to another: Samoa in 1925-6, Manus (Admiralty Islands) 1928-9, Arapesh, Mundugumor and Tchambuli (New Guinea) 1931-3, Bali 1936-8 and 1939, and Iatmul (New Guinea) 1938-9. In her subsequent writings she transformed the way western society looked at gender, childrearing, education, adolescence and sexuality by showing just how relative and culture-bound such things are. In the way she opened up an awareness of new possibilities in personal life she was at the forefront of the whole liberalization of western society, which found its fruit in the sexual revolution and the hippy era of the1960s, and in the modern forms of the feminist movement.

It was in New Guinea that she met Bateson, a scholarly giant both physically and mentally. Bateson (1904-80) came from the rarefied English intellectual atmosphere of Cambridge University, not Mead's world of the American East Coast. His father, William

Bateson, had been one of the leading geneticists of the turn of the century, an associate of some of the most famous scientists of the age, such as Darwin. This family background allowed Bateson to move between disciplines, which in turn made his work on Bali all the more complex and interesting. He had already completed a study of ritual and play amongst a New Guinea people that revolutionized the way culture could be studied, and after Bali he was to go on to make major contributions to the study of sociology (where he invented the idea of "frame analysis"), psychology (the "double-bind" theory of schizophrenia and alcoholism), cybernetics, and dolphins.

Mead and Bateson came together in awkward circumstances. In New Guinea they were carrying out separate fieldwork, Bateson on his own, Mead with her second husband, the stolid New Zealander, Reo Fortune. As things developed all three were caught up in an intellectual and emotional triangle, as Mead was drawn more and more to Bateson. She later described the period as "the closest I've ever been to Madness."[88] The guilt engendered by their relationship along with their cultural displacement and the intellectual strains of fieldwork combined to drive all three to desperation.

Bali was the welcome relief of this tension, the happy settlement of a difficult intellectual and personal situation. After a series of interludes in the United States and Great Britain, involving lengthy separation while Mead divorced and both arranged their careers, the two were married en route to Bali, where their story intertwined with the arrival of Charlie Chaplin on the island. Bateson and Mead had originally intended to marry in Batavia, but the Dutch authorities were afraid of the city gaining a reputation for immorality, as Bateson recalled: "Charlie Chaplin had come through the Indies three weeks ahead of us, hoping to get himself married. His divorces and marriages were always news, and they did not want to get a reputation there for that."[89] So Bateson and Mead were cast into the role of libertarians, like Chaplin, who in 1927 had been the source of a divorce scandal. In that case he had been accused

---

88. Howard,*Margaret Mead,* p. 154. See further James A. Boon, "Mead's Mediations: Some Semiotics from the Sepik, by way of Bateson, and on to Bali," in E. Mertz & R. Parmentier (eds.), *Semiotic Mediation,* pp. 333-57, New York: Academic Press, 1985.

89. Howard, *Margaret Mead,* p. 186.

in court of unheard of (for those days) sexual practices such as fel-
latio, accusations which moved the artists of the Surrealist movement to write publicly in praise of his preferences, which the judge
had called "abnormal, contra naturam, perverted, degenerate and
indecent."[90] No such detailed information exists on Bateson and
Mead's private pleasures, beyond the fact that their honeymoon on
a slow boat to Bali consisted of proofreading Bateson's first book
and planning new fieldwork methodology.[91]

That Chaplin should come to Bali says much about the island's
sexual reputation, especially for bare-breasted women. But then
there was a nightclub in New York called "The Sins of Bali."[92]
Chaplin was probably disappointed on that front, since the reputation has always been greater than the delivery. The only stories
about Chaplin on Bali tell of his parodic attempts at Balinese dancing, and of the way large crowds of children would follow him everywhere he went. Mead, however, was not fooled by this aspect of
Bali's reputation, and she wrote later that there was "Not an ounce
of free intelligence or free libido in the whole culture."[93] To her new
husband, Bateson, the regulation of daily life in Balinese culture
was an uncomfortable reminder of his own England.[94]

Like Chaplin, Bateson and Mead went to Spies for insight into
Bali. Chaplin later said he had read of Spies from Covarrubias's
book, and thought that his "fine, sensitive, clean-cut features and
the quiet manner" were not so much representative of Bali as "typical... of a German aristocrat."[95] Mead was introduced to Spies via
the vivacious American Jane Belo, then married to Colin McPhee.
Another mutual friend who suggested Bali as a fieldwork site had

---

90. "Hands off Love," app. in Maurice Nadeau, *The History of Surrealism,* Harmondsworth:
    Penguin, 1978.
91. Howard, *Margaret Mead,* p. 186.
92. Jef Last, *Bali in de Kentering,* Amsterdam: De Bezige Bij, 1955, p. 138.
93. Howard, *Margaret Mead,* p. 193.
94. Margaret Mead, *Blackberry Winter: My Earlier Years,* New York: William Morrow, 1972,
    p. 230.
95. Quoted in Rhodius, *Schönheit und Reichtum,* p. 365. According to John Stowell, Chaplin
    first met Spies in 1932, well before Covarrubias's book appeared, so his memory was not the
    best when he wrote to Rhodius more than fifty years later. Chaplin made at least two visits to
    be Bali, and was rumoured to have a collection of erotic Balinese art, but I have never been
    able to find any reliable information on this.

The cultural encounter: Robert Koke dancing the *joged*, by Louise Koke.

been Geoffrey Gorer, who had written his own travel book on Bali, and whom Mead hoped to turn from an amateur observer into another of her anthropological professionals.[96] Chaplin went to the Bali Hotel, Bateson and Mead went straight to Spies, where he was working on *Dance and Drama in Bali* with his co-author, Beryl de Zoete: "Walter Spies, fair and full of grace, looked up from his conversation with Beryl de Zoete,...and said, 'We'd given you up.'"[97] Mead later said of him that he "gave us our first sense of the Balinese scene."[98]

Here was Mead, the professional anthropologist, putting herself at the mercy of a gifted amateur. While the rigorously detailed observations and photographs of Balinese life which were to follow provided the data of Bateson and Mead's studies of Bali, it was Spies who gave a guiding hand to the direction those studies were to take: the study of unchanging Balinese "folk" life, and of Balinese art as a manifestation of the darker side of the psyche.

First, Spies guided them to see the real "folk" of Bali, to put aside the study of Balinese texts which interested Dutch scholars, and to discover instead the culture preserved and protected by colo-

---

96. On Mead and the new professionalism in anthropology, see James Clifford, *The Predicament of Culture,* New Haven: Yale University Press, 1987, p. 30.

97. Mead, *Blackberry Winter,* p. 223.

98. Howard, *Margaret Mead,* p. 191.

nialism, a "relatively untouched native life" as Mead put it.[99] They consciously avoided the study of Balinese high culture, for to Mead and Bateson, the study of a total culture was best served by ignoring the more sophisticated products of that culture. It was, of course, assumed that the "folk" were all artistic. In the context of a later article attacking the divorce of art and life in America, Mead was to repeat the "everyone is an artist in Bali" line, for the sake of cultural contrast.[100] In fact she thought the art was overdone, that the island "teemed with excessive ritual," a remark somewhat akin to Noël Coward's poetic observations to Charlie Chaplin:

> As I said this morning to Charlie
> There is *far* too much music in Bali,
> And although as a place it's entrancing,
> There is also a *thought* too much dancing.
> It appears that each Balinese native,
> From the womb to the tomb is creative,
> And although the results are quite clever,
> There is too much artistic endeavor.[101]

For Bateson and Mead the problem of ritual and artistic excess was a symptom to be subjected to the analysis of cultural psychology. Balinese culture was seen as part of the over-regulation of daily life, acting as a kind of straitjacket.

Mead had a taste for the bizarre, cultivated by following this interest in artistic excess. Like her contemporaries, the artists of the Surrealist movement, Mead collected items of "primitive" Balinese art, deliberately choosing works which were grossly exaggerated or strange to western eyes. Her collection of Balinese art is vastly different from the refined paintings chosen by Colin McPhee, for

---

99. ibid., p. 190.

100. Margaret Mead, *Blackberry Winter*, p. 232; "The Arts of Bali," in Jane Belo (ed.), *Traditional Balinese Culture,* pp. 331-40, NewYork: Columbia University Press, 1970 (orig. pub. 1940).

101. Quoted in Frank Clune, *To the Isles of Spice,* Sydney: Angus and Robertson, 1940, p. 317. It is not entirely clear whether Coward and Chaplin were actually on Bali at the same time, according to John Stowell's research.

example, which now sit beside Mead's collection in the vaults of the American Museum of Natural History. McPhee, as a musician, sought the best examples of cultural refinement, which he traced to the courts as the centers of cultural production through patronage. Mead had no interest in this narrower aspect of culture, which she considered to be less important than the culture of daily life as it was transmitted through families. The excesses and transgressions she chose in Balinese art were meant to show the way into the mind of Balinese culture.

One of the crucial moments in their study of Bali came when they photographed a mother teasing her little son by playing with his penis, something their knowledge of Freud led them to pounce upon. This, they asserted, was typical behavior, which allowed a profound insight into the way Balinese culture worked. In their joint book, *Balinese Character: A Photographic Analysis,* and in a later article by Bateson, they analyzed the implications of this genital play in full.[102]

This teasing was part of repression, they argued, a cultural repression that broke down the personality of each Balinese into a kind of cultural schizophrenia. On the one hand, people would be calm, harmonious, and almost too restrained. On the other, they would be prone to culturally controlled outbursts that allowed them to express the otherwise hidden aspects of their personalities. Bateson and Mead saw the witch and the kris dance above all things as examples of these outbursts. In the text of the book the figure of the witch was quite explicitly the teasing mother. As Mead saw it, when Balinese men sought sexual partners they looked for the little dancing girls, but the dancing girl turned into the *Rangda* witch.[103]

Mead's fascination with the witch did not end there. Out of all the members of the Bali set, Mead encouraged the brilliant and observant Jane Belo, to do what was also pioneering work for anthropology at the time, to follow up the "wild" aspect of Balinese culture in

---

102. Gregory Bateson & Margaret Mead, *Balinese Character: A Photographic Analysis,* New-York: New York Academy of Sciences, 1942; Gregory Bateson, "Bali: The Value System of a Steady State," rep. in his *Steps to an Ecology of Mind,* St Albans: Paladin, 1973, orig. pub. in 1949.

103. *Balinese Character,* p. 36.

studies on trance and the *Barong* and *Rangda* dance.[104] These studies produced unique insights into the nature of trance behavior and have been of special interest to anthropologists of ritual and dance, and they tended to confirm the general thrust of Bateson and Mead's own arguments. They should, however, be viewed in the context of the pre-existing fascination with trance and the *Rangda* held by all the members of the Bali circle. With Spies, Mead, Belo and others spent much of their time commissioning special kris dance performances, not just for academic documentation, but for personal entertainment. Others from the Spies circle joined in filming the performances, which were held during the day and substituted (at the suggestion of Balinese) young girls for older women.[105] It is not simple coincidence that these small parts of Balinese culture were elevated to the status of emblems for the whole culture.

In *Balinese Character* the harmonious side of Bali's image also had a part to play, but was overshadowed by the couple's interest in the bizarre, an interest in which Mead dominated. In a separate article Bateson argued that harmony was the essence of what he called the Balinese "ethos." He argued, through the example of the teasing mother, through quoting Colin McPhee's idea that Balinese music did not have a proper climax, and through other examples that ranged across many aspects of Balinese life, that the Balinese character was directed towards the maintenance of what he called a "steady state." By this he meant that Bali's culture was different from those cultures which concentrated on conflict, or "maximizing the variables." In Bali, the emphasis was on avoidance of conflict, in short, on harmony.[106] This was brilliant solution to the problem of how societies can be seen to be static, but still have dynamism, how they change, but do not change.

One unintended conclusion from Bateson's article, a conclusion which fits into the context of the colonial preservation of Bali, is that the Balinese have no real sense of history or change, something he

---

104. Jane Belo, *Rangda and Barong,* New York: Augustin, 1949; *Trance in Bali,* New York: Columbia University Press, 1960.

105. See Mead, *Blackberry Winter,* p. 231; Howard, *Margaret Mead,* p. 201.

106. Bateson, "Bali: The Value System of a Steady State."

Tourism 1930s style, photograph by Robert Koke

The grace of Bali, photograph by
Robert Koke, 1930s

The dances of Bali: *janger* dance in the
1930s, photographed by Robert Koke

also argued in another of his writings. While both articles provide original insights into the relative nature of culture, they promote the idea that Balinese history is a non-event, a stasis not even interrupted by Dutch colonialism, something with which the theorists of the village republic would have agreed. Here the historical nature of anthropology relegated non-Europeans to being people without history.[107]

Both Bateson and Mead argued each of their theses quite carefully, with a great degree of sophistication and with breathtaking insight into many aspects of Balinese culture. They did not intend to reproduce stereotyped images of Bali. But both of them were working within a set of limits provided by the interests of Spies and others who had formed a profound image of Bali as a culturally developed, folk-based society in which the figure of the witch and the dancing girl were prominent before Bateson and Mead arrived. Bateson and Mead provided academic credence to that image, and ensured that culture and art would become the only topics in talking about Bali. History, economics, politics and other less savory topics were dropped or relegated to the margins of Bali's image. To Mead they were a "backdrop" for her vision of the real Bali.[108]

The Message Spreads

The Bali scene of the 1920s and 1930s was an escape from Europe and America, from the values of the West to a spiritually deeper and richer world. In the end, however, these values caught up with the expatriates.

It was not the Second World War, but Bali's reputation as a homosexual paradise, which ended the golden era of European Bali. When senior Dutch officials initiated a colony-wide crackdown on homosexual pederasty (it seems they were not worried about the heterosexual version), a few members of the Bali set were targets. The police searched houses, perhaps looking for naked boys under the beds, clamped down on the expatriates, and threw some into

---

107. Gregory Bateson, "An Old Temple and A New Myth," in Belo, *Traditional Balinese Culture,* pp. 11-36; see. Wolf, *Europe and the People without History,* Berkeley: University of California Press, 1982; and also Johannes Fabian, *Time and the Other: How Anthropology Makes its Object,* New York: Columbia University Press, 1983.

108. Interview Linda Connor, quoted in Howard, *Margaret Mead,* p. 404.

jail for good measure. Colin McPhee left Bali just ahead of what the Bali set regarded as a "witch hunt."[109] McPhee had reason to be worried, since there was great suspicion about his "adoption" of the ten-year old dancer Sampih.

Spies and Goris were not so lucky. In 1938 and 1939 they were tried and arrested for the offence of sexual intercourse with minors of the same gender. Spies, whose younger sexual partners were somewhere in their teens, made a virtue of necessity and used the solitude to produce some of his best works.[110] Goris, rumoured to have preyed on very young boys in the mountains, had no silver lining to his cloud. He did not have the influential friends who helped Spies get a lighter sentence, and served sixteen months in jail. His career was shattered.

By the Second World War paradise had already been lost. Spies and the other Germans were interned as enemy aliens, and the artist met his tragic end when a boat taking him to Colombo was bombed off Sumatra on 18 January 1942. Some of the expatriates saw the signs, and left Bali before the Japanese occupation at the beginning of 1942. Hotel operator Koke and anthropologist Bateson were to meet again under very different circumstances, when they worked for the forerunner of the CIA, the OSS, in mainland Southeast Asia, planning ways to mobilize local populations against the Japanese. The brilliant archeologist Stutterheim died in Batavia of a brain tumor, after he and many of the other westerners in the Indies had been put in prisoner-of-war camps by the Japanese. Some, such as the Dutch government linguist on Bali, Christian Hooykaas, were taken from these camps to endure the horrors of the Burma railway.

Ironically a fellow sufferer on the railway was an Englishman who would play a key role in restoring Bali's reputation in the 1950s, John Coast. Coast, traveler, writer, political analyst, theater impresario and champion of Southeast Asian political independence, came to Bali well after the heyday of the 1930s, but had joined the British army out of the same sense of adventure which had sent many to escape Europe. The same longings compelled him to stay in the East

---

109. ibid., p. 209.
110. Rhodius & Darling, *Walter Spies,* pp. 45-9.

John Coast at rehearsal for his tour of Balinese performing arts

and to join the Indonesian struggle for independence from the Dutch in the post-war years. Like many in the Allied forces, he felt that the war had been a struggle for freedom, and that it was gross hypocrisy simply to return to the old imperial ways after it was over. After the war Coast spent some time in Thailand, where he got to know many of the leading politicians of the day, then stayed in central Java, at the heart of the Indonesian Revolution of 1945-9, and then settled for a while on Bali.

While Coast was engaged in the struggle for Indonesian independence, Colin McPhee, the expert on Balinese music, was writing one of the best of the Bali books attempting to capture the lost paradise. His was an autobiographical account, *A House in Bali,* full of loving details about the music of Bali and about the brilliant musicians and dancers with whom McPhee had worked, particularly the young man, I Sampih, whose talents he had recognized when Sampih was still a boy and had nurtured through exposing him to the best dancers of the day.[111]

---

111. Originally published London: Victor Gollancz, 1947, repr. Kuala Lumpur: Oxford University Press, 1979.

In the post-war era Bali was one of many balms to soothe a traumatized world. In this era of renewed interest in both the East and the
Pacific, Broadway hits like *The King and I* and *South Pacific* gained
enormous popularity first on stage and subsequently on screen.[112]
The 1950s version of these ideal places was more removed from
reality than the 1930s images. As a kind of over-compensation for
the hell of the Pacific theater, a world of jungle warfare and tropical disease, Broadway and Hollywood produced images that would
try to recapture the lost world of the pre-war era. In doing this, they
created something that never was.

In the Hollywood of the pre-war era the Indies were regarded as
one part of the South Seas Islands, and were most memorably featured
as the place where the gigantic gorilla King Kong was founding the
film of the same name.[113] A map at the beginning of the film locates
King Kong's island in the same position as the Mentawai islands,
just off Sumatra. The image of dark-skinned primitives in this film
is also based in part on the culture of the Mentawai islands, which
had excited some anthropological interest in the 1930s. In the 1930s
Primitive art and culture were at the heart of both intellectual and
popular interest, featuring in the art of Picasso and the Surrealists as
well as the dances of Josephine Baker.[114] One aspect of this interest
in Primitivism was the emphasis on the sexual and magical aspects
of Bali. By the 1950s Hollywood was replacing them with more
idyllic pictures.

A film which marks the transition between the "primitive" view
of the Indies from the 1930s and the idyllic vision of the 1950s is
an adventure film of 1948 starring John Wayne called *Wake of the
Red Witch*.[115] The film was based on a racist and sexist novel of the
same name by Garland Roark,[116] and featured Wayne as a private

---

112.   These Rogers and Hammerstein hits were respectively made into movies in 1956 (dir. Wal-
       ter Lang, Twentieth-Century Fox) and 1958 (dir. Joshua Logan, South Pacific Enterprises,
       Twentieth-Century Fox).

113.   Merian C. Cooper and Ernest Schoedsack (dir.), RKO, 1933.

114.   On the aspect of this so-called "negritude," see Clifford, *Predicament of Culture,* pp. 177-
       9. Note that André Breton and other leading Surrealists included carvings from Indonesian
       cultures in their collections of primitive art.

115.   Edward Ludwig (dir.), Republic.

116.   Boston: Little, Brown and Co., 1946.

trader who ran foul of corrupt and nasty Dutch officials in Batavia. The scenes of the film set on Bali show the island as a composite of Indian and Pacific islands, à la *South Pacific*. In one particularly memorable scene a volcano erupts just as primitive Balinese (Americans in black faces) sit around in a circle chanting, an imitation of the *kecak* dance. The focus of the chanting is a strange pagan rite, directed at statues based on Easter Island figures.

The "Bali Hai" of *South Pacific* had nothing directly to do with the people who lived on Bali in the 1930s, but everything to do with Bali's image. When searching for an island, which would be the ultimate encapsulation of all the ideals of the era, the name Bali came readily to mind. Little matter that the island shown as Bali Hai was not in the right ocean, the name and the soothing sea-breeze-like notes of the hit song were enough. Those who might have wanted to visit Bali at the time would have found it difficult anyway. Despite the best efforts of the Dutch Government to promote tourism as a propaganda measure in their fight against Indonesian independence, Bali was in turmoil. The island was polarized into pro- and anti-Republic factions, both sides willing to fight to the death—not a healthy atmosphere for tourism. After the Revolution the turmoil in Bali continued, and in the 1950s the increasingly leftist outlook of the Indonesian Government did much to alienate tourists. In the late 1950s the number of Americans and Europeans on Bali could virtually be counted on the fingers of one hand.[117]

Since reality could rarely get in the way of image-making, Hollywood was now unimpeded. John Coast and a group of Balinese encountered Hollywood's image-making process at first hand. In 1950, the Revolution over and independence won, Coast headed for Bali armed with McPhee's book as his guide. With President Sukarno's blessing and the assistance of Balinese politicians who had been key figures in the Revolution, Coast set himself up in Dénpasar. His mission was to spread Bali's culture to the world, a mission that Sukarno enthusiastically supported.

Coast found a Bali in utter turmoil, where you had to sleep with

---

117.   Information from Hildred Geertz, who, with her then husband Clifford was one of the few westerners on the island in 1957-8.

a gun under your pillow. He also found McPhee's cook, and then the musicians with whom McPhee had worked, and finally he found Sampih. Sampih had been a child when McPhee first discovered him and took him to study under the great innovative dancer Mario. Now Coast found him a young man, his ambitions to be a star ready to be refueled.

The story Coast tells is one of achievement against adversity, as he gathers a dance troupe together, and then takes them on an amazingly successful world tour. The troupe consisted of the musicians of Paliatan, near Ubud, led by the famous teacher Anak Agung Mandera, Sampih, three little girls who had been carefully tutored in the beautiful *lègong* dance, and assorted other Balinese talents.

In England they received virtually equal status with the world's greatest ballerina, Margot Fonteyn. The little girls especially were the toast of Broadway, where *Variety* proclaimed them "the first Broadway hit of the 1952 season."[118] This was the time when *South Pacific* was at its height on Broadway, and "Richard Rogers came to pay a generous tribute to our visitation from the true South Pacific."[119] The three girls appeared on the Ed Sullivan show, and in Hollywood Sampih taught the *oleg* dance to Michiko, the dancer from *The King and I*. Also in Hollywood they met Katharane Mershon, the dancer, former Sanur resident and friend of Spies, Belo and Mead, who took the dancers to Disneyland. They also met the great novelist Vicki Baum, who showed them old films of Bali on Christmas Eve and shared her reminiscences of Walter Spies.

The troupe was in Hollywood when Bob Hope and Bing Crosby were making *The Road to Bali*,[120] the ultimate amalgam of images of Southeast Asia and the Pacific, which under the guise of humor managed to include, "cannibals, wild animals, and a giant squid, as well as Humphrey Bogart and Katharine Hepburn pulling *The African Queen.*" The plot, what there was of it, had Hope and Crosby fleeing from "a pair of matrimony-minded girls" in Australia to "a

---

118. John Coast, *Dancing out of Bali,* London: Faber and Faber, 1954, p. 201.
119. Ibid., p. 203.
120. Harry Tugend (dir.), Paramount, 1952.

South Sea island" (Bali), where they met Dorothy Lamour play-ing a beautiful princess, her famous sarongs combined with bits of apparel from Thailand, India and other parts of Asia. She, like all island adventurers, was seeking sunken treasure.[121] Coast tried to persuade the producers to put in a few token scenes of Balinese dance featuring the little girls. In the promotion of the film they were immortalized, the latter-day version of one of the symbols of Bali, dancing so beautifully in front of cardboard cut-outs of what Americans thought a Balinese temple might look like, in this ulti-mate version of the fantasy of Bali.

Yet the smooth narrative of John Coast's book had a disturbing aftermath. His book and his tour were there to "normalize" a Bali that had become once again a very dangerous paradise. His tour and the films of the time were trying to resurrect the 1930s image of Bali and hold it out as an international ideal. Coast saw himself as smoothing away the violence which had crept into Bali's image but his book ends on a far from soothing note. At the end of the story the dancers and musicians were suitably homesick, in an inappropri-ate environment for the authentic cultural representatives that they were. The last dedicatory words describe their return, when:

One day towards the end of February 1954, after the dancers had been back in Bali a year, Sampih was called to dance with the Pali-atan group in the palace of the Raja of Gianjar in front of President Sukarno.

He failed to appear. Three days later his murdered body was found in the Ubud river.[122]

Better an unreal, idealized Hollywood Bali than a Bali where a dancer elevated by western patrons from an early age can meet such a fate.

The post-war reconstruction of Bali's image went on gradually

---

121. Synopsis quoted in Bob Hope & Bob Thomas, *The Road to Hollywood: My Love Affair with the Movies,* London: Allen, 1977, p. 228.

122. This passage was not included in the American edition, which does, however, have a pho-tograph of Hope and Crosby with the Balinese dancers. Apparently Sampih's death was the work of a jealous husband.

at first, beginning with the publication of McPhee's book and continuing in the Hollywood treatments and then Coast's attempt to normalize the real Bali. After Coast, various of the survivors of the 1930s era began to publish their own accounts, or to revive the work of others. In 1960 Ktut Tantri (Surabaya Sue, etc.), the American woman who had travelled to Bali alone, had, along with Robert Koke, set up the Kuta Beach Hotel, and had been intimate friends with the foremost prince of the kingdom of Bangli, published her story, *Revolt in Paradise*. The book spanned the period from her arrival in Bali in 1932 (inspired by an early Hollywood film, *The Last Paradise*) to her role as a propagandist in the Indonesian Revolution. Like Coast she championed the Republican cause, broadcasting for the revolutionaries of Surabaya at the height of the worst fighting of the Revolution. She became a close friend of many of the leaders of Indonesian politics, particularly Amir Sjariffudin, who was executed in 1948 for his leadership of a Communist Party attempt to hijack the Revolution from Sukarno.

The academic apotheosis of Bali came later. First the Dutch published two translations of the best articles on Bali by Goris, Grader and others, saving them from the oblivion of Dutch academia.[123] Then, in 1970, Jane Belo published a collection of articles by herself, Mead, Bateson, Spies and others from the 1930s.[124] This book was published posthumously, as was McPhee's magnum opus, *Music in Bali*,[125] while Claire Holt's elevation of the story of Balinese art in the 1930s in her *Art in Indonesia* appeared only three years before her death.[126] Walter Spies's status as the hero of the 1930s was relatively unknown outside a small group of survivors of the era until a wealthy Dutch enthusiast, the late Hans Rhodius, published a collection of letters and memoirs of Spies.[127] After this

123. J. L. Swellengrebel *et al.* (eds.), *Bali: Studies in Life, Thought and Ritual*, The Hague: van Hoeve, 1960; *Bali: Further Studies in Life, Thought and Ritual*, The Hague: van Hoeve, 1969.

124. Belo, *Traditional Balinese Culture.*

125. Colin McPhee, *Music in Bali: A Study on Form and Instrumental Organisation in Balinese Orchestral Music*, New Haven: Yale University Press, 1966.

126. *Art in Indonesia: Continuities and Change*, Ithaca: Cornell University Press, 1967.

127. Rhodius, *Schönheit und Reichtum.*

The consummation of images of Bali: Bing Crosby, Dorothy Lamour and
Bob Hope in a scene from *The Road to Bali*, Paramount Pictures.

book Rhodius worked tirelessly collecting paintings, photographs
and information, founding and funding a Walter Spies foundation to
perpetuate the name of Spies, and supporting a film and other books
on Spies.[128] A similar foundation was started in the Netherlands to
promote the name of Bonnet. The survivors of the era, kept writing for many decades: in 1972 Katharane Mershon published her
account of Balinese rituals; in 1987 Louise Garrett Koke, wife of
the man who started the hotel industry at Kuta beach, published her
memoir, *Our Hotel in Bali.*

The books, films, foundations and other material have ensured
that the golden age of expatriate Bali lives on in the world's eyes.
In all this material there has been some smoothing over of the inconsistencies in the image. In particular the negative aspects of
Bali have been forgotten. One part of the construction of the post-
war image of Bali has been the creation of the illusion that what
is shown is the "real" Bali, through the device of distancing the

---

128. Rhodius and Darling, *Walter Spies.*

perceived Bali from the social circumstances that drew the image-makers together. Only recently has the homosexuality of Spies and Goris been publicly referred to. Many of the memoirs have been very selective. McPhee, for example, not only hardly mentioned Spies, he did not even acknowledge the existence of his own former wife, Belo, as if all his time on Bali was spent in a profound musical dialogue between himself and the Balinese. Likewise in her autobiographical account Ktut Tantri "forgot" much, for example her partner in the Kuta Beach Hotel, Robert Koke, whose wife took her revenge by "forgetting" Ktut Tantri in her own account of the period. Various Balinese who also helped Tantri do not get a mention in her book.[129]

The writings of the 1920s and 1930s and their subsequent elevation have given us an ideal Bali. Even at its height this image was never flawless, never without its contradictions, but nonetheless it has survived to become the dominant image of Bali. Fuelled by a rejection of aspects of European and American societies after the First World War, the idealization of Balinese society as the ultimate in artistic, harmonious culture has been raised to unprecedented heights in the decades after the Second World War. While we may no longer think of Bali in terms of bare breasts, it is still the land of dancing-girls and witches, of natural and cultural abundance, where the people live happily in tune with the gods.

Despite the violent and unsettled nature of life in Bali in the 1950s, there has been no return to the old nineteenth-century image of savage Bali. The interests of the Indonesian Government and international tourism have ensured that the memories of the golden age live on after the deaths of most of those who experienced it and even the demonic side of the 1930s image has faded.

---

129. On more profound aspects of selective memory and the disturbances and incongruities of the Bali image, see Boon, "Between-the-Wars Bali."

CHAPTER FOUR

Balinese Under Pressure, 1908-1965

While the westerners on Bali were enjoying their golden age, Balinese were experiencing a critical reorganization of their lives. By the 1920s and 1930s a variety of Balinese responses to colonial occupation and control had emerged, centered on ideas of Balinese culture and identity. Everywhere Balinese were rethinking what it meant to be Balinese, and putting up ritual and artistic defenses against a new chaos. On top of natural disasters came a total dislocation of everything around which Balinese had previously organized their lives: the states, villages, temples and rituals. Many Balinese were left with nothing to cling to and became outlaws; others gained access to education from the West and challenged the nature of their society. Many lived on the brink of survival, pushed into landlessness and starvation, while a chosen few thrived. In all of this some Balinese were in a position to influence the colonial authorities and the charmed expatriate circle, the image-makers of the period. Few of the participants in this process were aware, however, of the extent to which they were interacting to form a new Bali.

The idea, adhered to by both westerners and Balinese, that the island's culture was traditional, and hence unchanged, masked the changes taking place in Balinese society. Bali has been caught up in the "modern" world since the Dutch first came in the sixteenth century and changed the economic and political framework by which Bali existed in the Indonesian archipelago. The changes of the

Images from the island of fear: a *léak* or witch in the form of *Rangda*,
by I Gusti Madé Deblog, 1937.

twentieth century, the introduction of a bureaucratic administration
and western education, simply accelerated the process of change.
However, everything about the changes in Balinese society, even
the most revolutionary actions of the Left, have been traditional, in
the sense that they are in line with precedents handed down from
the past.

The political and administrative reforms introduced by the Dutch
strengthened the position of those who had once been the kings of
Bali, but in doing this, the re-formation of tradition widened fissures
in Balinese society. While kings and priests benefited from a reas-
sessment of what "caste" meant on Bali, members of lower social
ranks challenged those ideas, and challenged them in such a way as
to strongly polarize society. The colonial period initiated a debate
about the relationship between religion, art and social order, a debate that became increasingly violent from the 1940s onwards. The
resulting conflicts led to more deaths than had occurred during the
puputans by which the Dutch took over the island—so many more
that we can only estimate the number of killings from late 1965 to
1966 at around 100,000.

When the World Was Unstable

Old people still use the phrase "the time when the world was stable," *degas guminé enteg,* to speak of pre-colonial Bali.[1] Despite the prevalence of the idea that the Dutch takeover only affected a small part of the aristocratic élite, the invasion threw everybody's life into chaos. States, districts, villages, labor, and rice farming were all subjected to Dutch "rationalization," and in the process Bali was drastically reorganized. The net effect of all this was the impoverishment of Bali under the Dutch, or what scholars now call "the development of underdevelopment,"[2] that is, the idea that colonial exploitation and the reorganization of life which accompanied it has led directly to the continued poverty of Third World nations and the continued dependence of the Third World on the First World.

Dutch colonial order represented disorder to Balinese society, and the Balinese needed to evolve different strategies to cope with that disorder. These strategies varied from the royal response of restoring kingship and attempting to shore up its power with a new political and economic base; to the artistic and religious response of finding new ways to express Balinese identity, giving form to the tensions and conflicts of the period in order to exorcise them; to the radical political response of directly attacking the new, caste-based version of Balinese culture which evolved under Dutch influence.

The Dutch reorganization of Bali placed people in the position of being links in the chain of the colonial state,[3] a strategy which was necessary so that a handful of Dutch civil servants could rule a society of a million people (the population of Bali in the 1920s). The former royal families were the first links. Although they had lost their kingship, they were able, as the Dutch reorganized the island, to use their positions to restore some of their former power, becoming important administrators and large landowners.

Those few members of the royal families of Badung and Klung-kung who survived the slaughters of 1906-8 were sent into exile, to join members of other important Balinese families who were not

---

1. Also quoted in G. Bateson, "Bali: The Value System of a Steady State," in his *Steps to an Ecology of Mind,* St Albans: Paladin, 1973, pp. 80-100.

2. Interestingly enough the first scholar to document this was the colonial civil servant V. E.Korn, in his *Het Adatrecht van Bali,* The Hague: Naeff, 1932, p. 337, writing in a way that anticipated scholarship of forty years later.

3. This metaphor was made famous by the Indonesian scholar Taufik Abdullah, but was first used in relation to Bali by V. E. Korn in *Het Adatrecht van Bali,* p. 335.

willing to accept Dutch authority. The royal families who remained lost much of their power and authority. In all their actions they were closely watched by Dutch officials, whom the Balinese rajas were forced to think of as their "older brothers," making it clear for all to see that the Dutch were at the top of Balinese society.

On all levels, district heads, village leaders and corvée officials lost their jobs or had their work reorganized. Those who kept their jobs were now, like the kings, answerable to the Dutch, and had to become civil servants in the Dutch bureaucracy.

As colonists the Dutch were good at organizing society to suit their own purposes: they decided what everybody's social position and role should be, and acted accordingly. They also defined the extent of each of the Balinese states, creating boundaries which had never previously existed.[4] In every kingdom the number of districts and wet-rice irrigation associations *(subak)* were reduced in the interests of reform and administrative convenience. Suddenly people found themselves with new district heads, and part of new, larger, irrigation societies. Life thus became more impersonal, as the old patron-client ties that organized people in states were dislocated.[5]

Even on the village level, the level that the Dutch were supposedly preserving, there was massive change. The *bañjar,* units of households which worked together to carry out service to the palace or other ritual duties, were made into wards of the village, whereas previously some *bañjar* had in fact included householders outside the area of a village, and village and *bañjar* identity were quite separate. This rationalized the size of villages, and put the *klian,* who was an intermediary between the householders and the court, out of a job. People found themselves in new villages to which they had previously never had any connection. Thus were the old "village republics" restored.

People no longer worked for the palace but for the colonial state. Corvée labor was directed to utilitarian public works, away from the vanities of kings and their palaces. This meant people had to do

---

4. See "Grenzen der Vroegere Vorstenrijken op Bali (1922)," *Adatrechtbundels* XXIII, The Hague: Nijhoff, 1924: 24-5.

5. For these and other details of the changes, see Korn, *Het Adatrecht,* and Henk Schulte Nordholt, Een Baiische Dynastie: Hiërarchie en Conflict in de Negara Mengwi, 1700-1940, (unpub. diss.) Vrij Universiteit te Amsterdam, 1987, pp. 205-306.

a lot of free manual labor for the Dutch, work that did not have the spiritual returns of working for royalty. Suddenly all privileges were lost. Artists had to do the same corvée as everybody else, and members of clans that had previously had special status were relegated to being commoners. Painters and palace officials found themselves working all day on road gangs, for no pay, and were told that this was a continuation of their traditional duties.

Nature and the world economy conspired to worsen the situation. In 1917 there was a massive earthquake, which flattened whole villages, destroyed some of Bali's foremost temples, and damaged some of the most beautiful palaces; in all 1350 lives were lost. After that came mouse plagues and other forms of devastation of rice-crops, closely followed by a world-wide epidemic of Spanish influenza, which claimed tens of thousands of lives.[6] Soon after came the Depression, which hit Bali's exports. By 1934 pigs and copra, the two major exports, had fallen to a quarter of their former price, and Balinese coins, *képéng,* had been virtually halved in value. Hard on the heels of this came further mouse plagues and devastation of rice-crops. Many at that time lost their land holdings and were on the verge of starvation.[7] The charmed circle of expatriates, however, were oblivious to all of this.

The Dutch colonial ideal of law and order meant control and an appearance of peace for the Dutch and suffering for the Balinese. Balinese at the time saw this as an age of wage labor, when lower-ranking aristocrats appointed to official posts could terrorize and control the population through spies and violence, and could serve their own interests through corruption and sexual claims over pretty local women, but who nevertheless could not control the gangs of thieves and bandits created by the social dislocation.[8]

The Aristocrats Regroup

Former members of royal families, *brahmana,* and other aristocrats salvaged what they could of their dignity and power in the early

---

6. Schulte Nordholt, Een Balische Dynastie, p. 240.

7. ibid., p. 267.

8. This is the picture of Bali given in A. A. Pañji Tisna's novel, *Sukreni Gadis Bali,* Jakarta: Balai Pustaka, repr. 1965.

decades of the century. A select few managed to compensate for their loss of power by re-acquiring a central role in Balinese society through wealth and patronage. As political power changed hands, religion became one of the key foci of Balinese life. The aristocracy in particular were able to recast their role in society through religion.

Gusti Bagus Jlantik (1887-1968), who later took the title of Anak Agung Ktut Agung, was one of the most successful re-makers of tradition under the Dutch. Handsome, refined, incredibly bright, but very short, he was the epitome of a colonial raja and led the way in evolving a new style and a new image of Balinese society which could cope with rapid social change. It was his photogenic features, which were found in many of Thilly Weissenborn's photographs of Balinese aristocracy.

He was the nephew and adopted son of the old ruler of Karangasem, Gusti Gedé Jlantik, who had ceded his sovereignty to the Dutch. Gusti Gedé died soon after this, and in 1908, at barely twenty-one, Gusti Bagus came to the throne under difficult circumstances. As he tried to hold the proper cremation rituals for his father, Dutch soldiers arrived at the palace door to seize a number of his uncles, cousins, and leading officials of the state who refused to acknowledge Dutch supremacy. As a result of Dutch threats to shell the town of Karangasem he was forced to surrender these members of his family.[9] His relatives went into exile, he stayed, but with the reminder that any challenge to Dutch authority would lead to a show of force and his own exile.

Allowed to stay on with the title of regent, which the Dutch preferred to the title of raja, he worked to restore or preserve his father's powers. His response to the earthquake of 1917 was to lead the call for a revitalization of Balinese religion. He and his brother rajas of Gianyar and Bangli, the kings who had surrendered to the Dutch, worked in concert with various priests. Together they decided that much of the natural and social chaos of the time had arisen through neglect of religious duties.

---

9. See his comments in Katharane Mershon, *Seven Plus Seven: Mysterious Life-Rituals on Bali,* New York: Vantage, 1971, p. 330.

The king of Karangasem, Gusti Bagus Jlantik, with his wife and daughter in his palace, photographed by Thilly Weissenborn, *c.* 1923.

First of all this meant restoring the proper caste order, so that if everyone followed the moral precepts of their caste harmony could be created. Secondly the restoration involved more attention to the holding of rituals and the rebuilding of the many temples that had been destroyed during the earthquake. In this latter aim the kings and the religious authorities were helped by the enthusiasm of a number of Dutch civil servants. Through the support of these indi-viduals calls for restoration could be transferred into government funding, both for the temples themselves, and then for the ceremonies to be held in the temples.[10]

Gusti Bagus led the way for the rajas to reclaim their kingship as a spiritual duty to their people, and directly challenged the Dutch image of rajas as oriental despots or potentates. He asked the Dutch resident of Bali if he thought the Balinese princes were really so bad. "Certainly the Netherlands-Indies Government is a just ruler," he said to assuage colonial pride, "but it is only a ruler in relation to material interests." The Balinese princes, he argued, "were less mindful of these, however… they taught the people reverence for God and they gave the population the opportunity of allowing the souls of the dead to reach their destination by means of the cremations intended for this purpose."[11] As a king, he later said, his job was to "keep my thoughts on those things which will ultimately elevate my spirit."[12]

A religious response to the instability of the Balinese world helped to stave off more directly political responses. The call to revitalize religious observance was essentially a call to preserve the old order, or at least the power of the former rulers. This was linked to another form of response to the earthquake of 1917 and the other disasters of the era: a call from former subjects to restore the kingdoms.

In Klungkung this was to lead to the return of the heir to the throne and his surviving family from exile in Lombok, but only after twelve years of protest and appeal. The heir, Déwa Agung Oka Geg (1896?-1965), had been barely a teenager at the time of the *puputan,* but for all that he bore the scars of it for life: he had been shot in the knee by a Dutch bullet and stabbed in the side by a Balinese kris. The Déwa Agung and the other exiles learned much about traditional Balinese values in Lombok, where the Balinese community staunchly upheld their ideas of Balinese tradition due to the

---

10. See D. J. Stuart-Fox, Pura Besakih: A Study of Balinese Religion and Society, (diss.) Australian National University, 1987, pp. 348ff.

11. Quoted in Korn, *Het Adatrecht,* p. 341; trans, following Schulte Nordholt, *Bali: Colonial Conceptions and Political Change 1700-1940,* Rotterdam: Center for Asian Studies, 1986, pp. 36-7.

12. Mershon, *Seven Plus Seven,* p. 330.

majority presence of Muslim Sasaks. On his return the young man had formed a clear vision of what needed to be done to organize a proper kingdom. He carried this out with resolution using the full armory of traditional and modern power. The Déwa Agung could call on his descent from Dalem Baturènggong and his vast reading of Balinese literature to make himself Upper King and Upper Priest. In doing this he continued to be seen as an opponent of the Dutch, someone unwillingly put under their power. Later he was to marry the daughter of Gusti Bagus, a step that recreated an old relationship between Karangasem and Klungkung. Through this alliance the Déwa Agung was able to have his role acknowledged through the good offices of Gusti Bagus.

By 1929 the Dutch felt that all the former kings had been tamed enough to allow them to become autonomous rulers, or what the Dutch called *zelfbestuurders,* part of a new body, the Council of Kings. This was established in 1931, with Gusti Bagus as the chairman rather than the Déwa Agung. The council's role was to decide on policy matters for the whole island, and each king was to administer his kingdom in accordance with these decisions, but the Dutch retained a supervisory role in the process. The Dutch made it clear that they did not necessarily see the old order of royal precedence as the best one, and instead favored those kings who had belonged to families which had offered the least resistance to colonial takeover.

Gusti Bagus, that most intelligent of accommodators to Dutch rule, expressed the political reality of the new Bali through the architecture of his palace. Traditionally palace courtyards were named to represent the different kingdoms of the world over which Pañji, the cultural hero of the courts, strode. Now, instead of the names of ancient Javanese and Malay kingdoms, Gusti Bagus chose the names of the cities of the world, then being incorporated into the domain of Bali: London, Berlin, and "Maskerdam" (Amsterdam). To his traditional palace he also added new courtyards and buildings in the styles of the Chinese architects and builders of the courts of central Java, which he often visited, and of the Dutch public buildings of Java. Away from the capital, near the coast at the old port of Ujung, he built a magnificent pleasure garden. This was a large Dutch-style building completely surrounded by water and elevated to catch the cool afternoon breezes. On the hills around it were cosmic symbols, which expressed its central position in the world.

Gusti Bagus's actions were a contrast to those of rulers like the Déwa Agung who preferred to argue their position by cultivating "tradition." The Déwa Agung's projects of the time included repainting the ceilings of the old law courts of Klungkung, the Kerta Ghosa. Following this, he sponsored the rebuilding of the pleasure garden of the old palace of Klungkung, which had been razed by the Dutch in 1908. The new, larger pavilion of the pleasure garden was also decorated with the traditional style paintings for which Klungkung was famous. The commoner artists of nearby Kamasan village were enthusiastic participants in the Déwa Agung's emphasis on tradition, and their reaction is indicative of the support on most levels of society given to the efforts to make Klungkung the most traditional of all the regions of Bali.

Other rulers, especially those newly elevated by the Dutch, were much more blatantly "modern." Along with their traditional palaces they built fountains and buildings in what they called the "office" or *kantor* style, meaning the Dutch style.[13] Even the word "office" was a word for the new age, and Balinese from all walks of life began to name their children "Kantor."

All the kings were "traditional" in their attempts to maintain the link between their status, their political power, and the holding of grand rituals, rituals which were attempts to religiously put the world in order. Under the Dutch the kings maintained their former ritual functions, and expanded them where they could in order to impress their colonial masters. The colonial era left royalty with few ways to manifest their power. They were able to convert earlier ties into formal landholding arrangements by which they had power over sharecroppers, and they received colonial state incomes, but they did not have their former powers of life and death over subjects, and could no longer wage wars. All that was left to them was their ability to hold rituals, and the king of Karangasem held

---

13. Henk Schulte Nordholt, "Temple and Authority in South Bali 1900-1980," paper given at the 6th European Colloquium on Indonesian and Malay Studies, Passau, June 1987.

The colonial order: the King and Queen of Karangasem and their family with
the Resident of Bali and Lombok and his wide, various Dutch and Balinese colonial
officials, and the district heads of Karangasem (front left) and court priests (front right).
Included in the photograph is the young district officer Victor Korn.

the most spectacular of the colonial royal rituals in 1937. This was documented by both Balinese and westerners.[14]

The 1937 ceremony was completed by a rite of consecration, where Gusti Bagus Jlantik took on the full hereditary title of Anak Agung Ktut Karangasem. In 1938 the Dutch came up with a very colonial version of the consecration. They inaugurated all the kings as regents in that year, and gave official recognition to their titles, as a way of formalizing caste. The ceremony was held at the Mother Temple of Bali in Besakih, the restoration of which had also been funded by the Dutch, and kings and priests lined up with residents, assistant-residents and district officers to receive the holy water of the colonial bureaucracy.[15] Along with their new titles the kings were also given increased autonomy over the budgeting and internal affairs of their kingdom.

The style of rule evolved in such a way that the Balinese rulers became part of a colonial bureaucratic élite, just as the princes of Java had managed to do during their far longer history of colonial rule.[16] In the process most of these Balinese rulers had both entrenched themselves within the Dutch system and grown rich from it.

Theoretically the Dutch takeover of the island meant that all the land that had hitherto been part of the kingdom's system of payment for service became Dutch government land, and the small part of that land classifiable as private holdings could be kept by the kings. In practice it did not work out like this. Kings like Gusti Bagus were in an excellent position to see how the Dutch policy was implemented, and to interpret it in such a way as to retain as much land in their control as possible.

Later, in the late 1920s and 1930s, kings like the Déwa Agung were able to use their positions to re-acquire what they thought was rightfully theirs, both by reinterpreting Dutch policy, and by using their wealth and position to take over existing land. This takeover was facilitated by the Depression and the other disasters of the time,

---

14. Mershon, *Seven plus Seven,* pp. 257 ff.

15. See further Stuart-Fox, Pura Besakih; Schulte Nordholt, *Bali: Colonial Conceptions.*

16. See Heather Sutherland, *The Making of a Bureaucratic Elite,* Singapore: Heinemann, 1979; Schulte Nordholt, "Een Balishe Dynastië," pp. 211-12.

which forced poorer peasants to sell what land they had to pay their debts and provide sustenance for themselves and their families. To express what happened in these terms is, however, to ignore the subtle "traditional" basis of the takeovers of land. The kings and other people in the major officials under the Dutch had converted their kingship into patronage. Former subjects would come to them for protection when things were difficult, just as they always had, and the kings and other people in the palaces would lend money to the subjects to help them. When the Depression came along the subjects simply had to become tenants to the kings because they were so deeply indebted to them.[17] The Déwa Agung himself was able to become probably the largest landowner of all the kings, and certainly the most powerful, by the 1940s.[18]

Kings had been able to recover the economic basis of their power and make it look as if nothing had changed in "traditional" Bali. The way they did this was unofficially seen by Dutch civil servants as corrupt, confirming their idea of Balinese rulers as oriental despots. Rumors circulated of "abuses of power," and even that one of the rajas was a sadist.[19] The stereotype of Balinese kings was created by the Europeans themselves, who set Europe up as the example to be followed, and then privately derided the Balinese aristocrats if they "aped" European manners and culture and tried to present themselves on the same terms as European aristocrats.

Ubud: Political and Cultural Influence

The Sukawatis of central Bali were another royal family, which managed to operate very successfully within the Dutch system. It was in Ubud that the political dynamics of influence under the Dutch system met with the artistic changes going on at the time, and where

---

17. On the processes by which kings converted their position into landlords, see Schulte Nord-holt, "Een Balische Dynastië," pp. 267-80.

18. Geoffrey Robinson, "State, Society and Political Conflict in Bali, 1945-1946," *Indonesia* 45 (April 1988): 1-48, especially p. 45, n. 123. As a number of Klungkung people have observed to me, it is impossible to put any figures on the Déwa Agung's landholdings, since whenever official surveys were done he would order loyal subjects to put his land in their names. Korn, *Het Adatrecht*, p. 331, notes how nearly one-sixth of the rice land of Klung-kung was lost to its hereditary owners in colonial "reorganization."

19. See Schulte Nordholt, *Bali: Colonial Conceptions*, p. 41.

the western image-makers saw Balinese society most closely. The Ubud family established themselves as a political force through membership of the Batavia-based People's Council, which was the only national voice of Indonesians in Dutch rule of their East Indies, and through friendship with Spies and other Europeans the royal family made Ubud the cultural center of Bali.

At the end of the nineteenth century the patriarch, Cokorda Sukawati of Ubud, was one of the most powerful, and richest, princes of Bali. He controlled the greater part of Gianyar and virtually dictated to the king, advising him to seek Dutch aid. Sukawati sealed his influence by becoming a father-in-law of the royal house of Gianyar, and by marrying powerful members of the former royal family of Mengwi.

His eldest son, Cokorda Raka Sukawati, became the People's Council representative for Bali under the Dutch. The Dutch liked his work so much that they kept him on in 1934 when Balinese were pushing for a progressive commoner to replace him. At that time Raka was the youngest member of the council, a singular honor. The appointment served Ubud well. Since Ubud had not yet gained the status of a separate state before the Dutch arrived, the royal family had no right, in Dutch eyes, to sit on the Council of Kings. But as Bali's representative on the People's Council in Batavia, Cokorda Raka was nonetheless also given a seat on the Council of Kings. While this position could have enabled Cokorda Raka to be a progressive modern voice for Bali, he quickly reverted to an ultra-conservative, pro-Dutch role, which became a precedent for the other powerful aristocrats of Bali.

It was Cokorda Raka who first invited Walter Spies when Spies to come to Bali through an introduction by a Dutch scholar of music in Central Java, Jaap Kunst. Like other Balinese aristocrats the Ubud family had ties to the Sultan of Yogyakarta, for whom Spies worked as court musician. The 1925 visit by Spies sealed his relationship with Ubud.

Spies's first introduction to Balinese culture was to determine the course of the image of Bali, which Spies was to develop. Cokorda Raka showed Spies the *Sanghyang* trance dance, one of the burgeoning number of exorcisms performed in the aftermath of the earthquake of 1917 and the many economic and agricultural disasters which overtook Bali in the first four decades of this century.[20] Spies, however, was provided with the information that the little girls in trance were performing a *Ramayana* story, which may not have been entirely accurate at that time, although Spies was to promote the *kecak* or monkey dance to the rest of the world as a combination of the trance dance chorus and Indian epic narrative.[21]

In 1927 when Spies determined to live on Bali he went to stay in Ubud. Eventually he built one of his houses nearby, in Campuan, where the younger brother of the royal family, Cokorda Agung Sukawati, was born. As with many Balinese families, sibling rivalry split the Ubud dynasty. Relations between Cokorda Raka and Agung were not good during Cokorda Agung's school years, but they deteriorated in the 1920s when their father died and the two became involved in an inheritance dispute, a frequent cause of family disputes in Bali (although hardly a uniquely Balinese source of friction).[22] Later the relationship was to become even more strained, and it is hard not to take the genial Agung's side against his aloof, violin-playing brother who went to Java and became very much the model of an aristocratic colonial civil servant.

At home Cokorda Agung and the expatriate circle promoted an image of Ubud as the cultural center of Bali; an image in which the artist, I Gusti Nyoman Lempad (1862?-1978), played a crucial role.

Lempad was a genius: architect, engineer, sculptor, carpenter, draughtsman, and painter who lived to an extraordinary old age.[23] He and his father fled their lord of nearby Bedulu in the latter part of the nineteenth century and claimed the traditional right of refuge against an oppressive lord (*matilas*). The old Cokorda Sukawati took them in and had them build some of the most beautiful palaces and

20. See Schulte Nordholt, "Een Balische Dynastie," p. 242, on an increase in *Barong* mask making at this time.

21. Hans Rhodius, *Schönheit und Reichtum des Lebens: Walter Spies (Maler und Musiker auf Bali 1895-1942)*, The Hague: L.J.C. Boucher, 1964, p. 205.

22. Tjokorda Gde Agung Sukawati with Rosemary Hilbury, *Reminiscences of a Balinese Prince*, Hawaii: University of Hawaii Southeast Asian Studies, 1979, pp. 13-15.

23. On the life of Lempad see the film by John Darling & Lorne Blair, *Lempad of Bali*, Australian Broadcasting Corporation/Australian National University production, 1980. An alternative date for Lempad's birth is 1872.

temples in Bali, work which is hard to fully appreciate now because so many other architects and sculptors have imitated their style.

After his father's death Gusti Lempad continued and excelled at the work for the lords of Ubud. Around 1930 or '31 he began to draw, using a unique variant of the traditional style of Balinese art to produce works of great power, works which immediately impressed Spies and the other Europeans living around Ubud. Lempad's son, Gusti Madé Semung, was later to extend the family influence on the cultural reputation of Ubud when he became Jane Belo's research assistant. In the writings of the Europeans Gusti Nyoman Lempad became the father (or perhaps grandfather) of modern art in Bali, despite his humble nature.[24]

Although Lempad's artistic talents were central to the development of Ubud, he was not necessarily appreciated by the Cokordas of Ubud. Cokorda Raka reserved Lempad's daughter as a concubine, but did not marry her. In 1930 or 1931 another brother forced Lempad to borrow money against his rice fields to give to the Cokorda. When Lempad looked like losing his land Spies intervened to repay the loan.[25]

In the same way that Lempad guaranteed the artistic fame of Ubud, the jovial Anak Agung Mandera, a musician from the village of Paliatan, to the south of Ubud, ensured that the area became famous for dance and music. The old Cokorda Sukawati had ensured that the best teachers of dance and music from all over Gianyar were periodically brought to Ubud. Spies and Colin McPhee continued this tradition. In their research on Balinese music they sought out musicians from all over Bali, and brought them to the Ubud area not only to give examples of their music, but also to teach local musicians.

---

24. On other schools of traditional and modern art, see G. M. Sudarta, *Seni Lukis Bali dalam Tiga Generasi,* Jakarta: Gramedia, 1975; A. Forge, *Balinese Traditional Paintings,* Sydney: Australian Museum, 1978; A. Vickers, "Gusti Madé Deblog: Artistic Manifestations of Change in Bali," *RIMA* 14, 2 (1980): 1-47; H. Rhodius & J. Darling, *Walter Spies and Balinese Art,* Zutphen: Terra, 1980; D. J. Stuart Fox, "Pelukis Kerambitan yang Terlupakan," *Bali Post,* 9 August, 16 Aug., 23 Aug. 1981; Wim Bakker, *Bali Verbeeld,* Delft: Volkenkundig Museum Nusantara, 1986; H. I. R. Hinzler, *Catalogue of Balinese Manuscripts... the Balinese Drawings from the van der Tuuk Collection,* 2 vols, Leiden: Brill, 1986-7.

25. "Goesti Njoman Lempad — by J[ane] B[elo]," in Mead-Bateson fieldnotes, Library of Congress.

The growing artistic output of Ubud was one of many manifestations of a new identity for Bali. Bali really was becoming a cultural mecca, and people on different levels of society were struggling to find forms to express that cultural status. At the time when Spies, Bonnet, Mead and the others were fighting to maintain the ideal of a pure cultural life, a life of artistic activity related to the totality of society, Balinese artists were responding to colonialism by combining the styles of the different cultures which met on Bali.

The work of Gusti Nyoman Lempad of Ubud illustrates the way in which this mixed style emerged. Lempad was both a "pure" conservator of culture, valued for his genius by Spies, Bateson, Mead, McPhee and the others, and an innovative mixer of cultures. Painting on paper rather than the traditional (and much larger) cloth led Lempad to experiment with the single-scene format rather than use the multiple scenes, which had previously been the basis of narrative painting. In this he was really continuing the work of nineteenth-century painters who had used European paper from as early as the 1810s to experiment with composition and the organization of narrative scenes.[26] Much of Lempad's work involved the same long narratives used by other "traditional" artists to express ideals of religious purity and spiritual quest in this world and the next, to tell of the boundaries between the material and the spiritual worlds.

Lempad formed a link between the nineteenth-century Balinese artists and the younger generation who began painting in the late 1920s. These artists were from all over Bali, but especially from Gianyar, Badung and Tabanan. Along with painters there were also sculptors, for example the *brahmana* Ida Bagus Nyana of Mas, whose sculptures feature thin, almost too-fragile, elongated lines which were masterpieces of technical display, or I Cokot of Jati, whose carvings are bizarrely twisted chunks of wood from which emerge horrible staring demons and startling magical symbols. Some of the new artists drew on hereditary training as puppeteers in

---

26. See John Guy, *Palm-Leaf and Paper: Illustrated Manuscripts of India and SoutheastAsia,* Melbourne: National Gallery of Victoria, 1982, p. 72 for an example from the beginning of the nineteenth century; A. Vickers, "A Balinese Illustrated Manuscript of the Siwaratrikalpa," *BKI* 134 (1982): 443-69 for a mid-nineteenth-century example; and H. I. R. Hinzler, *Catalogue of Balinese Manuscripts* for examples from the last decades of the nineteenth century.

the shadow theater, or, like Lempad, on training in architecture and sculpture. Others had access to the training in the arts given to members of the aristocratic and *brahmana* élites, and sometimes came from families, which had established themselves under the Dutch, either within the bureaucracy or as religious leaders. For these artists and their families, there was no real distinction between the traditional and the modern.

The language of art in 1930s Bali was mixed up with the language of tourist image-making. There was no real Balinese market for the new art, so of course when painters painted they did so with hypothetical tourists in mind; they painted to tell people about the "real" Bali. Most successful painters used the Balinese language of signs in this cultural dialogue, drawing on stories from the theater, literature or folk tales. The Bali of the painters was a Bali where tradition had to be continued, a place where rituals had to be held, and a frightening world of chaos, which needed to be exorcised.

The way in which Balinese painters worked for the tourist market, while also expressing their own cultural concerns, is highlighted by a disagreement between Spies and Mead about the sexual content of some of Gusti Lempad's paintings. Mead and Bateson first heard of Lempad from Bonnet, "who commented on the fact that this man who made such very obscene drawings was himself so shy and modest." Spies later told Mead that Lempad's obscenities had been "suggested to him" by tourists, but Mead, while crediting Spies with teaching Lempad how to "work with paper and paint" observed that, "none of these make the kind of point the special European pervert would think up to suggest," by which she meant that they did not cater to European tastes, but expressed Lempad's own obsessions.[27]

What were these scenes? One in particular stands as an emblem of Bali's reputation at that time. It is a graphic scene of pederasty showing an older man and a young boy, something very different from the bland carved heads of dancers most tourists took home. Lempad's painting was not an image dictated by tourist romanticism; like many of his other scenes it has a tone of violence. This

---

27. Mead-Bateson fieldnotes, Ubud, 8 Feb. 1938, Bangli, 21 Feb. 1938, Library of Congress.

violence is not what we might call sadism, but an aspect of Balinese sexuality made explicit in older texts, where sexuality and power often go together. In these texts the language of sex is one of war and conquest—of "piercing" and "stabbing" with "love arrows" so that the woman "dies."[28]

In Lempad's scene the power is of man over boy, and the expressions on their faces are not of aggression and pain so much as of emotional extremism. This is not the kind of thing supposed to happen in everyday public life; it is a moment on the boundaries of Balinese emotional life.

Lempad's work was not necessarily intended as some kind of puritanical censure of his friend Spies, although one Ubud local who was a teenager at the time recalled how he and his friends were warned to keep clear of Spies. Lempad was making a more general comment on the Bali of the time, where sexuality had been made into a topic of public interaction, something by which Bali was known, and a feature of Balinese interaction with others. Lempad, at least in part, was connecting pederasty with the age of instability in which he found himself. It was not morally wrong, but its public importance was a symptom of an age of indulgence where the moral order was undergoing rapid change.

Other artists responded to the moral rearrangement of Bali through the depiction of rituals and magic. The same cremations, which drew the attention of tourists, became part of a visual conversation about the nature of Bali. Such things as cremations had been selected as important by tourists and writers, which in turn compelled the Balinese to address the meaning of these aspects of their culture. Rituals were obviously important to both sides, but for different reasons.

For the tourists the cremations were all about spectacle; for the Balinese painters they were about conflict and harmony. In Batuan, the village where Bateson and Mead did at least some of their fieldwork, the artists of the 1930s depicted many ritual scenes, paying explicit attention to moments within the ritual that revealed social

28. See A. Vickers, The Desiring Prince: The Kidung Malat as Text (diss.), University of Sydney, 1986.

Cremation, depicted in the Batuan style by Ida Bagus Madé Jatasura, 1937. This painting was collected by Gregory Bateson and Margaret Mead and described and analyzed by Gregory Bateson in his article "Style, Grace and Information in Primitive Art."

tensions and aggression. Bateson and Mead's comments on the paintings they collected make some of this content explicit. The painters saw themselves as painting "what Bali was like," and presenting this information to the tourists, but it is not clear how the buyers of these paintings interpreted their purchases.[29] The paintings often depicted images of harmony, and Bali as a harmonious society, but the harmony of Bali was one born out of conflict and

29. See G. Bateson & M. Mead, *Balinese Character: A Photographic Analysis;* Bateson and Mead fieldnotes, Library of Congress; for Bateson's analysis of a Balinese painting, "Style, Grace, and Information in Primitive Art," in his *Steps to an Ecology of Mind,* St Albans: Paladin, 1972; for a reinterpretation of this in the light of comments by Batuan painters I have drawn on an unpublished paper by Hildred Geertz on Bateson's views and Batuan painting of the 1930s. See Hildred Geertz, *Images of Power: Balinese Paintings Made for Gregory Bateson and Margaret Mead,* Honolulu: University of Hawai'i Press, 1994.

out of balancing constant and strongly felt social tensions. This, as Bateson had seen, was the "steady state" of Balinese society. What was not clear to Bateson was the degree to which social tensions had been exacerbated by colonialism.

Bateson was concerned with locating an unchanging Balinese ethos, as he called it, but in looking at Balinese paintings he was looking at documents of change. The rituals that were held to be such a normal part of everyday life had in fact increased in frequency since the Dutch took over. Moreover the social relations involved in those rituals had been transformed, something that made it possible for commoners to increase the number of rituals they held.

In the nineteenth century commoners would often join royal rituals as followers, so that, for example, a royal cremation would be accompanied by the cremations of hundreds of commoners who could not afford rites of their own. The royal power mechanisms and the *brahmana* priesthood kept control over rituals to ensure that commoners did not get above themselves by adopting signs of high status in other rituals. In the twentieth century the major constraint on commoner rituals has been money. Increasingly families found that they could hold rituals in as grand a manner as they liked, provided their neighbors did not deride them too much for being pretentious. This has meant an upsurge in ritual holding in the twentieth century.

Exorcising the Age of Chaos

Another major theme for the artists of the 1930s was the dark side of the Balinese world. Many showed the same *Calon Arang* or exorcistic performances of the *Barong* and *Rangda* dances which fascinated tourists and academics alike. Painters and sculptors, particularly the artists of Batuan village south of Ubud and the unique carver I Cokot, joined in the exorcism with depictions of witches, demons and the magical forces abroad in the world.

The age of instability that was the colonial era on Bali was an age of fear. Some artists painted almost to exorcise that fear, and their works were of a piece with the exorcistic dances and rituals that had increased dramatically in Bali from the early decades of the twentieth century onwards. By presenting fear in the concrete form of the *Rangda*, the embodiment of fear, artists and dancers could made it concrete and thus hold it at bay. This was true not only of these Batuan painters, such as Ida Bagus Madé Togog, but also of artists from other areas, particularly I Gusti Madé Deblog of Dénpasar (1906-86). Deblog, a short, quiet man with the look of a street-seller from the backblocks, was almost the perfect embodiment of the period. His birth coincided with the beginning of colonialism, and he lived in a royal center that in the 1930s, evolved into a colonial town.

His works were full of images of witches, weird beings and demons, and of violent clashes between the terrible forces at large in the world. His heroes, the kinds of heroes appropriate to this era, were the two half-demonic characters from the *Mahabharata* and *Ramayana* respectively: one of the five Pandawa brothers, the violent and aggressive Bima; and Hanuman, the white monkey general. These two, because they shared in the same terrifying power of the demons and witches, were the only allies of mankind. Deblog's paintings spoke of fear, of an era when only extreme results could put right the order of things.[30] The *Barong* and *Rangda* became the quintessential Balinese figures, not because they had always been so, but because the era of instability was in drastic need of exorcism on all levels.

The Development of Social Conflict

Bali from 1908 to 1942, then, was an island of social tensions and conflict for the Balinese. The atmosphere was one of demonic exploitation, an atmosphere in which magical, political, religious and economic issues became inseparable. One of the prime examples of this was the issue of caste, ostensibly a religious way of describing order, but a major political and social issue as well.

The Dutch froze caste on Bali, and in so doing created a struggle for status as people jockeyed to be classified in the highest caste groups.[31] The struggle was converted into a physical one because the issue of caste created an alliance between Dutch colonial interests and the ruling group of Balinese, an alliance which was challenged

---

30. Vickers, "Gusti Madé Deblog."

31. Korn, *Het Adatrecht,* p. 176; Schulte Nordholt, *Bali: Colonial Conceptions.*

by educated commoners who saw their education as being at least as important as the old status titles, which they now saw as "feudal." The challenge to caste arose under the Dutch, but really crystallized after the Japanese occupation upset colonial power relations and prompted the maturation of Indonesian nationalist sentiments into a fully-fledged nationalist revolution. In the period after Indonesia gained its independence in 1949 the various forces that had emerged in Balinese society clashed over the direction Balinese identity, culture and religion should take. In this context the struggle between different groups in Balinese society took the form of a political struggle between Right and Left, a fight which the Left lost in the bloodiest of ways.

By legislating and by classifying people's social roles according to caste the Dutch created something that had not previously existed: a rigid hierarchy. Now the only hope of movement up the hierarchy come from the ability to legally back up claims in court. One of the jokes of the time was about *gusti ponnis* or "verdict Gustis," commoners who tried to get titles in the Dutch law courts. Many families sponsored the writing of genealogies that further supported claims to caste status. This new outpouring of genealogies was based on royal genealogy writing, but spread the practice to all levels of society.

The Dutch did not understand the details of Balinese society, and in order to freeze caste they needed the help of the *brahmana* high priests to explain and simplify the system, hardly disinterested parties. Just as the Dutch adopted kings to nominally head the Balinese social order, so they gave the priesthood a special role in explaining Balinese religion and society. A number of priestly families were singled out as particularly important advisers. Of all the former kingdoms Klungkung had the highest spiritual authority in Bali, but from 1908 to 1929 it had no king, so the family of the Geria (priestly house) of Pidada, a house that had arisen during the reign of Klungkung's Virgin Queen, was selected to provide the highest spiritual advisers. The Dutch chose Ida Wayan Pidada of Geria Pidada to advise them as to the rights and duties of the various castes. His profound learning and the prestige of the house as advisers to the highest kings made him a natural choice. All the Dutch authorities, even later researchers such as Korn, depended on him and his priestly brethren to give the most expert advice, ignoring others with some claim to expertise, such as the various types of commoner priests, and even the female priests from the *brahmana* caste.

The male *brahmana* advised the Dutch not individually, but formally, as judges in the traditional courts. These courts had lost their former role as tribunals at which the king officiated, and became courts of caste law, or canon law as some Dutch called it. The power of life or death over the king's subjects was gone, but the courts still handed down their precepts according to the ancient law books and religious works. They decided who could use which title, and what the proper moral duties and ceremonial rights were for each caste.

So it was Balinese, not Dutch, who determined the practical details of colonial policy. The Dutch after all saw the whole nature of religion and caste as a big mystery, and were satisfied with simplified explanations, which fitted into their administrative structure. The priests had great freedom within the confines of Dutch rule to determine how Balinese society should be organized according to their ideal model of caste. In this they were assisted by the former rulers, particularly the king of Karangasem, who supported the prestige of the *brahmana* priesthood.

The transition to Dutch rule and the imposition of the priestly ideal of caste was not bloodless. In the first decade of Dutch rule a number of cases of resistance to Dutch rule arose, in which the priestly courts were asked to make determinations. These cases all revolved around the corvée labor which commoners were asked to do for the state. It was the priestly courts that determined who was a *sudra* or member of the lowest caste, the people who had to carry out the corvée. A number of commoner kin groups, which had formerly been quite important, rightly felt that they were being savagely demoted in status. Their struggle to maintain status was the forerunner of larger struggles over caste and social organization.

In Karangasem the Bandesa and Pasek clans, which had previously provided many of the court officials, refused to carry out their corvée for the Dutch. They were forced to do so by armed guards. In Gianyar there were two different cases of resistance. The first in

1911 was from members of the *Pandé* (Blacksmith) group from the village of Beng. When they refused to toe the Dutch line, leaders of the so-called rebellion were put in chains and exiled.

The second case from Gianyar involved a number of villagers from Sukawati. In 1917, after the earthquake, which rocked Bali, 125 of these villagers felt that the former Age of Kingdoms was at an end, and that they no longer had to carry out any of their corvée. In a judgment from the priestly courts they were ordered to work, but still refused, and so a district officer was sent with an armed brigade to challenge them. After a warning the officer ordered the brigade to open fire. Four villagers were killed immediately, a fifth died later, and seven others were wounded. Thirty of the survivors fled to make a new life elsewhere.[32] Peasants like the rebellious villagers of Sukawati, who had been shot for their troubles, were starting to feel that the old order had disappeared, but were unwilling to conform to the new requirements.

The judgment of the priests on the Blacksmiths of Beng says a great deal about what was going on in this remaking of traditional Bali. The Blacksmiths had always been one of the dissident groups in the caste system. They had refused to acknowledge the four-caste scheme, and thus refused to accept the holy water of the *brahmana* priests. In the judgment on them the three priests of north Bali, with advice from Ida Wayan Pidada of Klungkung and three priests from Gianyar, let it be known that the Blacksmiths were really *sudra.* Their claims in court to be considered as *satria* or members of the second caste were denied, and the court made determinations as to the terms of address other Balinese used to the Blacksmiths in everyday life (whether they were high-caste terms or not) and on the number of roofs they could have on their cremation towers, another sign of caste. The court ruled they were not entitled to the seven roofs that they had been using. On their refusal to use the holy water of the *Brahmana* priests, the court decided that they were really of the residual category of "Original Balinese" or *Bali Aga,* and so this

---

32. Report in the *Javansche Courant* 44 (5 Juni 1917), cited in Lekkerkerker, *Bali en Lombok: Overzicht der Literatuur omtrent deze Eilanden tot Einde 1919,* Rijswijk: Blankwaardt en Schoonhoven, 1920, p. 400. The other cases are discussed in Schulte Nordholt, "Een Balische Dynastie," p. 223, n. 62.

did not represent a major issue.[33] Here, as elsewhere, the priests' knowledge enabled them to refer to special categories to sort out anomalies in the system.

When the new, revised version of caste was put into place it was the members of the three upper castes, the *triwangsa,* who gained. The old courts had overflowed with people, the abundance of whom represented the living power of the king. In those courts commoners played many roles, and could often be village heads or even senior state officials. Besides these commoners, there were the members of the *triwangsa*—distant royal relatives, brahmans who did not become priests, assorted hangers-on—who could be fitted into the hierarchy of the palaces in roles ranging from senior state officials to pages and retainers. Under the Dutch there were only a limited number of state offices available, as heads of taxation, opium overseers (until opium could be phased out), and so on. Hundreds missed out, and many found niches elsewhere as village heads. This was because the Dutch image of the upper castes was as the top of society in terms of position and power it was right for them to occupy all the high offices before commoners. This meant that commoners descended from state officials of the pre-colonial era lost not only status, but also the land that went with those positions. There were individual conflicts between commoners and aristocrats for positions, but the aristocracy always had the new version of tradition and the law courts on their side.

Nationalism and the Challenge to Caste

Official positions put the kings firmly back into the state, but for these kings to maintain their credibility and traditional loyalties they also needed to work through bodies, which were not so obviously Dutch. The contradictions in their double game were becoming apparent to some of the educated Balinese who were impatient with the claims of "tradition" used to bolster the positions of royalty and the priesthood and who challenged the royal equation of title

---

33. For the documents on this case and a complete discussion of the many issues involved, see Jean-François Guermonprez, *Les Pandé de Bali: La Formation d'une <<Caste>> et la Valeur d'une Titre,* Paris: École Française d'Extrême-Orient, 1987, especially app. C.

with superiority. From this new educated élite, formed mainly in the northern capital of Singaraja, came two generations of leader who were to form the backbone of revolutionary Bali from the 1920s until 1965.

In the 1920s the raja of Karangasem, Gusti Bagus, was instrumental in establishing religious reform organizations intended to direct the nature of religious change according to the precepts of caste. The first of these in south Bali was more or less a college of *brahmana* high priests that aimed at getting people to follow the duties of their caste. A second organization in Klungkung, established on the initiative of Gusti Bagus, aimed to preserve caste, and supported this aim through the collection and teaching of traditional knowledge based on a study of manuscripts.[34] Likewise in Ubud the royal family established their own organization for studying traditional literature.

These new organizations were set up because caste was being directly challenged in north Bali. In 1925 a twenty-year-old teacher from the Blacksmith clan, Nengah Métra of Bratan, Bulèlèng, became the leader of a religious reform organization, which aimed to overturn the old feudal ties of caste in the name of progress. Nengah Métra was committed to the new ideal of modernization. He was one of the first to receive a good formal education under the Dutch, and through education, he and his fellow teachers felt they had a chance to carve out a place for all Balinese in the new society of the Netherlands East Indies. Like most of the first generation of Balinese teachers, he had been trained in Java, and worked with Javanese teachers.

The Dutch were not initially worried about the contacts trainee teachers might establish, since up until 1915 they could get few Balinese even to go to school. Peasants were excluded from all but rudimentary education, and were too busy working with their parents to stay alive, while members of the upper castes were worried that attendance at school and participation in games such as leap-frog

---

34. See Korn, *Het Adatrecht,* p. 175; Anak Agung Gedé Putra Agung, "Balinese Kingship under the Colonial Period: Education, Patron-Clients, and Social Mobility, 1908-1938," paper given at the Balinese State and Society Workshop, 1986.

might infringe their status: people of lower caste might raise themselves physically higher than their superiors, or might not use the
proper respectful language to them in the school-room.[35] Eventually
the inducements of modernization, and a bit of coercion where necessary, increased school attendances, but introduced the extra factor
of allowing "harmful" outside influences to penetrate. By sending
teachers to Java to train, by having Javanese teachers, or by sending
graduates outside Bali to work, there was a real danger that Balinese
would come in contact with some of the subversive nationalist ide-
alism then developing in Java. Thus in the 1920s the Dutch set up
more schools in Bali, but tried to staff them with Balinese teachers
and to ensure that those who left school would be able to get civil
service jobs on Bali.

New ideas of equality and of the value of education made commoners involved in schools unhappy with the idea of caste and the
privileges of aristocracy. In 1921 the traditional ruler of Bulèlèng,
Gusti Putu Jlantik, set up the first religious reformist organization,
which was oriented towards education. It was superseded by the
organization *Santi* in 1923, of which Nengah Métra became one of
the leading members. Two years later at a meeting of *Santi* in the
house of the *brahmana* district head of Bañjar, Ida Gedé Suwandi,
things erupted. Ktut Nasa, one of Métra's closest friends, launched
a tirade against caste values, saying how it was the adherence to
old-fashioned feudal values which had made Balinese religion rot-
ten to the core. Fanatical members of the upper castes like Ida Gedé,
he said, did not deserve to have respectful language used to them.
Those who really deserved respect were those who had earned it
through the enlightenment (the word he used was *budi*) of education, not through birth.

Nengah Métra, Ktut Nasa, and a third friend, Nyoman Kajèng,
together with a number of others formed a breakaway commoner
group, called *Suryakanta,* and refused to accept the idea that they

---

35. See Anak Agung Putra Agung, *Perubahan Sosial dan Pertentangan Kasta di Bali Utara 1924-
1928,* (unpub. M A thesis) Universitas Gajah Mada, 1974, p. 18. See further I Gusti Ngurah
Bagus, "Surya Kanta: A Kewangsan Movement of the Jaba Caste in Bali," *Masyarakat Indonesia,* 2, 2 (1975): 153-62, and *Pertentangan Kasta Dalam Bentuk Baru pada Masjarakat
Bali,* Dénpasar: Universitas Udayana, 1969.

were *sudra,* a term they found insulting. In reply the hard-liners who considered themselves *triwangsa* (members of the three upper castes) organized their own new society, *Bali Adnyana.* The two groups waged war through their respective journals and at public meetings. The *Suryakanta* group pursued their arguments on many fronts. They saw education as the key means of enabling the population to develop and modernize. On the subject of religion they argued that the rulers' emphasis on holding large-scale rituals was a waste of money, and that the peasantry would be better served by simplifying ceremonies and joining co-operatives.

Nengah Métra made an even more dramatic attack on caste when he married a *brahmana* woman. This totally outraged the members of *Bali Adnyana,* who held that the principle of caste marriage dictated that women of rank should only marry men of equal or higher status. They then arranged for the Dutch to banish the couple to Lombok.[36] The Dutch were particularly fearful of potential subversive forces at that time, since from late 1926 to early 1927 the Indonesian Communist Party (PKI) had been responsible for a series of abortive rebellions which threatened the very foundation of Dutch colonialism. Even after he came back from exile, Métra remained active, and it was he who was chosen by leading Balinese in 1934 as a replacement for Ubud's Cokorda Raka Sukawati on the People's Council, a move blocked by the Dutch.

While Métra's exile was in force, and with the encouragement of the Dutch, who opted for a hard-line policy of squashing dissent, the aristocracy regrouped. The raja of Karangasem's new organizations, especially the educational institution in Klungkung, were aimed at reconciling all groups to the idea of caste. Likewise King Gusti Putu Jlantik of Bulèlèng had never been a strong supporter of *Bali Adnyana,* but nonetheless worked hard to defuse any potential clashes. To this end he fostered an alliance of traditional groups who supported the Dutch Kirtya Liefrinck-van der Tuuk, the foundation for the preservation of traditional Balinese knowledge named after the enlightened heroes of Dutch colonialism on Bali.

Gusti Jlantik donated many of his own manuscripts to this august

---

36. For a full account of this see Putra Agung, "Perubahan Sosial."

body, and helped in the collection and copying of other manuscripts. In doing this he helped to disabuse the radicals of the north of the idea that members of the upper castes were keeping secret knowledge for themselves, and therefore dominating Balinese religion, but at the same time he managed to co-opt Nyoman Kajèng, one of the leaders of the formerly dissident organization *Suryakanta* and thus a close associate of Nengah Métra, into working towards the politically safe goals of education and knowledge. Along with other leading intellectuals who operated in and around the Kirtya, Kajèng enlivened public discussion about popular traditions both through his research and by analyzing and summarizing traditional literature and religious teaching in cultural magazines.

The Kirtya was thus made into an expression of the harmonious or egalitarian nature of Balinese religion in the new Dutch state. Through this organization its members came in contact with a number of the Dutch scholars of the time, particularly Roelof Goris and his successor as language adviser at the Kirtya, Christian Hooykaas. These scholars helped foster self-confidence and a strong belief in the viability of Balinese culture amongst the intellectual élite of the colonial era, a confidence that was always a double-edged sword. While it contributed to the harmonious image of Bali, this confidence was also part of nationalist self-awareness, which ultimately challenged Dutch rule. Although reading old manuscripts and debating points of theology may not sound very radical, they provided the basic elements of Balinese selfhood as Balinese leaders defined their cultural identity to other Indonesians in the nationalist context. A number of Balinese associated with the Kirtya even went a step further on the classical path of nationalist identity and wrote novels in the Balinese and Indonesian languages, consciously presenting their work as models of Balinese culture.[37]

The intellectual developments going on around the Kirtya in the

---

37. The foremost modern author in Balinese was an employee of the Kirtya, Gedé Srawana *(nom-de-plume* of I Wayan Bhadra), *Mlancaran ka Sasak,* originally published as a serial in the Kirtya's magazine, *Djataju* (1935-9), repr. Dénpasar: Yayasan Saba Sastra Bali, 1978. From the 1930s until the 1950s he was the author of many articles and booklets on Balinese literature and religion in Dutch and Indonesian. In Malay/Indonesian the foremost Balinese author was A. A. Pañji Tisna, son of the raja of Bulèlèng.

1920s were connected with religious developments in the field of education. While some of the new schools, foundations for religion and study groups based on the use of traditional literature, were linked to the maintenance of royal power, others had specific ties to the educationally-based nationalist groups, which were then emerging in Java. Interestingly enough not all members of the aristocracy took a totally pro-Dutch outlook, and some were at the forefront of introducing Indonesia-wide nationalist thought to Bali, where it merged with the new intellectual interest in Balinese traditions fostered by the various movements, organizations and foundations already mentioned.[38] In doing this, Balinese nobles followed the example of royalty from other parts of Indonesia, with whom the Balinese royal families had links. Gusti Bagus Jlantik of Karangasem for example, was very close to the princely house of Mangkunegara in central Java, and his sons and daughters went to school in Java.

The double-sided nature of the aristocracy, leading the way in taking advantage of Dutch policy while being at the forefront of anti-Dutch nationalism, was not really so contradictory. The same impulses were present in both pro-Dutch attitudes and pro-nationalist sentiments, and these were impulses shared with other Indonesian aristocrats, particularly the central Javanese aristocracy. The Balinese aristocracy, the *brahmana* and the important group of educated commoners were all in the new position of needing to be able to explain social status and roles and the meaning of Balinese religion in terms explicable to other Indonesians, and to westerners in the form of tourists and colonizers. The language they needed was the language of western education, but they also had to use this in a way that made use of their own cultural values, which they presented as a consciously articulated tradition.

Caste became one of the cornerstones of Balinese culture because it could explain social status by reference to religious beliefs. Beyond this the intellectual leaders of Bali needed recourse to other

---

38. See Sukawati, *Reminiscences,* p. 13, for links between Ubud and the nationalist lawyer R. P. Singgih. Singgih also wrote an account of his "Impressions of Bali" in the magazine he edited, *Timboel* 3 (1929): 201-2, 213-14, 223-4, 247-9, 278-80, 296-7. On Singgih as a nationalist, see John Ingleson, *The Road to Exile The Indonesian Nationalist Movement 1927-1934,* Singapore: Heinemann, 1979.

internationally-recognized ideas about the worth of Asian religions to express their culture. They found such ideas in the influence of Theosophy. By the 1930s Theosophy was well established in Indonesia, and both Dutch and Indonesians were avid scholars of eastern religion. Some of the Dutch scholars associated with the Kirtya shared that interest, and were in contact with like-minded Javanese members of religious, cultural and educational organizations. When India's leading writer and intellectual leader, Rabindranath Tagore, like Gandhi a representative of the meeting between Theosophy and nationalism, came out to the Netherlands East Indies, he was taken to both ancient Hindu-Buddhist temples on Java (especially Borobudur) and to Bali, where Goris and others acted as his guides.[39] Theosophy was a convenient system through which Bali was fitted into the world of Indian cultural influence, the "mystical East," as a source of wisdom.

The Dutch, Javanese and Balinese here and in their broader interests in Theosophy, Indian religion and Javanese and Balinese culture were trying to elevate culture and religion from their Balinese contexts and relate them to what they considered authentically Eastern patterns. This gave Balinese religion far greater importance than if it was isolated from the cultural worlds of Java and India, and in this sense the legacy of very early scholars such as Raffles could be turned to Balinese advantage. Balinese religion became authentic and authoritative on international terms, and the Balinese kings and princes could take their place on the colonial scene on equal terms with the princes and sultans of Java, or even of India. Ironically here Balinese were involved in the same kind of elevation or idealization of culture as the tourists, colonial scholars and expatriates of the 1930s, but for different ends.

The Second World War and Its Aftermath

The colonial period on Bali, which ended with the Japanese invasion of 1942, set the stage for a conflict between forces in Balinese

---

39. *Timboel* also had features on Rabindranath Tagore's visit to Java and Bali. Goris's successor, Hooykaas, was a friend of the Javanese nationalist, founder of Budi Utâmâ and the Taman Siswa educational movement, Ki Ajar Déwantârâ. Hooykaas also taught many of the children of the Balinese aristocracy while he was a teacher in Yogyakarta.

society conceived of as those who were feudal against those who embraced the modern. The harmonious idea of Balinese society which was fostered by the Dutch and encouraged by common attitudes towards education and religion in the 1930s, was shown to be a facade by the sweeping victory of Japan. During and after the Japanese occupation there was an increasing polarization of Balinese society, exacerbated by the political divisions of Indonesia as a whole. The climax of these tensions was another kind of *puputan,* the killing of hundreds of thousands of Communists and Communist sympathizers after 1965. The period between 1942 and 1965 saw a consolidation of ideas of "culture" and "tradition" in the images of Bali. For most of the participants in the conflicts and struggles of the time the question of what Balinese culture was and who controlled it was of the utmost importance.

If the upheavals of colonialism inspired fear amongst Balinese, it was nothing compared to the terror of Japanese rule. Initially the Japanese were welcomed as liberators and heroes of the struggle against imperialism. The majority of villagers only started to worry about the Japanese as the war progressed and food shortages became endemic.

Japanese pre-war propaganda had fostered the idea of a "Greater Asian Co-Prosperity Sphere," and of Asian identity. For many nationalists, whose chief goal was getting rid of the Dutch, this appeal to fellow Asians was all-important. These same nationalists were to suffer later.

Many members of the élite of Balinese society remember the Japanese period as one of brutality, as the military used force to bolster their authority. One of the major religious leaders of north Bali was beaten and hung upside down for days for his unco-operative activities. Elsewhere in Bali there are stories of torture and atrocities, such as the man from Klungkung who was punished by having his legs cut off.

The main brunt of Japanese violence was borne by members of the aristocracy whom the Japanese regarded as feudal and collaborators with the Dutch. Japanese brutality took an even more extreme form in other parts of Indonesia, where many traditional leaders were executed. This did not happen in Bali, however, partly because the Japanese found that they needed the aristocracy to run the island, for the Dutch had left the traditional rulers in such a position that they were indispensable. The younger generation of Balinese royalty took advantage of Dutch support to foster new roles under the Japanese. The young son of the raja of Gianyar, Anak Agung Gedé Agung, who had studied law in Batavia, was given a high civil service position before being made to take over the running of Gianyar in place of his uncooperative father.[40]

As part of their anti-colonial stance and their emphasis on "Asianness" the Japanese promoted Balinese culture. This had the dual effect of strengthening the pro-Japanese war effort and bolstering Balinese feelings of identity. The Japanese held a number of art shows, and leading modern artists like Gusti Madé Deblog were awarded prizes for their work. In the long run, because Balinese culture was so strongly identified with religion, and in turn with caste, any support for Balinese culture aided the cause of the very feudal rulers the Japanese opposed.

While the war progressed Indonesian nationalists could do little but watch Japanese planes take off on their bombing missions to Darwin, or suffer as the basic necessities of life became harder to obtain from 1944 onwards. When the war ended the time came for the Japanese to deliver the carrot, which they had held out to Indonesia: Independence.

The nationalists hoped that the Japanese promises would be backed up with the delivery of arms for the struggle against the Dutch. Sukarno and the other national leaders had proclaimed independence in Jakarta at about the time that the allies were dropping the atomic bomb on Hiroshima. When Japan surrendered the allies demanded that Japanese weapons be handed over to them, and not given to the Indonesians. Mountbatten's Southeast Asia Command was to step in and hold Indonesia until the Dutch could arrive to reclaim it. In some cases the Japanese went along with the agreement and fought mercilessly to stop the Indonesians taking their weapons. In Bali as in other parts of Indonesia many Japanese were

---

40. George Sanford Kanahele, The Japanese Occupation of Indonesia: Prelude to Independence (unpub. diss.) Cornell University, 1967 says that Agung was trained as a military officer by the Japanese, although Agung's autobiography makes no mention of this.

sympathetic to Indonesian independence, and turned a blind eye or put up only token resistance to the nationalists when they raided weapons.[41]

Feudal Monarchs For the Dutch

The period between the Japanese surrender of 1945 and the landing of Dutch military forces to reclaim Bali in 1946 was a crucial one for the direction Balinese society was to take. During this period Bali was without a single center of power, as each former kingdom tried to reassert its importance while an interim Republican administration struggled to gain recognition both within and outside Bali. Kings vied with other important families in each state in factional conflicts over whether to join the Republic or remain pro-Dutch, and even within families there were strong divisions along these lines. Thus while the Déwa Agung emerged as one of the most staunchly pro-Dutch rulers, with strong mechanisms of control within his state of Klungkung, one of his sons, Cokorda Anom Putra, became a Republican.

When the Dutch came back in force after a period of chaos, their staunchest supporters on Bali were for the most part the rajas, some of whose fathers or grandfathers had died fighting Dutch rule. This pro-Dutch stance was not adopted by all the Balinese aristocracy; many members of the younger generation had been quite happy with the interim period of Republican administration on Bali. What followed, however, was an intimation of the violence inherent in the opposing forces in Balinese society, a violence which was to see the death of at least 2000 Balinese in the next few years.[42]

The leaders of that interim administration were imprisoned as soon as the Dutch arrived. Some Balinese chose to take the Republican fight underground, a decision reinforced by the harshness of the Dutch repression of resistance. The leader of the militant anti-Dutch Republicans was another member of the lower aristocracy from Mengwi, Gusti Ngurah Rai. He and his followers fought a series

---

41. For details of the end of Japanese rule and the beginning of the struggle for independence, see Robinson, "State, Society and Political Organisation," p. 36, and Nyoman S. Pendit, *Bali Berjuang,* Jakarta: Gunung Agung, 1954 (repr. 1979).

42. For this estimate, see Robinson, "State, Society and Political Organisation," p. 2.

of battles against the Dutch which culminated in a heroic fight to the death in the hills. Ngurah Rai and ninety of his supporters were surrounded in the area of Marga, and rather than surrender they invoked the traditional stance of the *puputan,* which meant they were all massacred.[43]

By calling this last stand a *puputan* Ngurah Rai consciously invoked tradition against the Dutch. In nationalist thought, as exemplified by the writings of prominent leftists, the *puputan* of 1906 had become as potent a symbol of Indonesian resistance to the Dutch as the long and bloody Aceh War which raged from the late nineteenth century until the early decades of the twentieth century.[44] Ngurah Rai's last stand marked Bali's coming of age as a force in the Indonesian nation, and is commemorated with both traditional-style monuments at Marga and the naming of the international airport at Tuban after this hero.

The holding of a *puputan* against the Dutch during the revolution shows that it was not only the pro-Dutch rulers who claimed a monopoly on Balinese tradition. One of the major reasons that the rajas supported the returning Dutch was that the Dutch represented the restoration of traditional Bali, in line with the decision to grant limited autonomy to the traditional rulers in 1938. The zeal of the nationalist youth, the *Pemuda* who were the vanguard of the Revolution, represented uncertainty. With the Dutch there was at least assurance of continuing the political and economic power structures carefully constructed during the pre-war colonial period, which had become synonymous with "traditional culture."

There was no developed nationalist policy on Balinese culture. One extreme of the *Pemuda* continued the anti-caste line of the north Balinese *Suryakanta* movement, while another saw any evocation of Asian tradition as a challenge to western imperialism. In the light of their post-Revolutionary actions, most pre-Republican Balinese could be said to have located themselves somewhere in the middle of this spectrum.

---

43. Pendit, *Bali Berjuang.*

44. My thanks to Helen Jarvis for information on Tan Malaka's interest in the *puputan.* For a more recent view of the role of the *puputan,* see Pramoedya Ananta Toer, *Jejak Langkah,* Jakarta: Asta Mitra, 1986, pp. 158-85.

The legacy of the *Suryakanta* movement was a tradition of education and the appreciation of learning as a social force, a legacy which was perpetuated in the northern capital of Singaraja, where Nengah Métra had returned to teach, after his exile on Lombok; where intellectuals such as Métra's friend Nyoman Kajèng worked in the Kirtya Liefrinck-van der Tuuk; and where practically the whole group of political leaders of Bali in the 1940s and 1950s went to school. At the major Dutch school in Singaraja the young men and women of Bali had a chance both to be inspired by teachers such as Métra and to form networks which could be carried over into guerrilla organizations in the Revolution. Métra himself took up arms for the Revolution, and died at the age of forty in 1946, shot down by Dutch troops. To commemorate his challenge to the caste hierarchy he was cremated in the style of a member of the *satria* or second caste by his fellow villagers of Bratan, the Blacksmiths clan area of the city of Singaraja.[45]

The aristocracy itself was wholly divided on the issue of Indonesian independence, and much of the population, willingly or not, tended to side with their various aristocratic patrons on the question. Virtually all of the political leaders of Bali at the time, including the commoner intellectuals, mobilized support by emphasizing their roles as traditional patrons, and factional disputes followed along the lines of patron-client networks. The split was such that brothers were pitted against brothers, as was the case for the two rulers of Ubud. Cokorda Raka Sukawati became president of the state of Eastern Indonesia or NIT (Negara Indonesia Timor), a pro-Dutch entity established as a compromise measure. When the Dutch realised they could not totally obliterate or even ignore the Indonesian Republic on Java, they attempted to set up various states in a federation headed by the Netherlands. The NIT was the most successful of these attempts, although republican wits interpreted the acronym to mean *Negara Ikut Tuan* (The Follow-the-Master State).

As President, Cokorda Raka worked closely with the Council of

---

45. Guermonprez, *Les Pandé de Bali*, pp. 104-5; see also Pendit, *Bali Berjuang*, p. 373 and Robinson, "State, Society and Political Organisation," p. 22, where I presume that Nengah Merta is a misprint for Métra, although there was another Nengah Merta who was the Lombok representative of Suryakanta.

Kings, which was the governing body of Bali, and in particular with his in-laws from the palace of Gianyar, amongst whom Anak Agung Gedé Agung had been appointed as raja to succeed his father, but handed over the position to his brother, so that he could become prime minister of the NIT. Anak Agung's role in politics has been fiercely debated by Balinese, and he has been called both a reactionary collaborator and a staunch patriot. The fact that he went on to become Indonesian Foreign Minister has made it difficult to assess his role in the Revolution, but he seems to have reacted to situations rather than taking control of them, which meant that at times he completely reversed his political stand.

At home in the Gianyar-Ubud area the staid and upright Cokorda Raka and the ambitious Anak Agung were zealous suppressors of resistance. The jail in Gianyar became the main site for the incarceration, torture, and sometimes execution of anti-Dutch Balinese. Cokorda Raka's brother, Cokorda Agung, found himself in this jail in 1946 after being interrogated by Anak Agung. "Just before we reached the prison they caught me behind the knees so that I fell forward. First they started with my cousin, beating him and then with myself also... I felt myself just like a dog as they beat us across the back and on the head." Cokorda Agung was lucky compared to some: his most grievous memory of this period was not his own interrogation but the execution of two of his close friends by Dutch troops. These were two brothers from the palace of Paliatan, just south of Ubud, who had been identified as the ringleaders of the pro-Republican group in Gianyar. Cokorda Agung's months of internment ended with the establishment of the NIT and a reconciliation between the Cokordas Agung and Raka.[46]

Anak Agung justified his anti-Revolutionary stance by the fact that he had been kidnapped by republican zealots early in the struggle, and was thus alienated from the cause, and by the fact that he later helped to save the Republic by supporting it in the NIT parliament.[47] This does not necessarily justify the brutality for which Dutch supporters in Gianyar were responsible. The most famous

46. Sukawati, *Reminiscences,* pp. 37-9.
47. See Robinson, "State, Society and Political Organisation," p. 43.

Ida Bagus Madé Jatasura of Batuan, as photographed by Gregory Bateson.

case of this was the public torture of a number of villagers of Batuan for supporting the Republic. These villagers, mostly *brahmana,* included some of the leading artists and dancers of the day.

The Republican influence had been introduced to the village by the artist, I Ngendon (1915?-47), a commoner teacher who had gone to central Java in the 1930s, where he associated with many of Indonesia's leading artists and intellectuals. Full of hope for the future he joined Colonel Ngurah Rai's regiment, and used his skills to make pro-Revolutionary posters. But the Dutch forces laid a trap for him, and he was captured and tortured, then taken back to his home village and tortured again until he was taken to the graveyard to die. The Gianyar royal family ordered the villagers of Batuan to publicly humiliate fellow villagers who had associated with Ngurah Rai. One of the most prominent of Ngurah Rai's supporters was Ida Bagus Madé Jatasura (1915-47), widely celebrated as one of the most talented of the 1930s painters. In Bateson and Mead's book on Balinese character we see a portrait of this relaxed, smiling young man at work, his unassuming good nature shining through as he sketches.[48] He, along with a number of his relatives and friends,

---

48. Gregory Bateson & Margaret Mead, *Balinese Character: A Photographic Analysis,* New York: New York Academy of Sciences, p. 102, ill. 1.

was whipped and derided in front of his home village and he died in Gianyar jail from the wounds he received.[49]

The split between the feudal and modern forces of Balinese society, which had hardened during the revolutionary period, was left unhealed after Indonesia gained independence at the end of 1949. The rajas of Bali played their part in gaining independence, and were able to retain some of their former pre-eminence. Anak Agung in particular rose to prominence on the national scene when he brought the government of NIT down in protest at the Dutch military action (the so-called "Second Police Action") of 1948, which also nearly destroyed the Republican Government in Java. This reaction showed the Dutch that their federal states were not as slavishly pro-Dutch as they had hoped, and contributed to the international pressure from the United Nations which forced the Dutch to the negotiating table with the Republic. From this position Anak Agung went on to a distinguished career in Jakarta politics and the Indonesian diplomatic service, before retiring to Gianyar to take over his traditional role as king.

Sukarno and the other new leaders of the republic of Indonesia had been able to create a new state after a long and faction-ridden Revolution. The Republicans had fought a long and difficult battle against the Dutch mainly in the Javanese countryside, and paradoxically had gained independence by diplomatic means just at the point when the Dutch were able to take over the Republican capital of Yogyakarta by force of arms. When the conflict was over Sukarno and the new parliaments, which rose and fell in rapid succession, had to forge a new unity not only with those from other parts of Indonesia who had taken sides with the Dutch, but also with Republicans who had disagreed with the Sukarno leadership. These included Republicans who had wanted to continue the armed struggle with the Dutch and were dissatisfied with the compromises made when the leadership negotiated a settlement. The early 1950s were thus difficult years when Sukarno struggled to wrest consensus out of conflict, and to hold together opposing forces.

---

49. *Patah Tumbuh Hilang Berganti (Kumpulan Riwayat Hidup Pahlawan P.K.R.I. Gianyar)*, Dénpasar: Markas Cabang Legiun Veteran Repubik Indonesia Gianyar, 1979, pp. 28-9 & 80-1.

Traditionalists, Neo-Traditionalists and Communists

While terrorist attacks, grudge feuds and revenge killings continued into the early years of the Republic, the struggle between feudal and modern forces took on increasingly subtle forms after 1950. Between 1950 and 1965 the conflict over culture moved into a struggle between political parties in Indonesia, culminating in the fiery clashes between the adherents of the Nationalist Party and those aligned with the Communist Party. Although the nature of the political forces involved had changed, the cultural issues on Bali were still those which had emerged in the pre-war years.

The political struggles of the time were complemented by economic struggles, and it was no coincidence that the leaders on both sides of Balinese politics, including the Communist leaders, were also the heads of large business concerns. As had happened during the Revolution, those who came from families of traditional leaders used their hereditary roles and pre-existent forms of social co-operation to gain leverage in the new context of the Republic. As one nobleman of the time asserted: "They've taken away the government from us—all right, we'll capture the economy."[50] A sense of being born to lead was transposed into entrepreneurial activities, as rajas and other power-holders set up hotels, small factories or transport firms, using those who would in the nineteenth century have been their dependent subjects as labor. The aristocracy was successful in this, and one of the major sources of social tension which grew into support for Communism was a perception that the upper castes had developed into a big business class.[51]

Political conflict in the early years of the Republic was based on positions achieved during the Revolution. With the victory of the Republic those in the strongest position politically were the members of the resistance. The most prominent of the members of this group was Bagus Sutèja, the leftist leader who went on to become Governor of Bali, the man who covered up Balinese bare breasts. A member of the marginal royal family of Jembrana in the west of Bali, Sutèja was the embodiment of Revolutionary fervor, the head

---

50. Quoted in Clifford Geertz, *Peddlers and Princes: Social Change and Economic Modernisation in Two Indonesian Towns,* Chicago: University of Chicago Press, 1963. All of my discussion here of changing economic roles is based on Geertz's analysis.

51. ibid., p. 133.

of those who wanted to keep the struggle going after the Round Table Agreement with the Dutch.[52]

Like many revolutionaries he was driven by a puritanical zeal. The decision to cover women's breasts in public was not made easily, considering that the Dutch authorities had tried and failed, and in the 1930s Balinese involved with the nationalist movement had also advocated such a cover-up.[53] Sutèja's decision was a direct challenge to the sensationalist tourism of an earlier age, a sensationalism which western writers wanted to continue, but which Indonesians considered would not do their claims to be a modern, progressive country any good. Sutèja's moral stance on this issue was part of his general passion for social reform and should be viewed in the context of the endemic corruption stemming from Jakarta, in which only the representatives of the Left were seen as untainted.[54] After his political demise, however, Sutèja was accused of all kinds of indulgences and abuse of his position by his victorious enemies.[55]

Sutèja was the embodiment of the left wing of the Revolution in Bali. He had been associated with the new generation of leaders educated in Singaraja, and had been made a district head by the Dutch when they returned, but was arrested for being too sympathetic to the Republicans. In 1949, with his good friend I Gedé Puger, he founded an organization to continue the Revolutionary struggle, and against him there emerged an alliance between members of the pro-Dutch royal families who had seen the light, and Revolutionaries who were more "neo-traditionalist" in their approach.

The first opportunity to air these differences came in 1950. The conservative forces in Bali, led by the remnants of the Council of

---

52. On Sutèja see Robinson, "State, Society and Political Organisation," and Max Lane, Wedastera Suyasa in Balinese Politics, 1962-1972: From Charismatic Politics to Socio-Educational Activities (B. A. Hons thesis), Department of Indonesian and Malayan Studies, University of Sydney, 1972.

53. These were the Balinese members of Partindo, see M. Picard "Tourisme Culturel" et "Culture Touristique." Rite et Divertissement dans les Arts du Spectacle a Bali, (these de doctorat de 3ème cycle) EHESS, Paris, 1984, p. 61.

54. See Jef Last, Bali in de Kentering, Amsterdam: De Bezige Bij, 1955.

55. See John Hughes, The End of Sukarno: A Coup that Misfired, A Purge that ran Wild, Sydney: Angus and Robertson, 1968, p. 179.

Kings, put up a case that the island should be designated as a Special Region (a status granted to Yogyakarta and Aceh), one in which traditional royal leadership could be maintained. Cokorda Anom Putra, a son of Déwa Agung Oka Geg but a supporter of the republic, was put up as a candidate for regional head. Sutèja and his allies had already been in the forefront of the movement to get rid of all powers remaining to the old Council of Kings, a stand which determined that Sutèja, not Cokorda Anom, would take the role of head of Bali. Cokorda Anom was elected over Sutèja by the provisional parliament of Bali, which had been dominated by the Cokorda's supporters in the Nationalist Party. But Sukarno intervened and vetoed the election, making Sutèja regional head of Bali, which was not to be autonomous, but part of the Province of the Southeastern Islands.

In 1959 Sukarno had to repeat his intervention. Bali was made into a separate province, but the regional parliament had elected another Nationalist with right-wing credentials, Mantik, as governor. This election was overthrown, and Sutèja was made governor in Mantik's place. For Sukarno the choice was between the conservative forces and the radical group, represented by Sutèja, who supported Sukarno's ideal of continuing revolution.

The Nationalist Party or PNI *(Partai Nasionalis Indonesia)* was Sukarnoist in many ways too, but as time passed it became more right-wing, representing the interests of land-owners. Some on the right took a purist, traditionalist stance, aiming to preserve what they understood by Balinese tradition. This group tended to support the PNI, although some areas, notably Gianyar, had been strongholds of the conservative Socialist Party *(Partai Sosialis Indonesia)* until it was banned by Sukarno at the end of the 1950s. Others took a neotraditionalist stance, developing tendencies begun by the reformist and educational organizations in the 1920s, and these formed a kind of left-wing within the PNI.

The neo-traditionalists continued with the reform of Balinese religion begun in the 1920s. They ranged from those who supported the revitalization of Balinese literature, to those who wanted to make Balinese Hinduism more like the "pure" Hinduism of India. Activities in these areas were manifested in the creation of a university in Dénpasar, the new capital of Bali, and the establishment of religious reform groups, of which one, the Parisada Hindu Dharma, has continued to the present day.

Another group developed to foster the establishment of a faculty of letters in Dénpasar. As justification for the Faculty of Letters, these intellectuals could point to their support by a Dutch man, the paramount scholar of ancient Bali, Roelof Goris. Goris, in a pathetic state since his imprisonment in the late 1930s, joined that group of Dutch who sided with the Revolution and chose Indonesian citizenship. The Faculty was established in the mid-1950s and in 1958 became part of a university named after the best-known king of tenth-century Bali, Udayana. Others involved in the founding of the faculty included an esteemed Javanese scholar of ancient literature and the *Kawi* language, Poerbatjoroko, and Sukarno's minister for Culture, Prijono, who like Poerbatjaroko had taken his PhD at Leiden University. The Right and the Left vied for control of the faculty, although one group in the PNI founded an alternative private university named after Marhaen, the mythical archetype of the peasantry in Sukarno's philosophy.

The faculty of letters group was at this stage closely linked with the Indian-oriented reformists. The heritage of Theosophy in Balinese intellectual life, combined with the emergence of India as one of the leading nations of the newly described Third World, made India a logical place to turn for the renewal of Balinese tradition. A number of young Balinese intellectuals such as the writer Nyoman S. Pendit, went directly to India to study. Pendit was also close to the leader of the Saraswati education movement, Gusti Tamba, who had also sponsored the first Indian teacher of Hinduism to come to Bali, Pandit Shastri.

The reformists came from a variety of social levels, both from the traditional authorities of the *brahmana* caste and from commoner groups such as the *Pasek,* who challenged the hereditary nature of caste authority. During the 1950s Balinese developed a new awareness of their origins. There was a great outpouring of commoners' dynastic genealogies, following the lead of the aristocracy in the late nineteenth century and the 1920s. With the writing of these genealogies came attempts to re-establish or strengthen clan ties, by setting up Bali-wide clan organizations to challenge the preeminence of the aristocracy. In the 1950s and 1960s these clan organizations were used as political networks to support the various parties, and as religious networks to be mobilized in arguments for the rationalization of Balinese religion, particularly where that rationalization involved challenging the central role of the *brahmana* priests in ritual. Even after political activity was banned in the late 1960s, political energies were maintained within the clan organizations and the organizations for religious reform.[56]

Initially all the factions of Balinese politics supported the first Hindu reformist organization, the Young Generation of Hindu Duty *(Angkatan Muda Hindu Dharma),* set up in 1957, but this organization soon split into separate groupings, each supported by a different political faction.[57] The organization advocated a more rational presentation of Balinese culture: rituals could be simplified, texts brought into line with their Indian originals, and the religion could be given a single divine focus in order that it could be more easily presented and explained to outsiders.

These reforms may sound like the kinds of response to the outside which are initiated by tourism or colonialism, but this was not the case. Although there were elements of continuity from the 1930s, the imperative for the proposals came from Jakarta. Balinese Hinduism had to be shown to be a religion of international status in order that it be given full legal standing. Like the other international religions of Indonesia, Christianity and Islam, it had to have a canon and a belief in one god.

---

56. On the clan organizations, see James A. Boon, "Balinese Temple Politics and the Religious-Revitalization of Caste," in A. L. Becker & Aram A. Yengoyam (eds.), *The Imagination of Reality: Essays in Southeast Asian Coherence Systems,* pp. 271-90, Norwood: Ablex, 1979. Boon's starting point is the important essay on religious change in Bali by Clifford Geertz. "Internal Conversion" in Contemporary Bali" in his *The Interpretation of Cultures,* New York: Basic, 1973, pp. 170-192. See further Anthony Forge, "Balinese Religion and Indonesian Identity," in J. J. Fox *et al.* (ed.), *Indonesia: Australian Perspectives,* pp. 221-34, Canberra: Research School of Pacific Studies, Australian National University, 1980.

57. See Sri Reshi (I Gusti) Anandakusuma, *Pergolakan Hindu Dharma* (2 vols), Klungkung: Satya Hindu Dharma Indonesia. Sri Rsi himself was a major figure in one of these organizations. Other supporters for the Angkatan Muda Hindu Dharma included Sutèja, I Gusti Putu Merta of the PNI, I Gusti Bagus Oka, former Governor of the Lesser Sundas, I Gusti Bagus Sugriwa, former guerrilla leader and the foremost expert in traditional Balinese literature, and Wedastra Suyasa, from the PNI left, Sutèja's deadly enemy. Sri Reshi and Wedastra were very close. For the political aspect of the reformists, see Lane, "Wedastera Suyasa."

The reformists worked closely with students of literature to show that Balinese Hinduism did indeed have a canon of texts, literary, ethical, and ritual. They demonstrated the belief in one god in Balinese religion by showing that the variety of the Hindu pantheon, with all its gods such as Siwa, Brahma, Wisnu and Indra, was in fact a manifestation of Sang Hyang Widhi or Atintya, the one Supreme Being. Sang Hyang Widhi was by no means a new figure in Balinese religion. He was principally the ultimate focus of the mystical meditations of the *brahmana* but the reformers made the symbols associated with him in that meditation into symbols of all Balinese religion. In practice this meant a slight change in the nature of Balinese temples. The symbol of Sang Hyang Widhi was the lotus seat or *padmasana,* the divine chair in which he was manifested in the priests' mediation. It was decided that all temples should include such a seat (most of them did not up to the 1950s), and further that the reformed Balinese religion should have its own urban temple in Dénpasar where everyone could worship and sermons (another innovation) could be regularly given.

There was no real conflict between the traditionalists and the neo-traditionalists. Both were active in the support of Balinese religion, which was almost synonymous with Balinese culture. The traditionalists, even if they did not accept the rationalization of rituals, were happy to have the new government in Jakarta grant proper recognition to Balinese Hinduism.

The most active of the traditionalists was the Déwa Agung, whose actions were directed at maintaining the position of the high kings of Klungkung in the face of change. He acted principally as arbiter and organizer of rituals, and in this role managed to have a great deal of influence beyond the bounds of Klungkung.

One of the areas of arbitration where the traditional role of the Déwa Agung came into play was in the upsurge of genealogy writing in the 1950s. As more and more commoner social groups started to rediscover their ancestry in a Bali-wide search for identity, they turned to traditional experts to help them find genealogical accounts of their origins. Since many of the stories of origin relate the dispersal of families or their loss of aristocratic status to events in Gèlgèl, the royal heirs to Gèlgèl in Klungkung were a natural source of authority. The Déwa Agung would visit temples and family groups to explain their origins, and relate to them the proper date of origin, temple festivals or other ritual details associated with their family stories. Often families would be referred on to him by other experts. One such was Dalang Ktut Rinda of Blahbatuh, whose great skills as a dancer and puppeteer and deep learning in traditional literature qualified him to discover genealogies for families by elaborating parts of already extant texts.

Ritually the Déwa Agung maintained his authority through close relations with a large number of high priests, and through the renovation of important temples and rituals. This was an activity which built on the cultural foundations of the 1930s established by himself and the raja of Karangasem. By the 1960s the Déwa Agung was more or less seen as the head of an informal council of *brahmana* priests, and it was said of him that he knew all the ritual texts so well that he could test and advise these *brahmana*. In 1962 he initiated the important renovation of one of the main temples of Klungkung, Pura Dasar in Gèlgèl, the name of which describes its function as the "Base Temple" of Bali. Pura Dasar is an important temple for all those who claim hereditary links to the royal family of Gèlgèl, as well as for the elevated commoner clan of Pasek. Its renewal strengthened the focus on Gèlgèl as the place of origin of most Balinese families, and boosted links between the Déwa Agung and important families such as the Sukawatis of Ubud.[58]

These resurgences in family histories and temple activities were topped off in 1963 by the holding of what should have been the greatest of all Balinese rituals, the centennial rite of exorcism of the eleven forms of the terrible god: *Ekadasa Rudra*. The greatest of all exorcisms was initiated by the Déwa Agung, and he set in motion a political chain of events which would have ensured his place as the paramount figure of traditional Bali were it not for the violent eruption of Mount Agung during the course of the ritual.

The magnitude of the ritual was so vast that it necessitated state funding, and therefore the support both of the reformist organizations and of the more leftist parts of the administration, including

---

58. See Sukawati, *Reminiscences*, pp. 63-8.

Sutèja, the Governor of Bali. Despite Sutèja's political position, he supported the ritual in the interests of Balinese culture as a whole, as did the reformists of the Parisada, whose attitude to the Déwa Agung's authority was ambiguous. When Mount Agung erupted, however, most of these supporters tried to have the ritual called off for the sake of the safety of the participants.

The ritual was held in the temple of Besakih, on the slopes of Mount Agung. Despite the rain of ash and stones from the volcano, this holy Mother Temple of Bali was relatively unscathed by the eruption. Not so most of the surrounding area of Karangasem and Klungkung. When the eruption reached its peak the lava flows wiped out whole villages, taking thousands of lives and utterly destroying houses, temples and rice fields. For over a decade afterwards some of the land in the path of the lava flows was stony wasteland.[59]

The Déwa Agung and his priest bravely stayed on to see through as much of the ritual as was humanly possible. His detractors thought the whole thing a failure, considering the devastation. In Balinese ritual thinking the eruption could equally be said to mark the success of the ritual. Great state rituals such as this are meant to bring about an age of harmony in the world, but the way they can bring it about is by harnessing and even accelerating the forces of chaos and destruction which precede the renewal of a golden age. In the eyes of many Balinese, the eruption was a manifestation of great change which could bring good results as well as bad.

The Communist "Puputan"

In the light of Balinese interpretations of the ritual at Besakih, the chaos of the period from 1963 to 1966 could equally be said to be a kind of ritual cleansing. In this case those cleansed were the Communists and other leftists who, in the eyes of the PNI, challenged the nature of Balinese tradition.

During the 1950s politics in Bali was mainly a contest between the Nationalists of the PNI and the Socialists or PSI. These Social-

---

59. For a description, see Anna Matthews, *The Night of Purnama,* New York: Jonathan Cape, 1965, and for photos, see Windsor P. Booth, Samuel W. Matthews, & Robert Sisson, "Bali's Sacred Mountain Blows its Top," *National Geographic* 124, 3(1965): 436-58.

ists were a conservative group, quite separate from the Communists. During the only national elections held in the Sukarno era, in 1955, they and the PNI gained most of the votes in Bali, with the Communist PKI lagging far behind, supported only in Sutèja's home region of Jembrana, where his cousin, Anak Agung Nyoman Dhenia was head of the Party. In the space of ten years this situation was to change dramatically, so that by 1965 Bali was one of the PKI's strongholds.[60]

The explanation for the change can be found in the increasing radicalization of politics over attempts at land reform throughout Indonesia. Colonialism had fostered landlord-tenant arrangements by which royal families could further their "traditional" hold over subjects through economic pressure. Sutèja, the PKI and even the left-wing of the PNI supported some kind of land reform which might alleviate the suffering of the peasantry, particularly as the rampant inflation and corruption of the Sukarno era brought hardship and famine on many small holders or landless peasants.

At the end of the 1950s Sukarno took control of politics in Jakarta. In the eight years from 1950 to 1958 there had been as many cabinets in Jakarta, and constitutional democracy in Indonesia was in disrepute. Sukarno proclaimed a new, Indonesian, form of democracy, "Guided Democracy," and in the process banned some of the political parties, including the PSI. This banning may have meant that disaffected PSI supporters were radicalized, and some went over to the PKI. The Communist Party held itself aloof from the corruption which many Jakarta politicians were seen to be caught up in, and undertook to do something about the promises of land reform which many politicians had made but not honored.

In the early 1960s a massive upsurge in membership of the PKI in Bali coincided with the Communists' push for land reform, the "Peasants' Unilateral Action," by which farmers were urged to take it upon themselves to claim the land of recalcitrant landlords. The Action achieved greater equity at the cost of heightening social

---

60. For an analysis of politics in Bali in the 1950s, see Lane, "Wedastera Suyasa"; and I Gusti Ngurah Bagus, "Bali dalam tahun limapuluhan," paper given at the Balinese State and Society Workshop, Leiden, 1986.

tensions, especially on Bali, where a handful (a few hundred at the most) of landowners possessed most of the land. Feeling was exacerbated by famine in 1964, when 18,000 Balinese were affected by a crisis which many felt could have been alleviated through a more equitable division of land ownership.[61]

Bali in the early 1960s was, according to those who lived through it, a place of tension and continual political rallies. Everyone was pressured to take sides in the growing split between the PNI and the PKI, and the split was construed in terms of the challenge to caste and to the old feudal order. In public rallies in Dénpasar, Sutèja and his more radical friend, Gedé Puger, the revolutionary from a wealthy Dénpasar family, exhorted their supporters to overthrow caste completely. They advocated marriage between commoner men and *brahmana* women, a policy with direct links to the *Suryakanta* reforms of north Bali in the 1920s. The PNI responded with village-based activities designed to create anti-PKI cadres, leading to direct attacks on the Left. All the parties organized numerous public meetings, and stepped up pressure on all members of society to become involved in politics. Violence erupted at many of these meetings; in July 1964, for example, there was a grenade explosion at one rally in Dénpasar, which led the authorities to attempt to curb the holding of rallies and to urge the parties to avoid "inflammatory speeches." Throughout the year small clashes occurred between PNI and PKI supporters over plots of land, and the PNI publicly announced that it would "meet illegal actions with force."[62]

In the villages farmers were urged to attack the greed of feudal landowners, and party cadres worked to get village officials on their side. The tensions led to splits in villages, temple congregations and even families. The basis of the dispute was still Balinese culture and identity, whether Bali should be a feudal caste society or not. The Communists did not advocate the banning of religion as a whole, and supported "traditional" dance troupes who would spread their message. Art became enmeshed with propaganda.

---

61. Rex Mortimer,*The Indonesian Communist Party and Land Reform*, Monash University, Center of Southeast Asian Studies, Monash Papers on Southeast Asia no. 1, 1972, pp. 16, 31.

62. ibid., pp. 52-3.

Although the challenge to caste led people to take sides as either *triwangsa* (members of the three upper castes) or *sudra* (members of the commoner caste), the real divisions were not always along these lines. Many intellectuals from the aristocracy or even the *brahmana* priesthood became members of the PKI or sympathized with its aims of greater social equality.

By 1965 the tensions were erupting into violence at many levels. Many PNI survivors of the period maintain that the Communists were against tradition, and in a sense they were because they would often try and stop or interfere with major rituals held by members of the aristocracy. The most important example came in 1965, just before events in Jakarta brought events to a climax. Déwa Agung Oka Geg, the raja of highest status who had labored hard for the preservation of old Bali, died. His cremation was to be an event which would be a tribute to his standing. The whole of Klungkung was mobilized and donated its labor and materials, and the highest level of cremation tower, with eleven tiers, was prepared. In preparation for the ceremonial procession to the graveyard, all the loyal subjects of Klungkung shaved their heads. On the eve of the procession the PKI massed its supporters outside the palace, ready to rush in and burn the tower and perhaps even the body, the ultimate insult which would totally destroy the ritual. The day was only saved when a loyal commoner family from the House of Tapean sent one of its members, a police officer, to get military support and summon PNI helpers. After a brief skirmish the PKI fell back and the ritual went ahead.

On 30 September 1965 an abortive coup in Jakarta took place, a coup which was associated with the PKI. Initially there was uncertainty—six leading generals had been brutally murdered by the Air Force officers who led the coup, and nobody was quite sure what was happening to Sukarno, or what his role might be. In the next few weeks a gradual fire of destruction spread across Java, fanned by reports of PKI atrocities and complicity, and supported by the military leadership under Suharto, the quiet Javanese commander who had emerged to put down the coup. After the "Peasants' Unilateral Action" and the political polarization of the preceding years, the PNI and other anti-Communists took it into their own hands to destroy the PKI absolutely.

On Bali the killings mainly took place between October 1965 and February 1966. They began in the north and west, where the Left was strongest, but by the end of this period the whole of Bali was a landscape of blackened areas where entire villages had been burnt to the ground, and the graveyards could not cope with the numbers of corpses.

The story of the destruction of one village is typical: "One evening the Communists had a meeting and the meeting was guarded by Communist soldiers." Troops and police arrived from a local center to investigate, and were met by PKI gunfire, which killed one of the police—typically in such accounts the PKI struck first, a way of justifying the killings as revenge or self-defence. The troops left to get supporters from Dénpasar, who returned quickly. "In a short time the whole village was surrounded, and they shot everyone and burnt the whole village."[63]

The wave of death was spread by black-shirted youths from the PNI who were so enthusiastic that Sarwo Edhy, the general left-wing Australian newspapers described as the "Butcher of Java," said of the situation, "In Java we had to egg the people on to kill Communists. In Bali we had to restrain them."[64] The fighting went from pitched battles to passive acceptance of death by the PKI. Leaders like Puger were rounded up and "cut to pieces."[65] Sometimes their houses, like the palace of Jembrana, were reduced to rubble, as if nothing should remain of the Left at all. If the real estate was valuable, as with Puger's house in the middle of Dénpasar, it was taken over the the military. Stories of the killings tell of magical battles going on as the Left was exterminated. One youth who took part in the execution of a PKI *padanda* (brahman high priest) described to an Australian tourist how his sword failed to cut into the priest's flesh, until another *padanda* could be brought in to sprinkle holy water and break his power, enabling the PNI killers to decapitate the first priest and hack him to pieces.

---

63. Sukawati, *Reminiscences,* p. 79. The main published description of the killings on Bali is Hughes, "Frenzy on Bali" in *The End of Sukarno,* pp. 173-83.

64. Quoted in Hughes, *The End of Sukarno,* p. 181.

65. Sukawati, *Reminiscences,* p. 80.

The military distanced themselves from the killings. They simply went into each village and produced a list of Communists to be killed, which was given to the head of the village to organize.[66] In most cases villagers carried out this veiled "order" because they knew if they did not they could be accused of being Communist sympathizer, so sometimes the killers were PKI members trying to cover themselves. In one or two cases whole *bañjar* (wards) refused to allow the village death-squads in, but these were rare exceptions. People who had been approached by the PKI to join or who had some family link to the party would sit in their houses as bands of youths went by, trembling for fear that the gangs would stop at their door. There are many well-documented stories of killers and family members of victims going mad, and the trauma has been passed down to the generation not even born when the mass-murder took place.

After the initial struggle the killing took on a dispassionate tone. Those identified as PKI dressed in white and were led to graveyards to be executed, *puputan*-style. Said one Balinese observer, "There was no personal hatred in any of this. There was no torture. It was all very orderly and polite."[67] The main justification was that the PKI would have been just as bloodthirsty had they won. This kind of fatalistic approach was repeated in other parts of Indonesia, and everywhere the favored form of execution was decapitation, perhaps deliberately harking back to Indonesian headhunting traditions, although the legacy of Japanese militarism can also be seen in this, since the favored weapon was the samurai sword. By February the jails were filled to overflowing and every night the black-shirted youths would load up military trucks with more people to be executed in the graveyards. Some of the imprisoned, such as those rounded up into a warehouse above a big Chinese store in Jembrana, were killed in their places of internment.

---

66. R. A. F. Paul Webb, The Sickle and the Cross: Christians and Communists in Bali, Flores, Sumba and Timor, 1965-7," *Journal of Southeast Asian Studies,* 17, 1(1986): 94-113, especially p. 98.

67. Quoted in Hughes, *The End of Sukarno,* p. 179. Further information from Balinese informants on the killings has been supplemented by personal communications from Michael van Langenburg, Helen Jarvis and Margo Lyon, all visitors to Bali in 1966.

The estimate (and we can only estimate) of the number killed is between 80,000 and 100,000.[68] The number may have been much higher, and those who are willing to speak of this time of horror describe corpses blocking the rivers and mass graves. The killings provided a pretext to settle old scores. For example some Chinese in Bali and Java were executed both because China was associated with the PKI, and because Balinese were jealous of Chinese business successes and felt that these businesses were involved in economic exploitation during the periods of massive inflation. Understandably, few Balinese want to relive this time in conversation and most, like survivors of other conflicts, prefer to block it out of their memories. Many Balinese agree with the view that the whole killing was the culmination of all the problems of the preceding years, "a sort of mystical cleansing of all the island's problems and ills... By ridding the island of Communists, they believed that all the other problems would somehow be removed, too."[69]

Even after the President who came to power by leading the killings, Suharto, had fallen from power in 1998, people on Bali remained reluctant to discuss the killings. Whereas in other parts of Indonesia there have been attempts at reconciliation, in Bali, where the families of victims still live as neighbors of the killers, this is not possible. Victims whose story has been published have been subject to harassment by police or local thugs.

The slaughter that came after 1965 was the end-point of a series of conflicts and issues from the colonial period. Even the element of land tenure, the economic basis of resentment and factionalism, had its roots in the colonial transformation of Balinese society. As terrible as the events of 1965 and 1966 were, they need to be understood in the long term as part of a series of events and disputes over the idea of Balinese culture. After 1966 nothing could be the same, and the removal of so many people, combined with the fear of a recurrence of such violence, led to a kind of "pacified" Bali.

Although the killings of 1965-6 could be said to be the last gasp

---

68. Hughes, *The End of Sukarno,* puts the figure around 80,000, but notes that reliable sources had it that 40,000 were killed in just two weeks.

69. Anonymous Balinese, quoted ibid., p. 176.

of "ferocious" or "amok" Bali, what was at stake, according to the participants, were the same "religion" and "culture" identified and idealized by the westerners who were interested in "preserving" Balinese tradition. When Balinese acted in terms of "culture" from the 1940s onwards they were not slavishly following the colonial agenda by any means. What they were doing was using the terms by which Bali had been defined for different ends. The image of Bali as the island of culture has not been disputed by any Balinese, including members of the Communist Party. Some, like Sutèja, tried to make that culture more "respectable" by banning bare breasts; others, like the members of the Parisada Hindu Dharma, acted to give that culture international respect by showing how much it was related to Indian Hinduism. Specific aspects of that culture, such as "caste" titles and rituals, were part of a continuing series of power struggles, going on in Bali even before the arrival of the Dutch. After the terrible moment of the anti-Communist massacres, Balinese became afraid to express conflicts in a public, political, fashion. The killings signaled the end of a period of overt social tension, since with the removal of a generation of leftist intellectuals and activists, they created an unchallengeable consensus about what Balinese culture should be.

CHAPTER FIVE

Indonesian Bali

After the Indonesian Revolution, when the archipelago achieved independence from the Dutch, Bali officially became part of the Indonesian Republic. Under Indonesia's first two presidents, Sukarno and Suharto, Bali was given an important role in national development. For Sukarno, Bali's primary role was in the development of a national culture: he made Bali the mother culture of Indonesia; he Indonesianized Bali at the same time as he Balinised Indonesian culture. For Sukarno there was no problem with this dual relationship, but for Balinese, the period of independence has seen a struggle between local control and the central control of Jakarta.

The struggle for control also meant creating a blander image for Bali. Just as the political violence of 1950s and 1960s Indonesia had to be cut out of the tourist image, so the most extravagant images of Bali as the "Island of the Demons" were airbrushed out of the new world of late twentieth-century tourist capitalism.

Under the less flamboyant Suharto regime, Bali became prominent in economic development planning: tourism realized its potential as a vital source of foreign exchange, and Bali became the prime tourist destination in Indonesia. In regulating tourism the Indonesian Government, especially its agencies in Bali, strove to preserve Balinese culture from what they saw as the threat of tourism. Tourism in their eyes brought with it all that is bad about modern life and modernization, but could be a force for good if properly managed. Under both presidents the image of Bali went from being a Western to an Indonesian image, consolidated in a policy called

"Cultural Tourism." This new policy drew as much on Indonesian stereotyping of westerners—Occidentalism—as on the Orientalism that shaped Bali's image.

Under both presidents, culture remained Bali's defining feature, and tourist advertisers and marketing authorities gave the colonial image of peaceful and artistic Bali a new lease of life. This image of cultural richness has never been challenged as the defining characteristic of the "real" Bali. Westerners, Balinese and other Indonesians repeatedly asked the question: "Can Balinese culture survive?" This validated Cultural Tourism as a policy, and for a brief period in the 1980s, now seen by Balinese as a golden age, this policy was an effective tool for giving Balinese control over their island and bringing prosperity, at least to some. But like all golden ages, it did not last.

Bali has gone from being one of the most densely populated islands on earth to one of the most densely toured islands. The figures in themselves look very ominous, showing that there are as many tourists to the island as there are Balinese. But if ritual and artistic activities are any indicator, Balinese culture is being strengthened, not weakened, in the age of tourism. The question about Bali's ability to survive tourism has been asked since the late 1920s. Indeed the question itself is part of the image-making process by which Bali is seen as a paradise. By seeing Balinese culture as fragile we help to reinforce its uniqueness and importance for those who go there as tourists, and in the minds of Indonesian planners in Jakarta, and for Balinese on all levels of society.

Concern about Bali's cultural survival is based on a number of different premises: that there is a fixed, authentic and unalterable Balinese culture; that it should be maintained and protected to stop it becoming unstable, inauthentic and un-Balinese; and that preserving Balinese culture is in the interests of the Balinese, who can be considered as a homogeneous entity. In both pre-colonial and colonial times Balinese culture constantly changed and responded to the rest of the world, and absorbed Javanese, Dutch and other influences when these accorded with the interests of powerful groups in Balinese society. That process has not stopped in the post-colonial period. Balinese culture both gives and receives cultural influences and in the process some, like Sukarno and the national élite, gain; others, like the Balinese villagers who are excluded from official patronage and tourist networks, lose.

In the sixty years since Indonesian independence the tourist image of the 1930s has been revived and enshrined as the only possible image of Bali. Bali's role as the paradise of paradises served the interests of Sukarno's nation building and Suharto's development policies. Tourist agencies, romantic hippies, filmmakers and travel writers have all reinforced the image of paradise in their various ways. On Bali itself the image of Balinese culture has been successfully used by the local élite in the shaping of a new ruling class. By defining Balinese identity in terms of opposition to and threats from tourism they give the impression of speaking for all Balinese, of representing the real Bali. No society is really as homogeneous as this, and most often those who invoke tradition speak only for small interest groups.

Sukarno's Theater State

"The eyes of the world are on Bali," exhorted Sukarno, the dynamic president of the new Republic of Indonesia in October 1950. Addressing the revolutionary youth of Bali who wanted to continue their struggle in factional fighting and revenge, he challenged, "You want to be the heroes of the Revolution... but where in your *Ramayana* or *Mahabharata* do you find heroes who murder with daggers in the dark of night, and when have Krisna or Arjuna ever taken their anger out on women?"[1]

So President Sukarno spoke of his dilemma over Bali. On the one hand he supported the idea of continuing the fervor of the Revolution to build Indonesian culture, but on the other he saw that the culture of Bali was being directly threatened by that revolutionary fervor. Sukarno wanted to use Balinese culture as a rich reserve for the nation, but he did not want the essence of that culture to be disturbed in the process. He both used Balinese culture for Indonesian ends and preserved it by maintaining the image of Bali as a place of harmony.

---

1. Quoted in Jef Last, *Bali in de Kentering,* Amsterdam: De Bezige Bij, 1955, p. 7, as the dramatic opening to Last's account of 1950s Bali. Last was present in the audience of this meeting.

Sukarno (1901-70) was an enigmatic figure. His Javanese school-teacher father and Balinese mother imbued him from an early age with a sense of the worth of their cultures. Unlike many of the leaders of the Indonesian nationalist movement he was not educated in the Netherlands, but in Surabaya and Bandung, the major cities of Java after Jakarta. There he came into contact with all the important leaders of the early nationalist parties, Muslim, Communist and Socialist alike, and was taken as a pupil by his first father-in-law (the first of five), Cokroaminoto, the fiery leader of the Islamic nationalists. From Cokroaminoto, Sukarno gained an incredible ability to speak to all Indonesians, to create some kind of unity out of the cultural diversity of the country, and to tell his audience what they wanted to hear.

When he exercised the leadership qualities taught by Cokroaminoto, he was jailed and exiled by the Dutch, but afterwards Sukarno led Indonesians to nationhood. Up until the mid-1960s he was the indispensable leader of the country, yet he was also an egomaniac, and a man prone to fits of depression and inconsistency. Many saw him as a visionary whose will to create Indonesian independence was the guiding force of nationalism from the 1920s onwards. Others, basing their arguments both on his collaboration with the Japanese during the Second World War and the endemic corruption of Indonesia in the 1960s, saw him as an unscrupulous dictator.

At low points in his career his will failed him and he backed down in the face of pressure. He was prepared to do deals with the Dutch in an attempt to avoid exile,[2] and likewise he sacrificed the lives of thousands of forced laborers in Java for the sake of achieving Japanese support for independence.[3] Towards the end of his rule his passion for women and the good life and his lack of interest in things economic distanced him from his people, who were suffering under rampant inflation and the political polarization of society. His once-handsome face was bloated by disease, and he found that the elements of his personality which were once so attractive to

---

2. See J. D. Legge, *Sukarno: A Political Biography,* Sydney: Allen and Unwin, 1972, p. 136, and John Ingleson, *The Road to Exile: The Indonesian Nationalist Movement, 1927-1934,* Singapore: Heinemann, 1979, pp. 216-22.

3. Legge, *Sukarno,* pp. 149-80.

Indonesians—his flamboyance and his use of sexual conquest as a metaphor for his own power—now earned him public criticism and turned popular support towards the Army and its backers. When the Army took power in the wake of the abortive coup blamed on the Communists in 1965, Sukarno was totally unable to raise support for his own position.

Before and during the Revolution of 1945-9 Sukarno had little time to travel for pleasure or to contemplate the subtleties of Balinese culture, but in the 1950s he was able to turn his attention to Bali, the homeland of his beloved mother. In 1950 the new Republic of Indonesia was established as a constitutional democracy with Sukarno as a President with limited political power. This period gave him time to work on the development of the "theater state" of Indonesia,[4] whereby he used theatrical display, art, architecture and his own magnificent oratory as a means to create the cohesion that the other mechanisms of state organization had not managed to foster. This groundwork undertaken in the 1950s was put to good use after 1958 when he made himself more powerful by declaring Indonesia a "Guided Democracy." According to Sukarno, this was an authentically Indonesian version of democracy, where the chaos of government by unstable parliamentary coalitions was replaced by the firm hand of the President as a national father figure who would direct and appoint the major instruments of state power. In the tense atmosphere of Indonesia in the early 1960s most of Sukarno's real power was derived not from the workings of state instrumentalities, but from a dangerous balancing game between the powers of the Communist Party, which in the 1960s claimed an affiliated membership of 27,000,000, and the Army.[5]

Indonesia was so diverse that it needed Sukarno's rhetoric and symbolism to hold it together and to counterbalance the tendencies

---

4. The term "theater state" is used by Clifford Geertz of Bali, in his *Negara: The TheatreState in Nineteenth Century Bali,* Princeton: Princeton University Press, 1980. Geertz's fieldwork experiences of Indonesia were from the 1950s. Benedict Anderson's "The Javanese Idea of Power," in C. Holt (ed.), *Culture and Politics in Indonesia,* pp. 1-69, Ithaca: Cornell University Press, 1968, is likewise a theory of "traditional" Indonesia formed during the Sukarno era. Both essays can be interpreted as arising as much from the Indonesian circumstances of their production as from the Balinese and Javanese material they seek to analyse.

5. See Legge, *Sukarno,* pp. 358-84.

towards the division of Indonesia posed by CIA-backed separatists, Islamic fundamentalists, and regional ethnic loyalties. In order to present the appearance of "unity in diversity" (the national motto), Sukarno called upon all the readily identifiable elements of culture in Indonesia.

Sukarno's speeches were delivered in the mixed language of Indonesia's identity. Although he spoke fundamentally in Indonesian, he borrowed from Dutch and other European languages to demonstrate his command of the concepts of nationalism and colonialism, and combined these with terms from the languages of the different regions of Indonesia so that he spoke more directly to people from a variety of ethnic backgrounds. As a patron of the arts he supported the development of a modern, truly Indonesian culture, which would synthesize regional cultures such as those of the Javanese, the urban cultures of the major cities, including elements of Chinese culture, and elements from the modern West.

Typical of the cultural symbols constructed during the Sukarno era were the monuments which still stand in Jakarta: gigantic and exaggerated Socialist Realist statues, expressing the struggles of the new Republic, or the huge phallic tower and gold flame of the National Monument. Set in the main square of the city, the Monument draws on Hindu-Javanese ideas of the phallic divinity of Siwa, ruler of the gods and symbol of fertility, and on the international symbolism of the flames of hope and national spirit.

Sukarno drew on commonly understood aspects of the Hindu-Javanese past such as references to ancient kingdoms and he looked to Bali to provide another dimension to the cultural repertoire of Javanese symbolism. In his speeches he would make reference to the stories of the shadow theater or *wayang,* as a way of calling upon a well known but nevertheless profound set of images and ideas. As the speech to the revolutionary youth of Bali shows, he saw the *Ramayana* and *Mahabharata* stories, which were the basis of the *wayang,* not just as a Javanese tradition, but as a mythology through which he could appeal also to Balinese.

The *wayang* was only one part of the cultural heritage of Indonesia upon which Sukarno drew. He and many of the ideologues of Indonesian nationalism called on the idea of the great historical empires of Sriwijaya and Majapahit to provide precedents for the creation of the modern state of Indonesia.[6] He and others like him were also strongly aware of the Javanese Messianic idea of the Just Ruler or *Ratu Adil* who would come and sweep away colonialism and establish a golden age. Sukarno, of course, saw himself as the "Just King," and in appealing to this idea he used some of the magical symbols of kingship commonly understood in Indonesia. In particular he let it be known that he had a number of magically charged heirloom krisses, both Javanese and Balinese, in his possession, krisses that linked him to some of the most famous kingdoms in Indonesian history. The mystical power of the weapons was reinforced in the public imagination when Sukarno miraculously survived numerous attempted assassinations, including a grenade attack and a strafing of the presidential palace in Jakarta by dissident Air Force officers. The same popular rumors that maintained the mystique of the President have it that when Sukarno lost his power in 1965 these krisses magically disappeared.

Sukarno's aim was to create a genuinely Indonesian culture that would blend elements of tradition and modernity. In order to do this he tried to abstract general principles from the different cultures he knew. Javanese culture was to be a kind of father culture, Balinese culture a kind of mother culture. A song of the time from the old-fashioned *kroncong*, a Portuguese-Dutch style of music using guitars and violins in a mixture reminiscent of jazz and Hawaiian music, describes Bali's as the original *(asli)* culture of Indonesia, and that is how Sukarno saw it. The view of Bali as the cultural museum of the ancient Javanese empire of Majapahit was largely created by Dutch scholars,[7] but the nationalists adopted this view, treasuring Bali as the inheritance of a period when the archipelago was an internationally important state, the kind of state which Sukarno wanted to recreate.

Theosophy, which Sukarno learned from his father and from the Indonesian élite of the 1920s and 1930s, provided a sense of the great mystical spirit of Asia, of which the spirit of Indonesian

---

6. See S. Supomo, "The Idea of Majapahit in Later Javanese and Indonesian Writing," in A. Reid & D. Marr (eds), *Perceptions of the Past in Southeast Asia,* pp. 171-85, Singapore: Heinemann, 1979.

7. ibid.

culture was one part.[8] Bali, where the important elements of the Hindu arts of ancient Java were so strongly preserved, was a shining example of one part of Indonesian culture. Sukarno thus ensured that the nineteenth-century European view of Bali as a museum of ancient Java was continued in Indonesian state mythology.

Sukarno's Bali

Bali had many roles in Sukarno's new Indonesian Republic: he encouraged Indonesians to go there, supported Balinese artists, and could use Bali as a show-place for international guests, which included everyone from Nehru to Robert Kennedy to Ho Chi Minh. During the Sukarno years some of Indonesia's most important artists, writers and intellectuals took an interest in Bali. Sukarno's minister for culture, Prijono, played an important role in providing the infrastructure for these developments, and he travelled around with Sukarno selecting artists, and if the rumours are true, even sharing lovers, in the quest for cultural development. Those artists whose interest in Bali continued after the demise of Sukarno included Affandi, probably the foremost modern artist of Indonesia, and Sutan Takdir Alisjahbana, the father of modern Indonesian language and literature. The houses of both can still be found on the island, and they spent as much time there as anywhere else in Indonesia.

Affandi was one of many artists whose work received state patronage, and some of his paintings hang in the national collection started by Sukarno, a collection in which the two most prominent subjects were Bali and naked women.[9] Affandi himself painted cock-fights, beautiful Balinese women, Balinese worshipping at temples, the *Barong* and *Rangda* dances, and idyllic beach scenes, all rendered in his powerful expressionist style.[10] The other non-Balinese Indonesian artists whose works were collected by Sukarno painted the same subjects, as did the European- and American-born artists

---

8. Legge, *Sukarno*, pp. 24 & 52.

9. Lee Man-Fong, *Lukisan-Lukisan dan Patung-Patung Koleksi Presiden Sukarno dari Republik Indonesia,* Tokyo: Toppan, 1964.

10. See Claire Holt, *Art in Indonesia: Continuities and Changes,* Ithaca: Cornell University Press, 1967, pp. 200-54; Popo Iskandar, *Affandi: Suatu Jalan Batu dalam Expressionisme,* Jakarta: Akademi Jakarta, 1977.

who settled in Indonesia after the Revolution and took up Indonesian citizenship. This last group, which included Bonnet, provided direct continuity between the pre-war images of Bali made under colonial conditions, and the Indonesian images of Bali.

Despite the upheavals in Bali from the 1930s to the 1950s, the dominant image passed on from this period was of Bali as a paradise. Instead of the dynamic and tension-filled scenes of the 1930s, found in the paintings of Batuan or of I Gusti Madé Deblog of Dénpasar, the national collection included those works of the 1950s described by one commentator as "increasingly naturalistic or decorative," generally "weak and often insipid."[11]

The more subdued Balinese art of the 1950s could be seen both as a response to the times and as the influence of Indonesian and European artists working on Bali. The quietistic nature of 1950s Balinese art was a kind of wishful thinking, an attempt to impose harmony on the turbulent times through which the artists were living. While the artists of the 1930s had depicted tensions that were still partially hidden, by the 1950s the conflict within society was all too readily apparent and in many ways there was no need to depict it.

Because the European and Indonesian artists working on Bali in the 1950s were concentrating on that same peaceful Bali, Balinese artists came to see the standard content of market scenes and dancing girls as the images which should be shown to the outside world. The market for such scenes was small: the foreign visitors to the island (who were largely government sponsored), and Indonesians from other islands, who began to follow Sukarno's lead in turning attention to Bali. In one sense it would have been unpatriotic to portray Bali as anything but harmonious, because that would have been a negative comment on the success of the Revolution.

Ubud, with its foreign-born artists loyal to the Republic, and particularly its ruler Cokorda Agung Sukawati, was given patronage and attention by Sukarno. At the same time he also encouraged the revolutionary side of Bali through Governor Sutèja, the Savonarola of Bali.[12]

---

11. See Holt, *Art in Indonesia,* p. 184.
12. Last, *Bali,* p. 46.

The Cokorda was visited a number of times by Sukarno and Prijono during this period, and occasionally would assist in the running of cultural displays or events for the benefit of foreign dignitaries.[13] On official visits by overseas heads of state or ministers, or on pleasure trips by Sukarno, the official party would be greeted at the airport by Balinese dancers, usually from Ubud or somewhere else in Gianyar. Sometimes they danced traditional martial dances or the *Lègong,* which was practically synonymous with Bali.

Dancers often complained, however, that at other times they were more or less ordered to perform so-called socialist dances, which consisted of a fairly simplistic series of movements meant to echo Socialist Realist painting and sculpture, and supposedly based on the daily lives of the peasantry. They included the "fishermen's dance" (fishermen casting their nets) and the "weavers' dance" (with motions imitating weaving and spinning). Balinese dancers found that the new style required little of the virtuosity and skill of classical dance but nevertheless performed for the sake of Bali's reputation.[14]

Sukarno had dances staged at the special palace he constructed in the mountains at Tampak Siring. Sukarno's and Sutèja's daughters performed here, helping legitimize the *lègong* as Bali's great symbol. They also helped to raise the status of female dancers, who had hitherto been regarded as akin to prostitutes. The palace was built around a renovated Dutch rest house, in marvelously lush surroundings, overlooking the holy spring and village bathing place. It was one of three main palaces the President used; the others were the "Freedom Palace" in the main square of Jakarta, and the old Dutch Governor General's palace in the cool hills of Bogor outside of Jakarta.

Sukarno's palace had one flaw: by building above a temple he was tempting fate, for such audacity sets the owner of the house above the gods.[15] The same error had already been made by two

13. Cokorda Gedé Agung Sukawati with Rosemary Hilberry, *Reminiscences of a Balinese Prince,* Honolulu: University of Hawaii, Southeast Asia Publications, 1979.

14. Ruby Sue Orenstein, Gamelan Gong Kebyar: The Development of a Balinese Musical Tradition, (unpub. diss.) University of California at Los Angeles, 1971.

15. Commented upon by Willard A. Hanna, *Bali Profile: People, Events, Circumstances, 1001-1976,* New York, American Universities Field-Staff, 1976, p. 113.

other noted experts on Bali: Walter Spies's house at Campuan was built above a temple near the confluence of two rivers (always a magically-charged spot in Bali), and Colin McPhee built his house in nearby Sayan on part of the land of a death temple.[16]

For Sukarno details such as the location of a palace were irrelevant compared with the broad plan of creating the Indonesian national theater state with its pan-Indonesian cultural underpinnings. In carrying out this plan aspects of Balinese culture compatible with the other cultures of Indonesia were taken out of context and elevated in state thinking. That way, elements of "old" Bali such as the *wayang* could be integrated with elements from "new" Indonesia, such as the paintings of the non-Balinese artists, or the socialist dances, without creating any apparent disharmony.

Balinese arts and dances were highly exportable aspects of Indonesian culture. The process of popularizing certain aspects of Balinese dance and music was furthered when performers went sent overseas for cultural missions. During the 1950s the Gong Belaluan, the orchestra from the area around Dénpasar's Bali Hotel, was the best known of the musical groups, building on their pre-War fame, and they often travelled to Russia, China and other countries Sukarno was courting. Unfortunately the orchestra fell apart over a factional dispute in their ward, leaving the way open for Paliatan-based musicians to fill the gap. John Coast's tour of Europe and America with the dancers and musicians of Ubud-Paliatan was one of many such trips which had Presidential sponsorship. Bali's greatest artists of the 1950s, for example, I Nyoman Kakul of Batuan, the genius of dance whose supple performances were captured on film by Henri Cartier-Bresson, and I Ktut Rinda of Blahbatuh, who combined dance skills with scholarship, writing and puppet plays to transform theater in Gianyar virtually single-handedly, were sent as well to more exotic locations such as Czechoslovakia to spread the message of Indonesian culture.

In picking out the essence of Bali, exemplified by its art and rituals, and elevating it to the national level, Sukarno, then, was quite consciously participating in the image-making process, which

---

16.   Colin McPhee, *A House in Bali,* Kuala Lumpur: Oxford University Press, 1979, p. 90.

had already begun in the colonial era. Unlike the foreign colonial powers, however, Sukarno could never be accused of using the images inherited from the colonial era to exploit Bali, for his aim was to integrate this island into the modern Indonesian state, in which Balinese culture would be accorded a great deal of status, and people from the Balinese ruling class could become members of the Indonesian ruling class.

Most Balinese were equally eager to be integrated into the new state of Indonesia, even if the price they had to pay was dancing the dreaded socialist dances. Both the Left and the Right in Balinese politics (the groups represented by the PKI and PNI respectively) keenly supported Sukarnoism. There was, however, a conservative middle ground that criticized the President. Anak Agung Gedé Agung, the prince of Gianyar and Indonesian Foreign Minister in the mid-1950s, was one of that group of critics allied to the conservative Socialist Party of Indonesia (PSI) who used attacks on Sukarno's cultural policy as a vehicle for more general criticisms of Sukarno's extravagances. To the Agung, Sukarno was undermining Balinese culture, a claim which implied that he, Anak Agung Gedé Agung, was the strong voice of tradition. For his opposition, in 1962 Agung was jailed along with leading members of the PSI, including Sutan Sjahrir, the former prime minister who had played a prominent role in the struggle for independence as a leftist student leader of the 1930s, a key figure in resistance to the Japanese, and a pragmatic parliamentary head.[17]

For people like the Agung it was Sukarno's attempt to dictate the direction Balinese culture should take, not Bali's cultural role in modern Indonesia, that was in dispute. It was one thing to be anti-Sukarno, but nobody was anti-patriotic and, unlike other parts of Indonesia, there was never any talk of Balinese secession from the Republic. For Balinese peasants too, pride in independence meant being able to stand side by side with other Indonesians. They could at least fill their pockets with self-assurance, even if they had no economic gain out of being Indonesians.

---

17. Cf. Hanna, *Bali Profile,* p. 112. Hanna's main informant on contemporary Bali was Anak Agung Gedé Agung, so the view of Sukarno presented in this book is one-eyed and right-wing.

The Sukarno era laid the groundwork for tourist planning. Sukarno's Minister for Culture, Prijono, helped coin a new, Sanskritized, word for tourism—*pariwisata*. The term drew on a *Kawi* term for the free wandering of gods, princes and princesses, but sounded nobler than the Malay "*melancong*," which sounds like what one does on an idle stroll, or "*bertamasya*," a term of Persian origins, which means something like "sightseeing." In line with this new approach, a Balinese, Nyoman S. Pendit, was commissioned to travel to the United States to learn about the systemization of tourism. His report became a standard text in tourist planning and tourism education, and in it he presented the term "Cultural Tourism" as one of the options for shaping the industry. Unfortunately, the report came out in the middle of Indonesia's political upheaval and was sidelined, like its author, by Suharto's takeover.[18]

Tourist Development

Although it fell to Sukarno's more prosaic successor, General Suharto, to establish mass tourism on Bali, he really built on what began in the Sukarno years. Suharto, the farmer's son who rose through the ranks of the military, took a more low-key approach to Indonesian culture and cultural display than his predecessor. Being deeply interested in developing the style of the old courts of central Java as the national cultural style, he did not give as much emphasis to other regional cultures as Sukarno. Despite this, he preserved Bali's special place in Indonesian culture by emphasizing the common cultural basis of Javanese and Balinese religious beliefs.

In 1957 there were only three significant tourist hotels on Bali, the Sindhu Beach Hotel at Sanur, the Kuta Beach Hotel at Kuta, and the Bali Hotel in Dénpasar, all owned by the government's national tourist agency. Then in 1963 Sukarno started the multi-storied Bali Beach Hotel at Sanur, using Japanese war reparation money. The Bali Beach was only finished after Sukarno's fall from

---

18. Interviews and correspondence with Nyoman S. Pendit, 1994-8. See his *Pengantar Ilmu Pariwisata*, Djakarta: Djembatan, 1965, which was subsequently published in 1967 as *Ilmu Pariwisata: Sebuah Pengantar Perdana*, and went through a number of expanded editions, Jakarta: Pradana Paramita, 1994. Also Pendit, "Pariwisata bermula dari tamasya," *Suara Karya* 10-9-1997: 13 & 15.

power, however, and symbolically, it was Suharto's government that reaped the benefits of Sukarno's planning.

The initiation of the luxury Bali Beach Hotel was just the first step in Sukarno's grand plan to develop tourism. Major developments took place in the Sanur Beach area, and then expanded to the present tourist centers of Kuta and Ubud, in a way that the government could not always control. The regime of General Suharto came to power just as the tourist boom was taking off, and has sought to control and regulate that boom for the good of the Indonesian economy and for the sake of Balinese culture, two goals which are not at all incompatible in government policy.

The early 1960s saw an upsurge in Indonesian tourist publications featuring Bali, and the first attempts to gain international support for the planning of tourist development. Sukarno's masterstroke for helping the tourist industry of Bali was to hold an international conference of travel agents on Bali in 1963 to coincide with the spectacular exorcistic *Ekadasa Rudra* ceremony at Besakih. The plan went awry when Mount Agung erupted, causing a major embarrassment for Sukarno and none-too-pleasant results for the Balinese. Still, many of the tourist representatives had already arrived in Bali and sampled some of its cultural wealth, so they could return to promote the island.

In the long term the disaster of 1963 and the anti-Communist slaughter of 1965-6 were only temporary setbacks to tourism on Bali. Since most of the coverage of the coup and its aftermath was centered on Jakarta, there was little in newspaper reporting to directly associate the destruction of Communism in Indonesia with Bali. If anything the end of the PKI was probably an asset in selling tourism in Bali to the American market. From almost no tourists in the 1950s, numbers slowly started to grow in the 1960s, fed by the post-war Hollywood images of "Bali-Hai," which in Sukarno's terms converted to an invitation to stay at the Bali Beach.

For many tourists the Bali Beach was too garish to be appropriate to the development of tourism on the island of paradise. Their criteria of good taste demanded hotels which had an element of Balinese style. The Bali Beach, however, was not a total encumbrance to tourist development. It catered to the type of tourist who craved all the comforts of a modern, international hotel and became the focus of Sanur as a tourist setting. To cater to different tastes smaller and cheaper hotels were established in the area, many at a respectable distance from the Bali Beach. Some of these were based on pre-war houses or small hotels, others provided the prototype of "bungalow" or "cottage" accommodation.

In the bungalow style each room was built separately as a self-contained and free-standing unit, with thatched roof, carvings, and other little touches to make it authentically Balinese. The Segara Beach hotel, which was subsumed by the Bali Beach, had pioneered this style. Established in 1956, its owner, the nationalist freedom fighter and friend of Sukarno, Ida Bagus Kompyang, had shown great acumen in recognizing the importance of providing a more personalized experience of Bali to tourists. He survived the purges of 1965 to take over management of the Bali Beach, and when his original hotel became part of the latter, he set up a new Segara Beach on the site of the Neuhaus brothers' pre-War aquarium. Gradually the bungalow style became the most successful of all the developments, and even the Bali Beach was forced to build a complex of bungalows at one side. Alit's Beach Bungalows established itself near the Bali Beach, while further down the Tanjung Sari grew from being a small and pleasant cheap hotel to being the large, sumptuous and still-pleasant complex it is today. Following the lead of the Tanjung Sari major hotel chains established themselves in the 1970s.

The Bali Hyatt was built on land originally owned by the Tanjung Sari and followed the Tanjung Sari's style of architecture and landscaping. Through clever use of open pavilions, thatched roofing and traditional carving the architects and landscapers created the impression of being faithful to Balinese culture, while still maintaining the standards and luxury of international accommodation. Around the major hotels beautiful gardens were established, featuring the most colorful of tropical flowers, especially the bougainvillea, a non-indigenous vine which provides spectacular sprays.

With the development of new hotels came the rebirth of the souvenir industry. A few entrepreneurs in the 1940s had struggled to continue the selling of art objects that had begun in the 1920s. One of the first efforts was part of the Dutch attempts to recolonize

Indonesia, when in 1946 the Dutch architect G. Koopman set up a shop in Sanur to continue the work of the Neuhaus brothers. He then encouraged Jimmy Pandy, a Eurasian who had worked for Thomas Cook, to join him, and together they stimulated others in the area. Koopman was killed in 1950 at the hands of local bandits motivated either by robbery or by nationalist revenge, but Indonesians continued his work.

By the early 1950s many Balinese were established in selling sculpture and paintings to tourists: Ida Bagus Tilem of Mas, a famous sculptor, went all over the island buying and selling from colleagues; a group of women in Klungkung who had been successful pre-War entrepreneurs continued their work; and a local cooperative in Dénpasar was the launching pad for a number of businesses in the main streets of the capital. One of the leaders of this development was the remarkable Ni Nyoman Rapeg, who set up the Sutji artshop in Jalan Veteran, Dénpasar, both through collaboration with suppliers such as Madé Tinggen in Klungkung, and through establishing new wholesale networks in Jakarta. From these beginnings the number of establishments that came to be called "artshops" increased exponentially.

The 1960s expansion of the airport south of Sanur, into the Ngurah Rai International Airport—named after Bali's heroic martyr of the Revolution—affirmed the expansion of Indonesian tourism. The bulk of the tourists were not the expected rich Americans that an emerging nation craved to boost its revenues, but the new breed of western middle-class youth—hippies. Bali was at the bottom end of the "Asian highway" which stretched from London and Amsterdam to Sydney, with every spot on the way a paradise of free love and cheap drugs. In terms of direct revenue these tourists were not exactly what the Indonesian Government wanted. In some cases they brought little or no money with them, and lived much of the time on goodwill and good vibes. Nevertheless, they formed the nucleus of tourist development.

Not being able to afford the plush Bali Beach, the hippies of the late 1960s and early 1970s preferred to stay in Dénpasar itself (mainly at the Adi Yasa Hotel), or on the beach at Kuta. In Kuta the informal arrangements of staying in people's houses developed into a semi-formal system of "home-stays," in which families were permanently geared to a flow of foreign guests. From two local food stalls, Poppy's and Madé's, a network of restaurants and pension-style accommodation (called *losmen*) grew. Kuta became a separate area for tourism, far enough away from Sanur or Dénpasar for the authorities to feel that any adverse influences were being localized and contained.

With the home-stays, the hippies who wanted to know more about Bali could also come into close contact with one group of Balinese on a day-to-day basis. Many strove for some kind of empathy with or understanding of Balinese, even if in many cases the lack of a common language led them to romanticize the Balinese lifestyle. These young people, who fostered an interest in Indian gurus and the use of drugs to achieve enlightenment, were, after all, the heirs to Theosophy. The pre-war image of Bali as a rich religious culture fed directly into hippy ideas about the mystical East. Those who were better read may even have come across the writings of Gregory Bateson and Margaret Mead on Bali. Bateson was at that time living in the hippy mecca of Southern California as one of its western gurus, while Mead's writings and public appearances had been important in developing ideas of liberation from the boringly puritanical mainstream of middle America. Both were active proponents of alternative lifestyles, of which Bali's culture was perhaps the most perfect example.

In the wake of hippydom came the "surfies," of which Australians have always been the largest group. Bali emerged in surfie mythology as the "cosmic trip" complete with magic mushrooms and dangerous waves. New Australian surfing magazines, notably *Tracks,* joined with magazines such as *Oz* to spread the word about Bali's beaches and lifestyle, while a number of Australian films showed the surf of Kuta in all its glory.[19] Bali's reputation continued to grow and by 1973 the restaurateurs and hoteliers of Kuta had perceived the need for better facilities for tourists. Within a few years the number of middle-range hotels, providing better rooms and even

---

19. One of the first surfing films on Bali was *Morning of the Earth,* made by the founders of *Tracks* magazine, David Elfick and Albert Falzon.

air conditioning at lower prices than Sanur hotels, had increased dramatically. In the late 1970s the hippies and the Australian surfies were overtaken by a kind of "swinging singles" youth scene, characterized by loud music, drunkenness, and commercially-savvy bars.

By 1989 there were hundreds of hotels, big and small, catering to the 400,000 tourists from all over the world who were pouring into Bali. With the burgeoning of the industry the tourist hype attached to Bali's image re-emerged in strength. Both the First Development Plan (*Repelita I*) and the World Bank master plan for tourist development of 1971 saw tourism as a money-earner for Indonesia and identified Bali as the showcase of Indonesian tourism.[20] The development plan involved consolidating the tourism established in the centers of Sanur, Kuta and Ubud, and limiting its growth through controlled expansion southward. Or, at least, that was the strategy.

In 1974, seeing the growing potential of tourism in Bali, the Indonesian Government sponsored a convention of the international tourist association, PATA, on Bali. PATA's first convention on Bali had been called off when Gunung Agung erupted in 1963, so this 1974 conference was Suharto's demonstration that he could fulfill what Sukarno had failed to do. At this convention the initial plans were laid out for further development on Bali. In the tourism master-plan projections were made about the growth of tourism and the number of hotel rooms or beds needed to meet that growth. An isolated luxury resort area was also planned for Nusa Dua, a beach spot south of Sanur. In fact most of the projections were overestimated, and the Nusa Dua complex took longer than expected to get off the ground. Only in the 1980s did Nusa Dua come into its own as the resort that could accommodate the President of the United States of America on President Regan's 1987 visit. Only since the late 1980s have the tourist projections been met, and then not consistently.

---

20. The full details of the processes of tourist development outlined here are discussed and analysed in M. Picard, Tourisme Culturel" et "Culture Touristique." Rite et Divertissement dans les Arts du Spectacle a Bali," (these de doctorat de 3ème cycle) EHESS, Paris, 1984, pp. 83ff. A revised English version has been published as *Bali: Cultural Tourism and Touristic Culture*, Singapore: Archipelago Press, 1996, and an Indonesian version, again updated, *Bali: Pariwisata Budaya dan Budaya Pariwisata*, Jakarta: KPG, Forum Jakarta-Paris École française d'Extrême-Orient, 2006. I have drawn heavily of Picard's work throughout this and the next chapter.

After Sanur, Ubud took off as a tourist spot using its reputation as an artistic center as the basis of its appeal. Walter Spies's former house at Campuan and the Cokorda's palace in the center of Ubud became the first forms of guest accommodation. Since most people were looking for an alternative to the stylish but slightly isolated nature of Sanur and the noisy sprawl of Kuta, the main focus of tourism in Ubud has been on providing smaller, more intimate forms of accommodation where foreigners can feel they are coming in close contact with the cultural riches of the area. Ubud managed to maintain that intimate feeling and cultural reputation by increasing the number of smaller-style hotels, which has meant that as tourist numbers increased the region of Ubud spread three or four kilometers south towards the village of Mas, and two or three kilometers east to Sayan, subsuming the identities of surrounding villages such as Paliatan.

Ubud still has a large expatriate population, but not one that can compare with the intellectual image-makers who gathered around Spies in the 1930s. Instead the multitude of artists and ageing hippies have been content to live off the golden age of the 1930s, modeling themselves consciously on Spies's role as a devotee of Balinese culture, but destined never to make the history or art history books.

After Ubud the only other major growth of tourist areas has been on the north and east coasts. In Bulèlèng a set of small coastal hotels was pioneered by the late novelist and former king of north Bali, I Gusti (Anak Agung) Nyoman Pañji Tisna (1908-78). Pañji Tisna used his palace at Lovina, to which he retired after conversion to Christianity in the 1950s, as the basis for a hotel. Following his lead a chain of smaller hotels spread right across the top of the island, depending mainly on the attractions of the dark sandy beaches and scuba diving for their income. In the 1980s another beach resort area developed in Candi Dasa, in the former eastern Balinese kingdom of Karangasem. There the reluctant instigator of tourist development was an intellectual and follower of Gandhi, Ibu Gedong Bagus Oka (1921-2002), whose husband held important political positions in the 1950s and 1960s. She had built a meditation center on a beautiful lagoon, and others, seeing the spot's potential, began to build small hotels around it. As is usual in Bali, the lack of restrictions on development resulted in building too close to the beach, which destroyed it, and the lonely lagoon was soon hemmed in by the walls of bigger and bigger hotels. Candi Dasa was mainly seen as an alternative for those seeking to get away from the main tourist haunts, and this search for alternatives has fuelled the sprawl of development through the island.[21]

The 1971 master plan included good provisions for shaping future development: no building (with the exception of the Bali Beach Hotel) should be taller than two-thirds the height of a palm tree, hotels should be kept one-hundred meters back from beaches to preserve them, and ribbon development—buildings spread along major roads—should be stopped. None of these provisions survived the 1990s.

Return to Paradise

The marketing of Bali since the 1960s has taken the paradise image of the 1930s and blown it up into an extravagant display of hyperbole. At the same time official government sponsorship attempted to keep the image of Bali respectable, so that by the 1980s some of the sexual and magical aspects of the island emphasized in the 1930s had been dropped.

While academics like to think that they can challenge popular stereotypes in favor of more accurate assessments of society, the resurgence of the 1930s image of Bali as a paradise went ahead despite an increase in scholarly studies of Bali in the 1970s and 1980s. Few of the significant numbers of scholars researching on Bali attained the kind of influence that Spies or Mead had in the 1930s. This lack of influence can be attributed to the position of western scholarship in the Indonesian state, and the lack of any ties between scholars and image-makers. In the 1930s western anthropologists and artists, even when they did not work directly with the Dutch colonial government, were part of a knowledge-gathering process in which western identity implied a position of power or authority.

---

21. For portaits of Ibu Gedong and other "characters" and important people from Bali, see Putu Setia, *Bali Menggugat,* Jakarta: Grafiti Pers, 1986.

Nowadays that privilege is largely lost: Bali has its own academics. Nevertheless, Balinese academics have been restricted by language: lacking access to publication in English, their audiences are national rather than international.

Only one western scholar who has written about Bali has been influential on an international scale: Clifford Geertz (1926-2006), once the leading figure in American anthropology, whose writings created whole academic sub-industries. Geertz was a personally shy and reclusive man, physically drawn in on himself, hiding behind a thick beard, while expressing in his writings a breathtaking range of ideas, all conveyed in marvelously complex, highly literary, prose. He wrote extensively on Bali, having researched there in the 1950s with his former wife, Hildred Geertz, under the influence of Bateson and Mead. Mead said of the Geertzes' work on Bali that they were "elaborating that middle distance that was so lacking in our own work."[22]

Many of Clifford Geertz's most important works on Bali, his studies of the nineteenth-century Balinese state, of the Balinese cockfight, or of Balinese ideas of personality, took the best of Mead and Bateson's writings as their starting point.[23] In Geertz's writings Bali was an example to be compared with other societies, an island made precious by its distinctive presentation of a number of cultural traits, particularly the obsessive holding of rituals. What he had to say about Bali did not have a direct impact on such areas as tourism, Balinese self-image, government policies, or popular perceptions of the island as a whole. Bali was, in his work, chiefly academic in all senses of the word: removed from ongoing economic and political forces and events, a culture of special interest in the intellectual study of cultures. This emphasis was not in itself a bad thing, since it avoided the interdependence of colonial ideas and anthropological writing suffered by earlier generations of western anthropologists. In many ways the process of abstraction was a logical outcome of the professionalization and the theoretical direction

---

22. M. Mead, *Blackberry Winter: My Earlier Years,* New York: William Morrow, 1972, p. 239.

23. The main book and articles are: Geertz, *Negara*; and the essays in his *The Interpretation of Cultures,* New York: Basic Books, 1973.

taken by anthropology under the impetus of Margaret Mead and her generation of scholars. As a consequence it is hardly surprising that even academic writing that directly challenges the ideas and stereotypes of the 1930s is totally ignored in favor of popular re-workings or republications of Miguel Covarrubias's *Island of Bali.*

The first Indonesian national attempts to market Bali came through guidebooks in the 1950s and 1960s. These actually drew on a few pre-War Malay examples, notably the work of Soe Lie Piet, a Chinese-Indonesian writer, and father of the famous scholar-activists Soe Hok Gie and Arief Budiman.[24] Veteran local tourism manager I Nengah Bendesa was inspired by nationalists such as Nengah Métra in the 1930s to commit himself to a new, independent, Indonesia. Bendesa remembers that, as one of the first guides for the Nitour Company in 1962, he found the lack of guidebooks a problem, as few were readily available in Bali. Bendesa's qualifications were that he had learned English at Gadjah Mada University in Yogyakarta. Having studied to be a teacher, he found the salary of Rp. 600 per month inadequate to live on, but the first time he tried his hand at guiding his English was so rough and his knowledge of the sights so slight that he was ridiculed by a German tourist. Disheartened, he enlisted to serve in the Irian Jaya campaign, was rejected and had another try at being a guide. This time he was successful, and a group of ladies from Palo Alto gave him a tip equivalent to his month's wages as a teacher. He used Miguel Covarrubias's *Island*

24. Soe Lie Piet, *Pengoendjoekan poelo Bali atawa gids Bali,* Malang: Paragon Press, 193?; *Melantjong ke Bali,* Soerabaia: Tan's Drukkerij, 1935; *Pengantar ke Bali.* Djakarta: Magic Carpet Book, 1954. Later examples include Elvanianus Katoppo, *Bali, Pulau Kahjangan* [Bali, Island of the Gods], Bandung: Ganaco, 1950, 2nd ed. 1958; the section on Bali in *Indonesia: An Invitation,* Bandung and The Hague: Ministry of Information, Republic of Indonesia and W. van Hoeve, 1956; *Bali: Island of the Gods,* Jakarta: Ministry of Information, Republic of Indonesia, 1957; *Bali: Where, What, When, How,* Jakarta: Nitour, 1958; *Bali and her Temples,* Jakarta: Ministry of Information, Republic of Indonesia, 1961; Abdul Hakim, *Dari Pulau Bunga ke Pulau Déwa* [From the Flower Island (Flores) to the Island of the Gods (Bali)], Jakarta: P. T. Pembangunan, 1961; Ananda, *A Handy Guide for Java, Madura and Bali,* Jakarta: Kinta, 1962; *Bali: Island of Temples and Dances,* Jakarta, Ministry of Information, Republic of Indonesia, 1962 (other edns 1963, 1967); *Tourist Guide Book: Djakarta, Bogor, Bandung, Jogiakarta, Surakarta, Bali,* Jakarta: Executive Command, 10th Anniversary of the 1st Asian-African Conference, 1965. Also from this time comes the more academic publication by R. Goris and P. L Dronkers, *Bali: Atlas Kebudayan Cults and Customs/ Cultuurgeschienis in Beeld,* Jakarta: Dept. of Information of the Republic of Indonesia, 1953[?] Dronkers was another of the Europeans who took Indonesian citizenship.

of Bali and some country guidebooks published by Japan Air Lines. Famous guide Nyoman Oka (1911-1993), and others who had a lot of contact with foreigners, were often given books that helped both their work and their English.

The Indonesian publications all focused on the "Island of the Gods" theme, ensuring that this would be the most enduring epithet for Bali. A host of different books, advertising campaigns and films have elaborated upon the theme. For example, in an early 1980s brochure from Garuda Indonesia—Indonesia's national airline—we are told that the island is "so beautiful it seems unreal." Brochures such as this one make full use of claims to be showing tourists the real Bali. You could visit Bali, it says, for a vacation, at "A resort with skyscraping hotels, self-service restaurants, all-night discos. All relentlessly diverting attention from the natural beauty of land-scapes, customs, ways of life." But, says the brochure, there is a real Bali experience beyond all these lesser, more banal attractions, "An experience that will outlive all the others put together. There is one place in the world that offers it: an island whose very name seems to convey an aura of magic." "Magic" here does not refer to the extreme and possibly menacing experience with which the writers of the 1930s flirted, the experience embodied in the witch, *Rangda,* but refers to "A favored sea-kissed haven of volcanic mountains, lakes and rivers, terraced rice fields, giant banyans, palm groves, of sun dappled roads that meander quietly past peaceful villages and markets ..." The catalogue goes on, from mountains to beaches, to the artistic life of Bali, with its "superbly graceful girls" and its Hinduism.

Promotions like this one have packaged Bali quite neatly, telling the tourist what to experience. They present a list of rituals, starting with a cremation ceremony, and outline the artistic pleasures con-sisting of dances, paintings from Ubud or the traditional art center of Kamasan, gold and silverwork, and stone carving. Such promo-tions provide a short catalogue of "special places to visit" which outlines the standard tourist itinerary: the sea temple at Tanah Lot in Mengwi, set on a rocky outcrop just off the coast; the Elephant Cave in central Bali; the holy springs of Tampak Siring (although Sukarno's palace there is not mentioned); the Turtle Island off Sanur; the Monkey Forest at Sangeh; and a number of scenic villages and temples, including Bali's Mother Temple of Besakih.

It is in the nature of tourism to reduce and encapsulate places and experiences to make them readily accessible. Who wants to hear intricate details about the more boring aspects of daily life or perhaps the negative aspects of life in a Third World nation when they can be told about "the essential Bali" in six pages of flowery prose?

So the paradise image of Bali snowballed from the 1980s, an irresistible and indisputable force: "Paradise hasn't changed for thousands of years," said a 1980s advertisement for the Bali Beach Hotel, "except to get better." And so another stereotype of the Orient left over from colonial days has been continued by the advertising agencies—Indonesian, European, American and Australian— who work for the various hotels and airlines involved in tourism on Bali.

Besides appealing to the "magical" and the "eternal" nature of Bali, these advertisements have been unstinting in their dredging up of clichés and praises: "Paradise begins and ends in Bali," the Garuda "Bali on Any Budget" brochure of 1988 told us, praising all aspects of the island, including "Bali's greatest asset," which is "the Balinese themselves, a serene, harmonious people," who are "spiritual in a pure and delightful manner." These spiritual and harmonious Balinese are the quintessence of both the mystical East and the smiling and friendly Pacific Islanders of earlier stereotypes. It may not be true to say that "paradise hasn't changed in a thousand years," but it is true to say that tourist images have not changed in over eighty years. The only difference is that Indonesians, not Europeans, must take the credit for these statements and images.

The major variation on the paradise theme became a campaign of the late 1980s through Garuda's promoting of Bali as an "élite tourist" destination. The tourist authorities in Bali and Jakarta began discussing how best to attract élite tourism in the early 1980s when they considered that mass tourism had reached an optimum level. The advertising campaign which followed was called "Bali as the rich and famous see it," with television advertisements showing us where David Bowie ate, Ronald Reagan stayed, and Mick Jagger went swimming. This campaign focused on the luxury resort of Nusa Dua, designed and decorated using traditional Balinese arts and crafts. "King Hussein of Jordan was so impressed, he stayed here twice as long as he'd planned," the accompanying booklet tells. Stunningly photographed displays of scenery and amenities invite us to do as the rich and famous have done. If we want to go beyond the exclusive resort, then an air-conditioned car can whisk us away to Ubud, where the artistic life of Bali impressed "Her Majesty Queen Elizabeth" so much, "she bought a painting for her collection."

This kind of advertising has emphasized a respectable Bali. Even photographs of the self-stabbing kris dancers from the *Barong* and *Rangda* dances are no longer used, and the title "Island of the Demons" has been completely dropped.

The overtly sexual image of bare breasts and the "Sins of Bali" have been taken away from official tourism, but are still present in the image of the island, including the strong gay sub-culture that is a mainstay of some of the Ubud resorts. Homophobia in Indonesia's Muslim-based public culture results in contradictory approaches to this issue, despite the importance of prominent gay figures amongst the expatriate community on Bali. Hysteria about AIDS in the 1980s was channeled into the idea that westerners could bring a new form of impurity to Bali, to complement diseases such as hepatitis reputedly brought in by hippies. As in other countries, blaming foreigners is always a safe option for politicians who are not competent to cope with problems.

By the mid-1990s local government was directly repudiating the idea that Bali should be a site of sex tourism, a response to anxieties about the regional precendents set by the Philippines and Thailand. Governor Ida Bagus Oka's 1990s strategy to restrict sex tourism was to prohibit making condoms available in hotels "because married couples do not need to use condoms. If you use condoms it means you are having sex with someone else or someone who is ill."[25] However many of these anxieties were based on the idea of sex tourists as male, and Bali has never been the subject of the grosser marketing of Thailand, where European tourists can select

---

25. Rahmayanti "Wawancara: Saya Berjanji Desa Miskin akan Habis; Ida Bagus Oka lanjutkan pekerjaan rumah lima tahun lalu', *Editor* 6,50 (11 September 1993): 68-73.

their holiday "partners" online. While Bali's traditional sex-trade center of Semawang expanded in the 1990s on the basis of North Asian tourism, this was never part of the public face of the island.

Balinese officials have either turned a blind eye to the early development of Bali as a site of female pleasure, or have been so blinded by sexism as to not know of its existence. In the soft-core pornography of the film *Emanuelle II*[26] Bali, along with Thailand, appeared as one of the backdrops of a badly-acted transnational orgy, with the chanting chorus of the *kecak* or monkey dance providing an arousing rhythmic display of the primitive passions supposedly seething on Bali. What is controversially called a gigolo industry developed in the 1970s as part of the Kuta beach scene. Initially it depended mainly on the large numbers of unattached Australian women visiting the island, and later expanded to include Japanese tourists. An Australian newspaper report, "Don't cry for Bali," made some observations about these young Australians, "usually on their first holiday abroad," who "fall madly in love with [these] undeclared gigolos," the "Kuta Cowboys."[27] By the 1990s Balinese men had been pushed aside by other Indonesians as Kuta Cowboys, while Muslims from other islands pretended to be Balinese for unsuspecting tourists. Balinese officials claimed to have only discovered anything was going on in 2009, when a Singaporean-made film on the topic appeared on YouTube. Discussion of the topic is still limited by stereotypes of both sides of the engagement.

The erotic and magical sides of Bali's image have been dropped by the Indonesian planning authorities through a combination of puritanism and anti-colonialism. On Bali itself the process has been helped by the various reformist religious groups, who have argued that while such sensational activities as trance and cockfighting are a feature of Balinese religion, they should be minimized or eliminated when they encourage attitudes counter to other aspects of

26. Trinarce Films, 1975 (starring Sylvie Kristel).

27. *Sydney Morning Herald,* 20 Aug. 1985, by Janet Hawley, the author of a number of astute and widely read feature articles on Bali and Australians who have lived there. Updated in the following decade with "Bali Gigolos," *Marie Claire (Australia)* No. 15 (November 1996): 46-50; and on the Japanese connection, Herry, "Pemburu Pria Kuta." *Tiara* 159 (16-29 Juni 1996): 114-120, for a critique, see Mary Ida Bagus, "Sows on Heat and Disoriented Boars—Straight Sex from Bali to Melbourne," *Melbourne Journal of Politics* (1997) 24: 69-93.

religion.[28] The Indonesian and Balinese have a justifiable interest in ensuring that their nation is not seen as a laughing-stock internationally, or as a kind of sexual curio for the satisfaction of voracious western appetites. They see the earlier image of bare-breasted, gay Bali as making the island into a passive object of foreign attention, whereas their interest is in representing what they perceive to be Balinese interests, which are best furthered by showing the Balinese as a group of happy, smiling people always ready to cater to the needs of tourists. The survival of the erotic and magical images of Bali is a testimony to the persistence of generalized images of the Orient.

The Threat to Balinese Culture, Again

The government tourist authority's shift from general marketing of Bali to advertisements aimed at élite tourism was one of a series of strategies designed to protect Bali from the perceived negative influences of tourism. Implicit in the notion of tourism as a threat to culture is the idea that tourism is a powerful force that can define culture. For most Balinese, tourism does not determine how their culture is organized on a fundamental level, but it is the arena in which public discussion over the direction of Bali's culture takes place. Thus important decisions about Balinese religion and art are made either by Balinese or by authorities in Jakarta with reference to tourism, either to treat tourism as a negative reference point when rejecting western influences, or to reaffirm state authority.

In the early 1970s the idea of Cultural Tourism—the idea that exposing tourists to Bali's cultural life in a manner controlled by government authorities would be beneficial for all concerned—was the main strategy for "protecting" Balinese culture. The shift to élite tourism signaled a perception amongst the tourist planners that the weight of tourist numbers was negating the advantages of Cultural Tourism, and that only by appealing to a more refined and select group could the necessary appreciation of Balinese culture be produced. Unfortunately there is one fallacy in the logic behind the

---

28. On the banning of cockfighting in Bali, see M. Picard, "En Feuilletant le < <Bali Post > >: à Propos de l'interdiction des combats de Coqs a Bali," *Archipel* 25 (1983): 171-80. For the banning of cockfights in the 1950s, see C. Geertz, "Deep Play: Notes on the Balinese Cockfight," in his *The Interpretation of Cultures,* pp. 412-56.

campaign: wealth and fame are considered to bring good taste and cultivation in a variety of Indonesian cultural traditions, but there are many examples to prove that this is not the case.

Beyond the issue of whether a particular tourist strategy can work or not lies a deeper problem of what constitutes culture and what exactly is a threat to culture. Balinese culture is now more or less synonymous with the image presented by the marketers of tourism and Indonesian Government agencies. The various groups associated with the service industry on Bali, together with artists, dancers, musicians and artisans, have a vested interest in the maintenance of that Balinese culture. Nobody on Bali would seriously think to challenge the idea of Balinese culture. Even those people who oppose tourism and see themselves as defenders of tradition are supporters of the idea.

In these public discussions "culture" is not the same as the anthropologists' broadly defined idea of "meaningful behavior," but the more narrow idea of formal religious and artistic activity. For present day anthropologists culture means many things, and usually embraces all the activities that give significance to people's lives: everything from mundane practices to major public ritual acts. Thus, for some—for example Clifford Geertz—culture is the ideals that serve as a model of society, but also a model for social life; for others, it is the processes of life, the accumulation of habits and knowledge built up over many generations, but subtly changed as they are handed on. The official discussions of culture in the context of tourism are confined to a very superficial level. Culture, as it is talked about officially by Balinese, other Indonesians and tourists, is not such things as fighting with one's relatives, making decisions about borrowing money, buying a motorcycle or listening to the radio, but wearing sarongs, holding cremations, or dancing in a manner prescribed by tradition.

The issue of whether tourism would destroy Balinese culture was a major topic of discussion for all the groups involved in tourist planning in the 1970s. Underlying both official and unofficial discussions was the notion that tourism would change the visible signs of culture. Threat and preservation were the two key terms, using the underlying assumption that up until the 1960s Balinese culture had not essentially changed for thousands of years. Although the problem sounded contemporary, these discussions were revivals of the anxieties held by writers such as Covarrubias that Balinese wearing trousers or using galvanized iron for roofing were participating in the destruction of their culture.

In the 1970s Bali's survival was to be assured through confining tourism to one small area. In the various plans a "tourism triangle" was conceived, with its points at Kuta, Sanur and Ubud. The government could limit the malevolent influences of tourism within this area, and the majority of Balinese could thus be protected from the need to"modernize" by copying western clothing, bad manners, or libertarian ways.

Even the containment plan for tourism could not allay all fears about Balinese culture. In 1971 World Bank planners predicted ominously that by 1983 Bali's "cultural manifestations will probably have disappeared." "But," they reassured, "Bali can still retain its romantic image and still be thought of as a green and sumptuous garden."[29] For the purposes of tourism, Bali's culture was not seen as essential, as long as the romantic image of the island remained.

Indonesians, particularly Balinese, were not as phlegmatic as this. They understood that cultural manifestations were more important to tourism than natural surroundings, and so responded officially through the establishment of a tourism board, and through attempts to channel the flow of tourism into Cultural Tourism. For some, Kuta's tourism provided one such example of how close contact between tourists and Balinese could be beneficial for both.[30] Unfortunately the accelerated development of Kuta in the 1980s destroyed any hope of such benefits.

Cultural Tourism combined exposure to Balinese culture for tourists and regulation of tourism by various authorities. From the early 1970s onwards the first manifestations of this policy started to appear. More or less simultaneously the respective religious and civil authorities erected signs in English in front of temples and

---

29. Quoted Picard, "Tourisme Culturel," p. 95.
30. ibid. See further I Gusti Ngurah Bagus (ed.), *Bali dalam Sentuhan Pariwisata,* Dénpasar, 1975.

government offices. The signs for the temples proclaimed that people dressed inappropriately (in shorts or other revealing clothes) were not allowed in, and likewise neither were menstruating women, whose presence in Balinese belief, as in Jewish and certain Christian scriptures, renders a sacred space impure. Although not including the prohibitions on menstruating women, the signs used for government offices prohibit the entry of those dressed in shorts, not wearing shoes, or those whose dress is generally untidy. The idea behind these signs is based on the assessment that many tourists regard the whole island as one big holiday center, where they should dress as casually as possible, and that tourists need to be made to appreciate local sensibilities.

Such signs are just the most obvious manifestations of attempts to regulate tourism. Tourist planning authorities supervise different aspects of the tourism industry by licensing all those involved in major tourist businesses, and cultural officials authorize dancers and musicians to perform for tourists. One of the mechanisms designed to preserve Balinese culture was the decision to categories Balinese dances and music as sacred or profane, with prohibitions on the commercialization of sacred dance and music. Commercialization is regarded by tourist planning authorities and Balinese artists, musicians and dancers as the major threat to their culture, degrading the standards of their art, and detracting from the religious purity of their work.

This fear of commercialization is not simply a matter for bureaucrats. It is a general issue for most Balinese, who hold various positions as to whether it would be better to keep tourists out of some areas of Balinese life altogether, or to allow more access for tourists to performances and rituals. In the major tourist areas few Balinese have any real privacy for the holding of rituals. Although people are usually happy to invite tourists they may meet to a wedding or other ceremony, there are often complaints and grimaces when, halfway through a ceremony in a temple, a tour bus pulls up and twenty or thirty people are shepherded through the middle of the proceedings. In this situation Balinese direct their resentment as much at the Balinese guides who have brought the tourists to the ceremony as at the tourists themselves. Most Balinese try to ensure that there is a balance between the private part of family ceremonies and the public displays such as the parade of the cremation tower and sarcophagus to be burnt, where it is important that things be bustling and crowded, or what the Balinese call *ramé*, busy. If a ceremony is busy it is successful, for it is an activity that has gained large-scale public participation and recognition, and the crowds have contributed to the dynamic energy of the ritual.

Tourists with any sensitivity at all and Indonesians from outside of Bali continue to express sympathy with Balinese in this situation and share their fears of commercialization. W. S. Rendra, the romantic Javanese poet regarded as his country's most public dissident in the 1970s and 1980s, wrote poems bemoaning the fate of Balinese as objects in the international tourist trade.[31] Tourist guidebooks and travel accounts have taken the same approach, offering the reassurance that the "real" Bali still survives, and bland statements about how the resilience of Balinese culture will enable the Balinese to resist any negative influences.[32] To back this up they offer photographs of half-naked or poorly dressed tourists sunning themselves or bargaining for trinkets while solemn ritual processions are going on.[33]

These laudable sentiments usually miss the point that Balinese culture is strong because of tourism, not despite it. Tourism defines what Balinese culture is in a context where such definitions have hitherto not been needed, and it defines Balinese identity within Indonesia. Balinese and other Indonesians talk about tourism in terms of "us" Balinese/Indonesians versus "them," the tourists.[34]

Tourism encourages Balinese to reflect on their own culture. Members of a culture usually learn and express their culture unconsciously—it is something they have grown up with, a matter of habit. Balinese culture has long been an object of study. For over a century various Balinese have had to make statements to outsiders,

---

31. Text reproduced as an appendix to Picard, "Tourisme Culturel," p. 448.

32. ibid.

33. ibid., p. 428, and Leonard Leuras & R. Ian Lloyd, *Bali: The Ultimate Island,* Ringwood: Viking, 1987, p. 226.

34. Picard, "Tourisme Culturel." Picard's analyses are far more extended and more subtle than the rough outline given here could show.

first Dutch scholars and civil servants, then tourists, describing their culture and the elements of their religion. This process of articulation has meant that the Balinese have had to be conscious about their own culture, producing both a sense of pride in their cultural identity as Balinese, and an ability to sum up what may be considered as the essential aspects of culture—such as Hinduism, caste, priestly rituals and dances—in a way that can be conveniently understood by others. Tourism is only one element in this process of externalizing culture,[35] and nowadays the Indonesian Government plays as big a role as tourism in the process, since the government requires formal rationalizations and criteria in order that cultural and artistic activities can be bureaucratically described and supported.

Art and Souvenirs in 1980s Bali

Those involved in the arts in Bali have played complicated roles in the interactions around Cultural Tourism. They have been the raw material for its content, and subject to government planning and control. Some artists have survived by maintaining the role of the arts as an intimate part of Balinese social and spiritual interaction, others have tried with varying success to deal with the economics from tourism. Some have found regular income in the performances of the *kecak* or monkey dance and the *Barong and Rangda* dance, held daily as part of the itinerary of tourists, or hastily produced unsigned works for quick, cheap sale. The luck of more specialized artists and performers varies according to knowledge of English, age, attitude and contacts with foreigners, and this says a lot about how the tourist industry has an impact on local society.

Ida Bagus Madé Togog was one example of a leading artist who did not fit into the tourist art scene. Togog (1913-89) was a mild and unassuming brahman, seemingly in a constant state of bewilderment about the pressures of life outside his cloistered household. The studiously meditative attitude of his caste concealed a deep warmth in personal interaction and a great excitement in sharing his

35. For a discussion of how tourism has speeded up the process of cultural and religious rationalisation elsewhere in Indonesia, see Toby Alice Volkman, "Great Performances: Toraja Cultural Identity in the 1970s," *American Ethnologist* ll (1984):152-69.

Ida Bagus Madé Togog of Batuan village, one of Bali's foremost artists.

knowledge, his art and his stock of fabulous tales. He began painting in the 1930s and knew Gregory Bateson well. In many ways his
life was torn between his desire to tell stories, orally and in paint,
and his training as a spiritual leader in the community, brought up to
become a high priest. Unwilling to go on because he felt unworthy
of the task, his energies were concentrated in his art. According to
Bateson and Mead, part of Ida Bagus Togog's feeling of unworthi-
ness was an unusual preoccupation with caste and status, resulting
from his youth when "he had broken a serious caste rule in stealing
the wife of another *brahman.*"[36]

He exhibited internationally and received numerous awards from
the state and national governments in recognition of his art. Nevertheless he painted as an expression of religious devotion, and out of
a need to express metaphysical issues in terms of stories from the

36. *Balinese Character,* plate 10, ill. 6. See further Hildred Geertz, and Ida Bagus Madé Togog,
Tales from a Charmed Life: a Balinese Painter Reminisces. Honolulu: University of Hawai'i
Press, 2005.

broad array of Balinese traditional narratives or from images of ritual life. His subject matter was neither easily recognized nor easily understood by tourists, since it was not the usual dancing girls, birds, fish, demons or lush scenery that fill paintings for the tourist market. Moreover he did not paint quickly and so did not produce works in bulk to be marketed. His patient attention to detail and meditative attitude to the work process meant that his works were large, complex, and necessarily priced above the usual range of tourist works. In his later years he was too old to travel from his home village of Batuan north up to Ubud in order to market his works directly to tourists, even if he had been interested in doing so.

Most of those tourists who came to see him did so as a result of his fame, which spread through the various scholarly studies of Balinese art, and not all of these people necessarily came to buy. Added to this was the fact that the family lacked inherited wealth (the older generation lost all their rice fields through gambling), and the end result is that, despite being a famous artist, he was nowhere near as prosperous as fellow villagers.

Ida Bagus Togog's caste did not, therefore, directly enable him to be elevated above commoners in any sense of economic power or influence. On the contrary, some commoner families in the village live more luxuriously from their earnings as artshop owners. One advantage did remain from his status as a *brahmana:* Ida Bagus could command the loyalty and respect of hundreds of people from all around the area who were traditional "pupils" *(sisia)* or ritual clients of the priestly house, and in times of need, or during rituals, that is still a very important resource for families of standing.

By comparison, another of Bali's greatest artists, the commoner I Nyoman Mandera (b.1946) of the artists' village of Kamasan, Klungkung, can rely only on his talent. Nyoman is a serious and gentle painter who has, in his work, attained a level of refined perfection that stands out in the five-hundred-year-old tradition of painting that has made his village famous. His elegant works have achieved international recognition, and through his talent he supports an artists' school for children and teenagers of the village in his own house, a school dedicated to, as he sees it, ensuring that the tradition of painting is kept alive for future generations. For this he receives often meager government support, but without traditional clients or wealth to call upon, his lifestyle is austere, a hardship compounded by a succession of serious illnesses he has suffered. Kamasan has the disadvantage of being outside the well-worn tourist paths, meaning that guides and artshops ignore the work of his school; without this market, Nyoman's work and teaching have an uncertain future. The village's plight is typical of many of those outside the Gianyar and Dénpasar areas where most tourist wealth is generated.

Dancers often manage to be more successful than painters in dealing with tourism. As with painters, there is a marked dichotomy between those who are not highly skilled but who perform frequently for tourists, and those who are regarded as expert dancers in demand for rituals and other kinds of activity. Probably the most successful dancer in the latter category is I Madé Jimat (1948-), a former fellow villager of Ida Bagus Togog. The son of talented painter I Nyoman Reneh (1910-1976) and the famous dancer Ni Ktut Cenik (1922-2010), Jimat has been highly praised by western scholars of dance since the early 1970s, and is an example of someone who combines tourist success with a traditional role.

Jimat was the subject of a film made around 1972, *Bali: The Light of Many Masks*,[37] which shows off his skills to full effect. His broad, handsome features adorn many books on Bali. He goes about his daily activities quietly, but his face carries the look of restless energy and the spark of genius which lights up his dancing. After the protracted illness and sad death of Jimat's fellow villager, I Nyoman Kakul, one of the greatest dancers of the 1930s,[38] Jimat enjoyed unrivalled fame for the mastery of his masked *topèng* performances and for the professional and highly gifted troupe he leads in performances of the classic *gambuh* dance drama. In the 1980s he travelled extensively all over the world, yet he still performs just as much for temple festivals or royal weddings at which no tourists are present at all.

---

37. Directed and produced by Karen Goodman & Wayne Lockwood, Bioscope 1981 (filmed in the 1970s).
38. On Kakul's life and artistry see Anna Daniel, *Bali: Behind the Mask*, New York: Knopf, 1981.

Jimat's reputation was spread through the Indonesian planning authorities' Cultural Tourism network. On the fringes of Cultural Tourism were the more intellectually inclined hippies and travelers of the late 1960s and early 1970s whose initial experiences of Bali led to film-making, writing of books about the island, or academic study, especially of music and dance. Films such as *Light of Many Masks* were the fruits of these interests, and they shifted attention from the typical tourist itinerary of temples and scenery to a kind of in-depth itinerary of key cultural figures. For those in the know, following Jimat around in performances and taking dance lessons from him became almost compulsory. Through tour guides and hotel networks in Ubud Jimat was also frequently asked to hold special performances for western visitors, either in Ubud itself or in his own house, which has a large performance and rehearsal area. This kind of public attention has been a mixed blessing for him. While it has allowed his family to prosper, it has also attracted the attention of fellow villagers who expressed resentment at people who "get above their station." Factionalism is an ever-present aspect of village life in Bali, the product of cultural encouragement of sibling rivalry, reliance on gossip as a basic means of information-gathering, and the sheer fact of having a large number of people living closely together, intertwined in each other's lives. For Jimat tourist success has meant becoming the focus of factional disputes in the village.

Scholars, both foreign and Indonesian, tend to play an intermediary role in promoting particular artists and dancers. Dance schools and theater studies groups have been particularly effective in bridging the gap between scholarship, performance and the promotion of Balinese performers overseas. Since the international study of Balinese theater and music goes back to the 1930s, it is to Gianyar, the center of that study, that modern scholars go. Hence, these students of dance and music were led to the up-and-coming talents of only one area, and Jimat and his contemporaries were sponsored by various overseas institutions to travel and perform so that the example of Balinese theater could be more widely appreciated. In the wake of scholarship has come more directly commercial sponsorship for travel to Europe, Japan and elsewhere.

Jimat's reputation developed at a time when government-sponsored bodies for the study and propagation of Balinese dance were in their infancy. Since the 1970s the government-run National Academy of Dance (STSI), now ISI, has been active in Bali, and has progressively gained importance in the public area of cultural activity. It is closely linked to a number of other official organizations devoted to the study, preservation and perpetuation of Balinese culture.

Much of what the Academy does in terms of teaching and research takes place independently from the activities of village-based dancers like Jimat, and to some degree many village-based dance experts are excluded from the official world of the academy and the other government institutions. This has happened not because of any particular policies, but as a secondary effect of the bureaucratic requirements of state-run organizations. Basically salary and status in any government organization is linked to education, since everyone who works in a government instrumentality, whether a university or an office of public works, is a member of the civil service. Many village-based performers, particularly older ones, have not been to school, or have only had the most basic formal education, so it is impossible for them to gain civil service positions which would reflect their status or what they have to offer students, let alone a position that pays more than a bare minimum in salary. Indonesia has no cultural treasure program such as that of Japan or Korea, where expertise is respected and recognized through state subsidy.

The Academy and the other official institutions have produced a civil service élite who play a key role in determining what Balinese culture is, and in government policy towards it. These are often younger men or women who come originally from different villages or areas in Bali with long artistic traditions, so they are not at all divorced from Balinese tradition. By combining their traditional background with formal education, including taking doctorates at American universities, they place themselves in the happy position of having the best of both worlds.

The Academy represents the future of the arts in Bali, and of culture as a whole. Its equivalents in the religious sphere are the government and private organizations which debate, sponsor and decide on the direction Balinese religion should take. As in other parts of the world, culture is dependent on government recognition and sponsorship, and the people who can mediate with that sponsorship are those who are qualified in traditional and modern terms, those who have their fingers on the pulse of what is identifiably traditional, but who have the qualifications and the expertise to utilize tradition in the modern world.

The existence of formal organizations which direct, or at least attempt to control, the nature of culture in Bali in no way means that Balinese culture is not properly "traditional," just more self-consciously so. The main difference between Balinese culture at the present day and in the past is that now Balinese culture is more self-consciously seen as culture, but it is no less real for that.

Traditional and Modern Élites

The former rulers of Bali, the kings and the priests, have adopted a variety of strategies to be able to maintain their former status within the cultural paradise of Bali. Although many of them are modern Balinese, with university degrees, international qualifications and recognition, and jobs outside of Bali, as a group they still maintain a healthy respect for tradition, which is after all the basis of their claims to status.

The heads of many former royal families have maintained something of their status through a combination of wealth acquired in the 1930s, access to tourist income, and membership of an Indonesia-wide élite. Such families often prosper through a division of labor: one member might become a member of Parliament in Jakarta, another might own a chain of hotels and artshops, while a third might continue to support rituals and maintain old patronage networks. A number of the prominent developers of the hotel industry thus have come from such families, such as as A. A. Pañji Tisna, former king of Bulèlèng, or Ida Bagus Kompyang, from a leading priestly house in Dénpasar.

Not all members of these families necessarily follow modern patterns of power. A fascinating example was Dalem Pemayun (b.c.1920-1998), the eldest son of Déwa Agung Oka Geg, the ruler of Klungkung through the colonial and post-colonial periods. After their father's death in 1965, the leading princes from the thirty-eight children, including Dalem Pamayun and his full-brother Cokorda

Anom, the former political leader and state head, divided the roles and esteem due to a traditional king between them.

Dalem Pemayun, or Ratu Dalem as he was known, did not have the kind of grand palace his position would suggest, and he and his immediate family and a few retainers occupied just one cool and leafy courtyard in a sprawling complex of royal dwellings, a complex with more than a faint air of decay. In his little corner of the palace this man, trained by his father in the vast store of practice and belief associated with the court, sat carving sacred statues and masks, visited by subjects who came to ask favors and advice of him. He was a thin man, with short-cropped hair, white with age, and a small moustache like his father's, an oval face made thin by diabetes, and the reserved manner befitting one who had chosen an ascetic life devoted to religion.

In 1980 he was ordained as a royal priest or *bagawan,* and this is when he took the title of Dalem, the hereditary title of the kings of Gèlgèl. The title showed his descent and the importance of his family, and its choice was controversial, since it had not been used for members of the Klungkung royal family in their lifetime. He was justified in his use of the title by the fact that most other royal and priestly titles in Bali had been devalued by overuse.

By being consecrated as a priest Ratu Dalem had opted to separate the secular and religious aspects of life in Bali, as the secular aspect became more involved with either tourism or with the role of Bali in the modern Indonesian state. He and his wives oversaw the holding of various rituals, and played important roles in the re-staging of the centennial exorcism known as *Ekadasa Rudra*, held in 1979 as a kind of New Order regime response to the holding of the ritual in 1963. Recognition of Ratu Dalem's role was still strong within Klungkung, although outside it some others, including the various organizations concerned with religion, only begrudgingly acknowledged his importance.

Most of Ratu Dalem's popular support was based on the maintenance of tradition—people still want to be seen as subjects of the king of Klungkung, because as subjects they share in the status of the former kingdom. When the Klungkung royal family held major rituals under Ratu Dalem's supervision, people from all over Bali provided goods and labor to confirm that they are in some way distantly related to the Klungkung royalty, or to emphasize being "traditonal" and receive the spiritual benefits of royal ritual and all its associated trappings. Although the position was left vacant for over a decade after his death, eventually one of his younger half-brothers was persuaded to return from his modern career in Jakarta and take up the position of traditional ruler, into which he was consecrated as the new Ratu Dalem in 2010.

The cremation of the great patron of the arts and prince of Ubud, Cokorda Sukawati, in 1979 was another example of how a former royal family could be united in the common purpose of paying respect to their patriarch and at the same time ensuring that the reputation and prestige of the family was displayed. The underwriting of the ritual by overseas film units ensured that the rite was truly spectacular. Rudolf Bonnet was cremated alongside his old friend, in a ceremony that confirmed the primacy of the royal family in the rise of Ubud as a major center in Bali.

Likewise when the grand old ruler of Dénpasar, Cokorda Pamecutan, was cremated in 1986 his family combined resources from tourism (they ran a major hotel and other businesses) with the loyal assistance of the extended Pamecutan clan and the important role of some of the late and venerable ruler's sons in regional government. These resources ensured that the ritual was a grand affair befitting the man's status as the last of the old generation of rulers, a staunch preserver of royal ceremony, and an astute politician from the 1930s onwards. There is always much talk of such cremations being the last royal cremation, but they seem to keep getting bigger and more spectacular as time goes on, as examples from the 2000s have shown. For aristocratic families tourism both directly and indirectly supports their public identity, and complements the role many family members have found in local or national government.

How to Succeed in Tourism

During the 1980s tourism shifted from being an economic option for Balinese looking for employment, to being the focus of the Balinese economy. Official statistics indicate that in the 1980s tourism accounted for around 20% of economic activity on Bali, or at the most

30%, while nearly 45% of the regional income was derived from agriculture, mainly rice-growing. By the next decade the majority of jobs were in tourist-related work, and agricultural was in sharp decline, and by the end of the century, hospitality made up nearly two-thirds of the island's economy, with agriculture shrinking to less than 20%.[39] Tourism has provided a living in a variety of other areas for tens of thousands of Balinese, to the point where poverty in Bali is associated with lack of access to tourist income.

Still, in the twenty-first century, as in the 1980s, tourism emphasizes the inequalities in Balinese life, and supports the cultural activities that are the focus of much Balinese attention. Tourism has created a new middle class that consisted initially of hoteliers, artshop owners and tour guides—a group with access to the consumer symbols of success, such as black BMWs. By the end of the twentieth century this class diversified into the related areas of property investment, taxi companies, building, catering, design, clothing manufacture, import-export, and all the other aspects of contemporary capitalist economy.

As Ubud gradually built up its tourist reputation in the 1970s a strip of artshops grew up along the road between Dénpasar and Ubud. These artshops provide the full range of tourist souvenirs for the visitor to Bali, whilst managing to blot out totally the attractive wet-rice fields which made the journey north to Ubud interesting. Nowadays the artshop is part of an entrenched system. The smaller street stalls of Dénpasar have been eclipsed, relegated to the upper storeys of a new and unattractive market complex.

The artshop owners usually commission paintings and carvings in bulk, looking for the most easily recognizable and therefore saleable styles. In recent times there have been various fads in the industry, one being for brightly painted carvings of fruit and banana

---

39. For a survey of the 1981 census statistics on Bali, see W. Donald McTaggart, "Some Development Problems in Bali," *Contemporary Southeast Asia* 6,3 (1984), pp. 231-45. See also Picard, "Tourisme Culturel," pp. 188-96. K. G. Bandesa and M. Sukarsa, "An Economic Survey of Bali," *Bulletin of Indonesian Economic Studies,* 16 (1980): 31-53, argue that tourism accounts for only 2-3% of economic activity on Bali, but this figure seems grossly reduced, and ignores both the relation of small industry (the production of handicrafts/souvenirs) to tourism and the fact that many people whose livings wholly or in part depend on tourism are not formally linked to the tourist industry. Figures for the year 2000, from the research of Nyoman Erawan, Bali's leading economist, taken from Michael Hitchcock and I Nyoman Darma Putra, *Tourism, Development and Terrorism in Bali*. Aldershot: Ashgate, 2007, p. 171.

plants. Whereas in the early 1970s paintings or carvings could be bought for few dollars each, by the 1980s the least expensive carvings had risen to the $15-$25 range, with paintings selling for $75 or more. Prices escalated rapidly as the waves of Japanese tourists sweeping the island liberally dispensed their yen. In the 2000s the struggle to maintain the market saw souvenir makers move into less and less identifiably Balinese products, including Aboriginal Australian digeridoos.

The market for tourist souvenirs has very little to do with art in the sense of high art, despite the generic title of the shops. The artists of Bali who are recognized by international scholarship rarely if ever produce for artshops. The artshops usually pay artists only 20-30% of a painting's sale price, sometimes less; so they rely on quick mass-production and copying of works by cheap labor rather than on the kind of slow inspiration required to produce the paintings Balinese artists value. The rest goes to the owner of the artshop and as commission to the guides who bring the "guests." Artshops are so plentiful that they would not be able to compete without agreeing to pay out at least 30% (or 60%, if you believe the artists) of any sale to the guides.

Tour guides developed as one of the most prosperous middle-class groups on Bali in the 1980s. The main qualification for becoming a tour guide is fluency in English, Japanese or one of the other main languages spoken by Bali's tourists. Given the difficulties of learning English in Indonesia's underfunded education system, this qualification is hard to come by, and highly valued. Tour guides often get their start by being employed in a minor capacity by big hotels or tour companies and working their way up the system. As guides they establish a relationship with artshop owners and other major figures in the tourist scene, forming an alliance that makes them into a tourist middle class, often jealously watched by fellow villagers or neighbors who do not have the same access to income from tourism.

Déwa Gedé (not his real name) is an example of how the professional tour guides continue to prosper. Coming from a palace or *puri* he has had the advantage of an education. This education, combined with his natural quick wit and charm, has allowed him to develop the skills required for dealing with groups of foreign travelers. Although academically distinguished, he has found that his fluency in English and Japanese have given him a far better means of supporting his family than the small salary and tenuous future which is the fate of most Indonesian university staff, a choice aided by bureaucratic obstructions which hamper his chances of becoming a lecturer. His work as a tour guide has enabled him to develop his section of the *puri* as a guest house, while buying land and building a house in the impossibly inflated property market of Dénpasar and supporting an extended family that reaches out to include his sister-in-law and a number of nieces and nephews with their own dependants. In this way he has made a major contribution to the sprawling extended family that typically fills the modern Balinese palace. One of the costs of this prosperity is the jealousy of fellow villagers, who scathingly deride Déwa Gedé's ties to a local artshop owner, a commoner whose family used a combination of inherited land, artistic networks and strong entrepreneurial talents to become one of the major economic forces of the village.

Others in this tourism-based middle class include restaurateurs and those who can regularly command substantial sums for tourist performances. While the larger hotel owners and managers are the wealthiest of Balinese, they are a fairly small group, and very big businesses such as these are usually owned by Indonesian companies based in Jakarta or by foreigner investors. The growth of this middle class has created a division between the "haves" and the "have-nots," perceived by Balinese as the ability or failure to get access to the tourist dollars promised in government planning and so frequently displayed in the spending-sprees of the tourists themselves. The have-nots are most of all those who do not speak English. Although villagers have many other forms of income, mainly from rice growing, tourist dollars are regarded as easy money, and the prosperity of the tour guides is a goal to which most Balinese aspire. Although the tourist industry is concentrated in the regions of Badung and Gianyar, young people come from all over Bali to be involved, either travelling daily to these regions, or moving permanently to centers such as Kuta. In addition, hotel owners and others who hire large numbers of people often follow a policy of employing networks of people from the one village, meaning that people move temporarily to Sanur, Nusa Dua or Kuta as part of a village group.

In the hierarchy of access to tourism there is an abundance of hawkers of souvenirs, with their cries of: "You buy my postcard—I give you cheap." By mastering the bare minimum of the relevant languages these people eke out a meager existence by getting small tourist items from local producers and travelling all over the island to sell them. The hawkers, often women, can sometimes make big profits by catching tourists unawares on the beach at Kuta or Sanur, or coming out of one of the places on the standard tourist itineraries such as temples, monkey forests and bat caves. Unfortunately the high profit sale is all too rare, and most of these sellers are consigned by overheads such as transport costs to these tourist sites, and by larger competitors to very small profit margins.

Those hawkers who come from the remoter villages of the north or east are unlikely to ever strike it rich. They are often people who have gone into hawking as a result of the massive changes in rice-farming practices that have resulted from the Green Revolution in Indonesia. In the late 1960s and 1970s Third World countries were encouraged to convert to new high-yield varieties of rice in order to increase production. For a country such as Indonesia, whose food supply is insufficient for its massive population, the introduction of these strains of rice was successful, and meant that the nation as a whole was able to move from importing rice to providing for its basic needs. This success has not been evenly distributed, however; changes in the way rice is harvested have meant that people involved at some stages of the growing and harvesting of rice have been displaced, and to supplement family income have had to set up in business either as petty commodity traders, food-sellers or hawkers to tourists.[40]

---

40. See Mark Poffenberger and Mary Zurbuchen, "The Economics of Village Bali: Three Perspectives," *Economic Development and Cultural Change* 29(1980): 91-133. More recent studies suggest that the view of agricultural development put forward by Poffenberger and Zurbuchen and other writers on this topic in the 1970s was overly pessimistic. See Anne Booth, *Agricultural Development in Indonesia*, Sydney: Allen and Unwin, 1988. As yet there has been little detailed research on the specific impacts of changing agriculture in Bali; besides the work of Poffenberger and Zurbuchen there are only unpublished studies of fruit growing in north-eastern Bali by John Wilkinson.

It is easy for tourists to forget that Bali is a part of a poor Third World nation. They never see those who do not have any access to tourist income, such as the poor villagers of the mountains who scrape out a bare subsistence living from growing less desirable forms of crops on terrain no one else can use; or those of the north who go out in fishing boats every day for a portion of a catch which is ever-diminishing thanks to competition from the high-tech fishing boats of East Asia. In north Bali some people can no longer receive a viable income from fishing, and try their hand at casual labor at rates of about $1USD per day, when they can get the work. Labor is abundant, work not all that plentiful, and people in such areas have been reduced to the indignity of living in rags, embarrassed to meet anyone because they cannot cover their nakedness.

Even in the rich rice-bowl of south Bali, the Badung-Tabanan area, people's livelihood is not assured. In the areas still dependent on rice-growing, farmers constantly talk about the availability of water, and the other elements needed to produce a good harvest. Overall, Indonesia has been successful in increasing its national rice production so that, mercifully, the famines that used to regularly strike such areas as West Java and Lombok are now a thing of the past. Still, for the rice farmers, production is always a delicate matter. When the monsoon rains are late the intricate balance of the water supply as it trickles down through the rice terraces can be upset. Those who live lower down in the irrigation system can get only just enough water to flood their wet-rice fields, especially now that the introduction of new varieties of rice means more crops per year and more demand on water. On an island such as this, with its lush tropical climate, water is strangely enough a rare commodity. Add to this the fact that the new varieties of rice are more subject to pests and disease than the old types of rice, and depend on plentiful supplies of goverment-subsidized fertilizer and pesticides, and you have a situation in which any one event—a rise in the price of fertilizer, the withdrawal of subsidies, a new form of virus—can reduce peasants to paupers.

In general, some of the poor have managed to share indirectly the benefits of tourism. As various groups in Balinese society have become wealthy from tourism there has been a kind of "trickle-down effect" by which others get to share in their wealth. On a daily basis the most prominent example of this is an increase in the number of women who run little roadside or market stalls *(warung)* selling all kinds of food and goods. Others who have prospered include the various kinds of priests who carry out rituals for families, villages and clans, particularly the priests who have traditional links to prosperous families.

Aside from indirect benefits, patterns of priesthood and religious leadership have continued without much influence from tourism. An example from the 1980s was the medium Jero Tapakan, a short, middle-aged widow from the mountain area of Bangli, whose life history was typical of the pattern of social mobility amongst those who are often called "folk healers." Although she was relatively successful later in life, her moon-shaped face was lined with the privations of a peasant life, and her spontaneous wit developed into the dry edge of one who had seen the ironies of life. In the 1960s she was a poor itinerant peddler forced to travel long distances from her home village in order to scrape out a living. During this time she was severely ill, but as a result, she received divine inspiration in the form of a period of "madness," which led to her becoming a medium and healer, someone to whom people from all over Bali come either for a cure from illness or to receive instructions from the gods or ancestors through trances. Jero Tapakan was a combination of peasant simplicity and astute entrepreneurial ability, presenting herself as a simple vehicle of divine will whilst cautiously building up a wide clientele and a significant reputation for her abilities. The relative prosperity that came with the large clientele was translated into upgrading the family courtyard and holding sizeable rituals connected with the family, although she could hardly have been called rich. She did not, for example, have access to the kinds of consumer goods that are the signs of success in the tourist industry.

Jero's pattern of upward mobility had given her a tenuous kind of security. Like most Indonesians she knew that the slightest change in her position—for example a sudden decline in her popularity—could plunge her back into the deepest penury. Other traditional healers looked jealously upon her achievements, and tried and blacken her name with gossip. Even worse, her son who was to succeed her in the practice of healing, predeceased her due to cancer, and so after her death the rest of the family were left with no source of income.

As with most Indonesians on the village level, her family's path to social mobility was cut off by the inabilities of a poor state to provide education for a population that had passed the 200 million mark by the end of the twentieth century, and by the petty corruption through which teachers and civil servants must supplement their inadequate incomes. Her life illustrated not only the persistence of tradition in Bali and the degree of social movement within Balinese society, but also the precarious nature of that social movement.[41]

Keeping the Balance

Professor Doctor Ida Bagus Mantra (1928-1995), Governor of Bali from 1978 to 1988, was the model of a successful brahman. During the decade of his governorship, this tall, plump and pleasant man presided over Bali's growing prosperity and the real boom in tourism on the island, but kept it under control. His family came from the Sanur area, which has maintained a strong reputation as a center of spiritual power and magic over the last two centuries. The family home is still preserved as a majestic version of a traditional priestly house, slightly isolated from the surrounding village and tourist developments, showing its opulence in a reserved and dignified manner. Governor Mantra was part of the generation of the Revolution which saw that the way to strengthen the identity of Balinese religion was to return to its Indian roots, and so he was educated in India, after which he became a university lecturer and served on various Balinese bodies that, in the 1950s and 1960s, aimed to promote the status of Balinese religion through presenting it as a branch of international Hinduism. He gradually rose up through the university administrative hierarchy to become Director General of Culture in the national Ministry of Culture and Education, and then Governor.

41. On Jero Tapakan, see Linda Connor, In Darkness and Light: A Study of PeasantIntellectuals in Bali, (unpub. diss.) University of Sydney, 1982; Linda Connor, Patsy Asch & Timothy Asch, *Jero Tapakan: Balinese Healer. An Ethnographic Film Monograph,* Cambridge: Cambridge University Press, 1986, and the four films which the book accompanies, *A Balinese Trance Séance, Jero on Jero: A Balinese Trance Séance Observed, The Medium is the Masseuse: A Balinese Massage & Jero Tapakan: Stories from the Life of a Balinese Healer.*

During his term of office he set a high moral tone for the island, and had a reputation for being above the corruption that dogged the lives of other public officials.

Governor Mantra towered over most other Balinese and had a commanding presence that reinforced his role as one of the most popular public leaders in recent Balinese history. He succeeded Governor Soekarman, a Javanese who was brought into Bali in 1967 as part of the pacification process that inaugurated President Suharto's New Order Government. For those Balinese who were worried that Bali would be swamped by Javanese cultural influences, the replacement of a Javanese governor with a Balinese was a welcome sign of the strengthening of Balinese identity—something that Mantra, with his academic background and his interest in Hinduism, actively emphasized. Governor Mantra consistently supported the activities of such culturally-oriented bodies as the Dance Academy, and sponsorship of traditional crafts by government bodies, for example through the use of traditional paintings from Kamasan village in the new Nusa Dua hotel complex. One of the crowning moments of his period of office was the holding of the exorcistic *Ekadasa Rudra* ceremony in 1979, when President Suharto put in an appearance to show how important Balinese ritual, religion and culture were to the Indonesian state ideal of "unity in diversity." Governor Mantra embodied the consolidation of ideas of culture and tradition in Bali.

Social control was probably the major interest of the Suharto's New Order regime. Administratively, it operated through a parallel structure of civilian and military bureaucracy. The armed forces presented themselves as having a dual function in society: to both defend the nation and ensure that society is properly regulated, so that on every level of society, from the central administration in Jakarta to local-level offices, there were military administrators working side by side with civilians. Living in a Balinese village, one was likely to frequently encounter military appointees as village heads, if the area was regarded as politically sensitive, or at least to be visited by military carrying out "volunteer" development work.

Bali's reputation as a former center of Communist activity, its population density, its high international profile, and its proximity to Java all meant that the government paid close attention to the island. Village activities, particularly around the time of national elections, were closely observed, and occasionally public performances or newspaper articles which might be construed as critical of the government were censored by local authorities.

For the most part, however, the army did not have to actively control the population. Balinese with influential positions in society found that a career in the government bureaucracy or the military was a boost to their own status, so they had a vested interest in government policy and in ensuring that there would be no public expression of discontent. The Balinese had, to a very large extent, been integrated into the national hierarchy. The Chief of Staff of the Army in the late 1980s, for example, was a Balinese *brahmana*. Although it is impossible to accurately judge such matters, in many ways the majority of Balinese were more loyally committed to Suharto's New Order Government and less likely to express dissent than many other Indonesians, including Javanese.

The New Order Government of Suharto equated all the negative aspects of modernization and social change with tourism and tourists, and the positive idea of tradition with the continuing identity of Balinese as a group. Aligning national and local governments as defenders of Balinese interests, made the actions and motives of both sacrosanct. Mantra's dexterity as an Indonesian politician was strongest in his ability to maintain the balance between Balinese cultural pride and national political pressure—to appear to play to the interests of the central government while keeping them at bay. Because of this, and the fact that he was able to limit major tourist developments, his rule is seen as the modern golden age of Indonesian Bali.

CHAPTER SIX

Bombings and Branding: Beyond Cultural Tourism

Since the end of the 1980s, the Indonesianized Bali of the New Order period has been replaced by a globalized Bali. In appearance this has been a very different Bali, one in which rice fields have been rapidly transformed into hotels and artshops, the green and pleasant landscape turned to concrete, and the once-verdant views blocked out. In the twenty-first century the Indonesian Bali of the Cultural Tourism policy has become harder and harder to imagine.

Bali became a major focus of international terrorism with the 2002 and 2005 bombings, turning it into a place of danger in the eyes of the world, and ironically echoing the image of Bali before the twentieth century. Balinese have since struggled with ways to cope with this new image, coming as it does in the mix of Indonesia's complex and rapidly changing politics. It is not so easy for Balinese to define their island using the old, standard images. An increasingly defensive stance towards the outside world has led Balinese to sharpen their focus onto essential elements of their culture, looking for fundamental definitions of their island as ethnically and religiously exclusive, a Hindu island for those of Balinese descent. At the same time "Bali" has spread globally, both through the widespread use of symbols of Bali, and through the increased migration and mobility of Balinese themselves. The many "Balis" of the twenty-first century have contributed to problems of branding Bali in an increasingly competitive tourist market.

Jakarta's Colony

Changes to Bali's image began with the building of large-scale resorts in the 1980s. These offered self-contained holiday packages, with all the eating, sleeping and entertainment available within the beautiful grounds of a beachside complex. Customers were able to enjoy to a range of water sports and other diversions without having to brave the outside world. This resort tourism has provided an experience very different from the encounters that hippies, surfies and backpackers had in the 1970s and early 1980s.

Bali's transition from the official policy of Cultural Tourism to the actuality of resort tourism began when the Indonesian economy was partially liberalized around 1988, and Bali saw a massive influx of finance, building and internal migration. Coming out of a regional economic crisis, Suharto had agreed to the demands of liberal advisors to deregulate aspects of the Indonesian economy. Loosening of financial and business restrictions not only stimulated foreign investment, but also paved the way for a massive expansion of wealth by those who were closest to the government, some of which trickled down to create a new middle class. Suharto and his close allies had been known for corruption from the time that Suharto, as a military officer, had been punished for smuggling in the 1950s, to the spectacular crash of the state oil company, Pertamina, in 1974. In the 1990s the scale of corruption increased to the point of undermining the whole of the Indonesian economy.

In 1988 another brahman, Ida Bagus Oka (1935-2010), succeeded Ida Bagus Mantra as governor of Bali. Oka has not been remembered as favorably as Manta. All of the problems of rapid change seemed to start with Oka's management. Although his academic background was similar to Mantra's, Governor Oka failed in the politics at which Mantra was so able. He could not keep the Suharto cronies at bay, and he struggled to deal with the inadequacy of Bali's infrastructure and lack of clear policy. Criticism of Oka reached a point where he was openly labeled as "Ida Bagus OK," since he rolled over and assented to all the demands of Jakarta. Despite serving as Minister for Family Planning and Population Control under Suharto's successor, B. J. Habibie in 1998-1999, Oka was later convicted of corruption and served a brief prison sentence until

Who profits from tourism? Ida Bagus Surya Dharma was one of the *Bali Post* cartoonists commenting on how Balinese were no longer getting the benefits from the tourism (*Pariwisata*) industry

the verdict was set aside.[1]

The boom of the late 1980s and early 1990s meant that members of Suharto's family and his associates increased their access to state monopolies and other channels of finance and power, and some of these were deployed in Bali. Development restrictions were forgotten as a series of luxury hotels was built, beginning in the formerly barren Bukit peninsula in the south, extending upwards through the once sleepy fishing village of Jimbaran, until it even intruded into the space of Tanah Lot, one of Bali's most sacred temples in the former kingdom of Mengwi.

Suharto's sons took the lead in building what Balinese referred to as "mega projects," gigantic resorts that could command top dollar, such as the Bali Cliff. International hotel chains and overseas investors were allowed in as long as they paid a percentage or gave part ownership to the Suharto cronies. Following that lead, it became fashionable for all the rich families of Jakarta to own a bit of Bali. Some of the shadier members of this élite found such

---

1. "Former Bali Governor and Cabinet Minister Ida Bagus Oka Succumbs to Stroke and Heart Disease," *Bali News* 3rd August 2010, Bali Discovery Tours, <http://www.balidiscovery.com/messages/message.asp?Id=5869> read 8th May 2011.

"investments" a good way to launder money, along with speculating in the market for the paintings of the 1930s expatriate artists who worked on Bali.[2]

One of Indonesia's most famous dissidents at the time, George Aditjondro, christened Bali "Jakarta's colony," and that was certainly how it felt to Balinese. Cartoons and popular writings by Balinese expressed disquiet about outside corporations squeezing Balinese out of the picture. The tourist development near Tanah Lot temple became a focus for the growing resentment of Balinese against the sudden ramping up of building and the takeover of what was once regarded as Balinese land. Given the tight political control of the time, the protests over this Bali Nirwana Resort and connected golf links were quite remarkable.[3]

Ultimately the development went ahead. Minor changes gave the appearance of respect for Hinduism, but the development signaled the end of the uneasy consensus of previous decades. Under the liberalization of the economy, the expanding Balinese middle classes were suddenly able to afford cars, eat at the kinds of restaurants hitherto frequented by tourists, and even become tourists themselves. While the New Order had promised development, everyone imagined that it would be pleasant, and lead to happiness and joint prosperity. From the 1950s until the 1980s, Balinese and other Indonesians maintained the 1930s image of Bali as the paradise of paradises both as a means of modernizing Bali through tourist development and of maintaining Balinese tradition. Bali was said to be genuinely modern, because it had become part of a global tourist world, while reforming religious and artistic traditions that were internationally respected. The kind of untrammeled development Balinese were suddenly experiencing in the 1990s threatened the stability of this image.

The Tanah Lot protests allowed Balinese to express their dis-

---

2. In revising the last part of this book I have drawn on Michael Hitchcock and I Nyoman Darma Putra, *Tourism, Development and Terrorism in Bali*. Aldershot: Ashgate, 2007.

3. Putu Suasta and Linda H. Connor, "Democratic Mobilization and Political Authoritarianism: Tourist Developments in Bali," in Raechelle Rubinstein and Linda H. Connor (eds), *Staying Local in the Global Village: Bali in the Twentieth Century*, pp. 91-122. Honolulu: University of Hawai'i Press, 1997. The other essays in this volume also give a fine view of social change in Bali.

"Bali hourglass," as ricefields disappear from the island,
1990s cartoon by Surya Dharma.

quiet over the loss of control over development, just as it presaged the fall of the Suharto government in 1998. The promise of development through Cultural Tourism was very much at odds with the new and very different tourist Bali that entered the twenty-first century. Ironically, the Asian Economic Crisis of 1997 that led to Suharto's resignation was also an economic stimulus to Bali, since it made the island a cheap destination again. The benefits to Balinese, however, were transitory.

Safeguarding Bali

In 2006, tourist authorities at Phuket, Thailand, proposed a sister "city" (or at least island) relationship with Bali, because of their similarities as travel destinations. According to Balinese sources, the Thai local government head stymied the arrangement because he thought it would lower Phuket's reputation.[4] After 12 October 2002, Bali's main identity had changed to that of "bombing target."

The Bali Bombings of 2002, with their 2005 repeat attacks, scarred the image of Bali, but more importantly had serious impli-

---

4. "Phuket is Proposed for Sister City Links with Bali Island of Indonesia" <http://www.thaivisa. com/forum/topic/65304-phuket-is-proposed-for-sister-city-links-with-bali-island-of-indone-sia/>, posted 06-04-2006, read 5th May 2011.

cations for Balinese self-perceptions as an entrenched and threatened minority in the Indonesian state.

Of the two sets of bombings, the first was the more serious, with 199 victims dead (plus the two sucide bombers), but the 2005 bombings, with only 20 deaths (and three suicide bombers) deterred those tourists who had believed that lightning never strikes twice in the same place, particularly Australians. Hitherto Australians had made up the largest proportion of tourists, and so comprised the largest number of vicitims, with eighty-eight killed in 2002. The effect on Australians was summed up by the quotation from a traumatized witness, "how can they do this to our Bali?" The bombings confirmed Bali's image as an innocent paradise, a gentle place now subject to hostility from Muslim extremists. The comment was double-edged, since it assumed that Australians had some kind of proprietary right over the island, treating it as a cheap extension of Queensland's Gold Coast. Australians had suddenly realised that Bali was actually part of Indonesia, something that had hitherto escaped the attention of many antipodean tourists. Unlike Bali, Indonesia had an increasingly negative image in Australian popular consciousness, although peversely, that negative image developed just as Indonesia was moving away from Suharto's authoritarian rule, and towards becoming the world's third largest democracy.

Bali had been advertised as a place of safety when riots and political violence gripped the capital and some remoter parts of Indonesia between 1998 and 2001, and foreign media summarized the whole nation as a place of terrorism and violence. Such, however, has been the strength of Bali's reputation as part of Australia's "pleasure periphery," as analyst Agnieszka Sobocinska puts it, that Australian tourism recuperated by the end of the decade. Despite official Australian government warnings not to travel to Indonesia, over 667,100 Australians travelled there in 2010, most of them to Bali.[5]

5. Agnieszka Sobocinska, "Innocence Lost and Paradise Regained: Tourism to Bali and Australian Perceptions of Asia," *History Australia* 8,2, (August 2011), an article which also updates the representation of Bali in Australia; see further Hitchcock and Darma Putra, *Tourism, Development and Terrorism in Bali*, chapter 10; and Mark Hobart, "Round Up the Usual Suspects: Some Radical Implications of Indians and Euro-American Media Coverage of 'Terrorist' Attacks," in H. Nossek, P. Sonwalkar and A. Sreberny (eds), *Media and Political Violence*, Cresskill, N.J.: Hampton Press, 2007.

For Balinese, recovery has been a different experience. Beyond the awful effects on those who lost family and friends or were injured in the bombings, the 2002 blasts were felt as a shared cataclysm across the island. The word "tragedy" was most often used in local media coverage, and Balinese have continued to describe the bombings as changing the nature of tourism forever.[6] These descriptions focus on the negative economic effects. Most people involved in the tourist industry have emphasized that when the tourists did come back, they did not fall back into the same spending and touring patterns, meaning that the income from their presence was not as widely spread as previously. Resort tourism influenced this effect, since more restricted contact with Balinese was reinforced by the image of security that enclosed hotels sought to promote. Compounding the post-bombing downturn was the advent of package tourism from Korea and China, where language difficulties allowed Korean and Chinese operators to keep a monopoly on their custom.

The bombings were perceived by many Hindu Balinese as part of a wider threat from Islam. Balinese unease about the island's position in the Muslim-majority nation of Indonesia had been building up since the 1990s, partly as result of Jakarta's "colonization" of Bali. These fears were more directly influenced by the increasing number of other, mainly Muslim, Indonesians taking up residence on the island. The redevelopment of Bali into an island of luxury resorts in the 1990s was not something Balinese did alone. Balinese could hardly refuse their fellow citizens entry to the island, but quickly found that dozens, then hundreds, then thousands of laborers were coming in from poorer neighboring islands, largely from the conservative Muslim areas of East Java and East Lombok. By the late 1990s, major road intersections were lined with shovel-wielding men, waiting to be picked up by passing trucks carrying soil and sand for building projects. This produced disquiet amongst Hindu Balinese. An escalation in crime, real or imagined, was blamed on Muslims needing to take gifts home at the end of the fasting month

---

6. See Hobart, "Round Up the Usual Suspects," and particularly Richard Fox, "Strong and Weak Media? On the Representation of 'Terorisme' in Contemporary Indonesia," *Modern Asian Studies* 40,4 (2006): 993-1052.

of Ramadan. Increased building of mosques, with loudspeakers that began prayers at 4 AM, gave Islam a high profile.

Already by the 1980s Balinese had been privately expressing anxiety about Muslim fundamentalism. It became known, or at least rumoured, that underground pamphlets were being published in Surabaya targetting Bali as an enemy of Islam. Such things could not be openly discussed under Suharto, since the New Order exercised a policy of tight censorship when it came to matters that included religious difference. Some Balinese saw Suharto's Javanese version of Islam as a protection against those who advocated a Muslim state, or wanted to introduce more Middle Eastern interpretations of the religion into a country that had hitherto guaranteed freedom for the practice of Hinduism.

In 1993, a series of temple robberies led to panic that poor itinerant Muslims were directly attacking Balinese culture. The reaction came in the form of a series of vigilante actions, in which Balinese temple congregations organized twenty-four hour watches, and tales began to circulate of the fate of poor unfortunate meatball sellers from Java who were not able to explain their presence in a village at night.

Although the actual number of robberies may have been small, the hysteria was great, and paved the way for the formation of paramilitary groups, *pecalang*, who came into their own with the fall of Suharto. The term used for these groups was claimed to be part of the reformation of Balinese tradition, since Balinese said that these *pecalang* existed in precolonial times as village police, although in fact they were more like spies and hitmen for the rajas of Bali.

Bali's darling of the 1990s was Megawati Sukarnoputri, Sukarno's daughter who rose to leadership of the Indonesian Democratic Party (*PDI*), the tame version of her father's political party. Megawati had a Balinese grandmother, and had spent time on the island, learning to perform the *lègong* for visiting heads of state. When her popularity became too obvious in the mid-1990s, Suharto's agents organized for thugs to throw her out of the party headquarters, and she eventually formed a breakaway Indonesian Democratic Party of Struggle (*PDI-P*). This party had an immense following on Bali, as the heir to the old Sukarnoist party, the *PNI*, so in the runup to the first Post-Suharto election in 1999, Megawati held a party congress on Bali. Not trusting the state authorities, security was put in the hands of so-called *pecalang*, whose membership was boosted by local criminal gangs, always the standby for political parties under Suharto. The legitimacy this gave to the vigilante groups helped cement their role in Balinese politics, to the point where the political maneuverings of any political party have come to rely on criminal thugs, or *preman* as they are called in Indonesia, as shock troops.[7]

Megawati herself was a bit of a disappointment to Bali. When she became president she did not deliver on the high expectations. It was her predecessors, the eccentric B. J. Habibie and the blind mystic Abdurrahman Wahid, who actually gave Bali greater political and economic self-determination through their legislation to create regional autonomy. In more recent elections her party has not received the support it might have once expected in Bali, and the party of her successor as president, the Javanese ex-general Susilo Bambang Yudhoyono, gained a significant following during his reelection campaign in 2009.

The use of thugs in Balinese politics was acceptable because they contributed to an idea of self defence. Early in 2002, even before the Bali bombings, the idea was given the grand neologism of *Ajeg Bali*, "Bali Standing Strong." The term caught on quickly, and fed into the notion that Balinese were losing Bali, as in the popular, anti-immigrant, saying "the migrant sells beef balls to buy land, while the Balinese sells land to buy beef balls."[8] Success was ensured by the championing of *Ajeg Bali* by the island's major media outlet, the *Bali Post* group, which expanded from having the island's main newspaper into having a television channel as well.

The October 2002 bombings gave meaning to *Ajeg Bali*. Although the vigilante groups were told to avoid a violent response to the bombings, more subtle intimidation, such as "sweepings" to check identity cards, let internal migrants know that they were not welcome in Bali.

7. Henk Schulte Nordholt, *Bali—An Open Fortress, 1995-2005: Regional Autonomy, Electoral Democracy and Entrenched Identities*, Singapore: Singapore University Press, 2007.

8. Quoted in Hitchcock and Darma Putra, *Tourism, Development and Terrorism*, p. 172, part of their detailed documentation of *Ajeg Bali*.

Thus the Balinese response to threats to their religion, ethnicity, and ownership of the island has been to emphasize or revive aspects of tradition. Balinese have become defensive about the appearance of change. As early as 2000, Nyoman Darma Putra and I published a collection of essays on social change dedicated to the late Professor I Gusti Ngurah Bagus, and in the media and at public seminars there was a strong reaction to the title: *To Change Bali*. Commentators at the launch stated that Bali should not be changed, but preserved. This seemed very much at odds with the original intentions of Balinese intellectuals who opposed the Dutch colonial idea of turning Bali into a "living museum." These were the progressive leaders who from the 1930s *Surya Kanta* movement to the political leadership of the 1950s strove to simplify rituals, ban the bare breasts that 1930s Western tourists were so obsessed with, and ban cockfighting. But by 2000, the "living museum" idea was starting to look attractive to some.

On the back of defending Bali, the police chief who led the hunt for the Bali bombers, Mangku Madé Pastika (1951-), became governor of Bali in 2008. Pastika came from the regency of Tabanan, notable for producing dynamic intellectuals and artists who distain the old "feudal" structures. Like most Balinese who have reached important state positions, he spent a lot of time outside Bali, and integrated into the Indonesian state structure, both in its earlier, Jakarta-based, centralized form and its more recent, decentered, version. In particular, Pastika survived the toughest posting in Indonesia, in West Papua, where counterinsurgency has been compounded by sometimes violent competition between the police and the military. The stakes there have been high, with both seeking to profit from the rich mining industry.

Pastika's popularity on Bali has had some contradictions. While he was police chief he built up an image of strength and determination amongst Balinese, but not all his actions fitted the Balinese mould. He spoke at *Ajeg Bali* events about the need for Balinese overseas to help buy back Balinese land, but at the same time he launched the most un-Balinese policy of (re-)banning cockfighting. There had been some conjecture in the 2008 elections that this would be his downfall, but a wide spectrum of Balinese supported him because his politics was less partisan, and he promised re-strengthening of Bali. One of his first moves had been to take on the herculean task of curbing excessive development, particularly the often illegally-built villas spreading throughout the countryside.

Another manifestation of "unchanging Bali" has been an attempt to gain UNESCO World Heritage status for the whole island. This began with (failed) moves to have Pura Besakih, Bali's most sacred temple, bestowed this status. Like most Balinese temples, Besakih has been the subject of extensive renovation and rebuilding. Although major alterations of style, material and aesthetics are usually not seen as real "change" by Balinese, the UNESCO criteria are a different matter. Balinese who did their homework soon realised that World Heritage Status would mean that they would not be able to keep adding to and modernizing the temple, and would lose control over it.[9] Nevertheless, other sites have been nominated, with mixed results, and conversations on the streets in the late 2000s mooted the idea of an island-wide nomination as a way of keeping out Islam.

Not wanting "to change Bali" may come from a number of causes: nostalgia for a Bali when traffic jams did not exist and life was simpler; or perhaps the idea that change always comes from the outside; or perhaps again the idea that there is some kind of cultural essence that can be preserved. For many Balinese the cultural essence is related to the features of Cultural Tourism, the dominant way of discussing culture as viewed by an outside "them," and consisting of temples, ceremonies, rice fields and people walking around in traditional dress. To maintain this "unchanged" cultural essence people are constantly renovating temples in grander and grander materials and style, holding bigger and bigger ceremonies, converting their rice fields into plots of land on which to build, and making "traditional dress" the uniform for hotel employees. Changing in order not to change is the island's biggest dilemma.[10]

---

9. Hitchcock and Darma Putra, *Tourism, Development and Terrorism*, chapter 7.
10. Thanks to Degung Santikarma for the last observation. He and associates were responsible for insightful commentary on the dilemmas of Bali through their magazine *Latitudes*.

Bali inside and outside Bali

Just as it is hard to find the "real" Bali on an island of renovated temples and disappearing rice fields, so are many looking for Bali outside the island. The Balinese diaspora can be found in many sites: in Melbourne or the Gold Coast of Australia where Balinese gamelan perform; in Asian resort areas where Balinese have been hired for their expert knowledge of the tourist industry; on cruise ships in the Caribbean where increasing numbers of young villagers find work; in Germany or the Netherlands where there are also substantial populations with their own temples.

As well as the many other Indonesians on Bali who are neither ethnically Balinese nor religiously Hindu, there are many varieties of "Balinese." There have been Muslim Balinese on the island at least since King Baturènggong gave his blessing to a settlement in his capital of Gèlgèl, where Bali's oldest mosque can still be found. Later Balinese rulers of Muslim subjects, such as the Lombok-ruling kings of Karangasem, supported extensive settlements centered on Islamic worship. The kings of South Bali hired mercenaries and hosted traders from the island of Sulawesi, whose settlements are still important features of the local landscape. In north Bali there are a number of villages that seem to be otherwise perfectly Balinese, until you find out that they are Muslim settlements.

Balinese Christians have also been around for a long time. During the 1930s, when the Dutch finally permitted reentry for missionaries, whole villages in parts of Tabanan converted to the religion hitherto associated with the West. A large Catholic congregation exists on the island, its most prominent sign being the Roman Catholic Church in the center of Dénpasar, with its beautifully carved Balinese-style angels and ornaments. Indonesians of Chinese descent moved to Bali after anti-Chinese attacks during the fall of Suharto, including a series of horrible rapes at the hands of military or paramilitary groups. The post-1998 increase in the Chinese-Indonesian population brought more funding for church building, particularly of evangelical Protestant churches, so that there are very large and prominent churches around Dénpasar.

Even within Hinduism, the old Balinese forms of the religion are subject to challenge and change. One Balinese friend remarked that she has no interest in visiting Indian Hindu temples in Singapore or India, since they have nothing that she would identify as belonging to her kind of temple, but there are many Balinese who want to re-Hinduize the religion. Successive waves of Balinese have been sent to study in India, and Balinese tour operators in the 1990s began to offer "pilgrimage" style tours to see the holy Ganges and other features of the Mother country of their religion. In the early 2000s an Indian cultural and religious center was established in Dénpasar.

The physical boundaries of "Bali" have always been problematic, since in the period from the end of the Javanese kingdom of Majapahit to the Dutch takeover, Balinese power has extended to include the Javanese regions of Blambangan, and Pasuruhan in the west, as well as the islands of Lombok and Sumbawa in the east. Jakarta has always had a strong Balinese presence (including a Balinese mosque in the old suburb of Angké) and, since the 1950s, a Hindu Balinese temple in the center of the city. Varieties of Balinese temples are also found all over Indonesia, such as the major Ubud-sponsored temple on the holy Mount Sumeru in East Java. Landless Balinese embraced the Suharto government's "transmigration" program and were moved to less densely populated parts of Indonesia. There they set up significant settlements, all with temples, in the Lesser Sundas, Sumatra and Sulawesi. Balinese had to leave a Hindu temple behind when Indonesians trashed and evacuated their former colony of East Timor in 1999.

One of the consequences of having Hinduism recognized as a national religion in the 1950s was that followers of indigenous practices in Kalimantan, as well as Majapahit remnants in the Tengger highlands of East Java, all included themselves under the Hindu banner, watering down its distinctively Balinese qualities. Some Balinese now want to define Balinese Hinduism, or Hindu-Buddhism, as separate from other varieties of Indonesian Hinduism.

Into the mix has come several newer streams of Hinduism. The Hari Krishna sect was already making village converts in Bali in the 1980s, and it has probably been most recognizable through the vegetarian food stalls catering to local clientele in many Balinese towns. So also the cult success of the Guru Sri Sai Baba found resonance amongst many modern Hindu Balinese, beginning with Balinese living abroad, who imported the practice to the island.[11] More personalized worship, such as that of Sai Baba, has the attraction of enabling people to stay Hindu but be free from the endless demands of offering-making and strict customary law.

Wayan from Bulèlèng exemplifies the appeal of Sai Baba. He moved to the south of Bali from the poorer north to find work in the tourist industry, but his experience eventually took him to the Maldives. He and his wife, a successful career woman in the Arts, now live in a modern housing complex in Nusa Dua. As a northerner, he is part of a culture that ignores the old formal hierarchies of caste, and as a modern Balinese he has had to be mobile. Sai Baba's teachings fit better with the more egalitarian and portable lifestyles of twenty-first century Bali.

Challenging custom-based identity has been a feature of new youth scenes. With prosperity, Balinese have been able to travel overseas, to become tourists themselves, and to consume the same kinds of products as other peoples. Reggae, Punk, Thrash and Death Metal have all developed on Bali since the 1980s, ulimately gaining local roots by incorporating aspects of Balinese religion and culture. These scenes have linked up with similar subcultures from other parts of Indonesia, leading to new compositions with Indonesian and Balinese lyrics and resonances. Such changes have been products of Balinese participation in international culture, much in the same way that Balinese have gone on to be professional surfers on the international circuit. Punk may not fit conventional Balinese ideas of essential cultural symbols, but it has nevertheless been thoroughly Balinized.[12]

Marketing Bali

Rapid changes in Bali's image have thus come from the increased intensity of tourism, from Bali's position in the Indonesian nation, and from the general effects of being in a globalized world in which

---

11. Leo Howe, *Hinduism and Hierarchy in Bali,* Oxford: James Currey; Santa Fe, NM: School of American Research, 2001.

12. Emma Baulch, *Making Scenes: Reggae, Punk and Death Metal in 1990s Bali,* Durham: Duke University Press, 2008.

contact, interchange and mobility are taking place at a more and more rapid rate. The official policy of Cultural Tourism has not been adequate as a vehicle to help deal with such change.

Cultural Tourism had been based on the premise that Balinese culture was under threat from the tourist gaze, but managing the flow and experience of western tourists could control this threat and turn it into an economic advantage. As resort tourism supersedes Cultural Tourism, this approach looks increasingly hollow. Most tourists see very little of Balinese culture, and even the growing expatriate community on the island is relatively insulated from exposure to that which made the experience of Bali so thrilling to the Spies set in the 1930s. Problems have arisen because the tourists are not only from Australia, the United States and western Europe, but are also Russians, Chinese, Koreans, and other Indonesians, all with very different expectations. The experience of Bali has changed, and the result has been a crisis in how to present Bali as a marketable brand in order to keep Bali's economy prosperous. Balinese-born national minister for Culture and Tourism, Jero Wacik, naturally has maintained Bali's central role in the national tourist agenda, but Balinese have been disappointed by the lack of clear policy to follow from this. The problem for Balinese in the travel business has not been the numbers of tourists, but finding ways to control the presentation of Bali, especially so that the benefits flow to Balinese.

In the 1990s, as the "mega projects" went up, the tourist brochures moved from the promotion of Balinese culture to selling "properties," i.e. rooms in luxury resorts. For tourists coming to Bali the impressions of Balinese culture became quite limited, and the emphasis shifted to staying in self-contained accommodation. The old problems of tourism in a poor country have remained: when tourists step outside their hotel areas they are assailed by heavy traffic and harassed by touts: "You want massage, you want special young girl massage, you want boy massage, just looking my shop, come just look, transport" etc. This kind of harassment has made resorts a welcome refuge from the street life of the island. When tourists are taken to see Balinese "art" it is the low grade products of the artshops, and their guides are only interested in taking them to places where major commissions are on offer. If tourists see beautiful landscapes the experience only comes after sitting through traffic jams, and if they see Balinese performances it is usually the tired old *lègong* and "welcome dance" of hotels and restaurants. There is little of the direct experience had by the hippies and surfies of an earlier era.

In coffee table books on Bali there has been a marked shift in attention from how Balinese live to the lavish lifestyles of expatriates. A growth in expatriate living in Bali was a product of late 1980s liberalization, when it became easier for foreigners to occupy property, usually on ninety-nine year leases. Ultimately this led to the villa industry of the 2000s as small independent living arrangements mushroomed. For those bored with resorts, villas have offered self-sufficiency. The villa developments have eaten up more and more land, and stretched the island's infrastructure very thinly. Such developments have tended to concentrate in the sprawling area to the north of Kuta, beginning at Seminyak, but moving out as far as Canggu as the living conditions have become denser and denser. Most of the longer-term expatriates in these developments live in isolation from Balinese village communities, an isolation reinforced by the fact that, unlike earlier generations of foreign residents, knowledge of Indonesian, let alone Balinese, is rare.

The resorts and villas have led to overdevelopment, and cultural and social relations have strained, along with the infrastructure. Commentary both by Balinese and outsiders on this problem has come to influence Bali's image. When *Time Magazine* published an article entitled "Holidays in Hell: Bali's Ongoing Woes," the official reaction from Governor Pastika was affirmation of the problems, not denial.[13] The article drew attention to the "frothing human waste" going "into the sea off Kuta Beach," before it went on to catalogue the woes of the island: "water shortages, rolling blackouts, uncollected trash, overflowing sewage treatment plants and traffic so bad that parts of the island resemble Indonesia's gridlocked capital Jakarta." The focus in such articles has often been on the experience of expatriates, rather than engagements with Balinese, so much attention has been devoted to fear of crime: "In January, amid a

---

13. Andrew Marshall, "Holidays in Hell: Bali's Ongoing Woes," *Time* Saturday Apr. 9, 2011.

spate of violent robberies against foreigners, Bali police chief Hadi-atmoko reportedly ordered his officers to shoot criminals on sight." Although some positive notes were sounded, such as the comment that "A new terminal at Bali's shabby airport is due for completion in 2013," the analysis was that Bali is heavily overdeveloped and over-touristed, with visits rising from 1.3 million in 2001 to an expected 2.5 million in 2011. And that is before a similar number of tourists from other parts of Indonesia is added in.

A product of the distance that resort and expatriate villa living creates from Balinese culture has been the perception that "Bali" can be reduced to a set of design motifs. These motifs are used as the decoration of hotel buildings and luxury home interiors. This perception is a problem for the image of Bali, since it turns the island into a set of floating signs that can be easily transported. This development is the paradoxical outcome of good intentions to promote Balinese culture through engagement. The earliest roots of a particular "Bali style" go back to the late 1960s, when Australian artist Donald Friend lived in Sanur and, in collaboration with local hotel owner Wija Wawarunto, commissioned a series of buildings and gardens both for private residences and for Wawarunto's exclusive Tanjung Sari Hotel.

The Bali style was further developed by Madé Wijaya, an innovative architect, again of Australian origin, but a long term resident of Bali who had converted to Hinduism and mastered colloquial Balinese. Wijaya's clever combination of extravagant decoration and strategic use of minimalism has come from his study of Balinese traditions of building and design. To this he has added elements from the arts of other parts of Indonesia, particularly Java and the eastern islands of Nusa Tenggara, and a strong sense of garden composition. The resulting mix of primitivism and sophistication made his name, having led to overseas commissions (famously, one from David Bowie for his home in the West Indies). Books on the style followed, creating a host of imitators. Now it seems *de rigeur* for any hotel in a tropical country, and some in not-so-tropical locations, to have thatched pavilions, small carved decorations and well placed "primitive" statues. Bali can be consumed everywhere.

Another aspect of the image of Bali that is more about foreigners

on Bali than about Balinese themselves has been the niche marketing of spiritual tourism. At the Bali Cultural Congress of 2008, held
in the Grand Bali Beach Hotel, Minister Jero Wacik gave an opening speech in which he offered his solution to improving the image
of Bali: a major Hollywood blockbuster. Although the delivery of
this was beyond Wacik's budget, Hollywood did duly oblige with
Eat, Pray, Love, starring Julia Roberts. This movie was based on a
self-discovery book by Elizabeth Gilbert, which had hit the top of
the bestseller lists after promotion on the *Oprah* TV show. In a shift
from the 1970s and 1980s image of Bali, the "love" that Gilbert
found in Bali was another tourist, not a Balinese.[14]

The making of the film created great anticipation in Bali, and
hotel operators rushed to raise prices when it came out. The hope
was that this would bring back the tourists frightened off by the
bombings. Tourist numbers did increase, but probably more because of the passage of time than a direct influence of the film, since
it flopped at the box office and in the eyes of critics. However some
women have been inspired by the book to come to Bali in search
of "spiritual growth." This has particularly proven to be a boon for
Ketut Liyer, the artist and traditional healer (*balian*) featured in the
book and film. Despite the somewhat condescending way that Liyer
was described in the book, he acquired a steady flow of customers
for the "renewal" offered as part of tours going under such titles as
"Spirit Quest."[15]

The film and book had plugged into an earlier vein of "spiritual
Bali," seen in the success of books such as Odyle Knight's 1998
Bali Moon: A Spiritual Odyessey. Her broad accent and sensible
dress reveal Knight as an everyday, unpretentious Australian. By
writing directly from her experiences, she, like Gilbert, has spoken to a wide audience. Of her experience of Bali, Knight said "I
believe in destiny. My life has revolved around Bali for the last 20

---

14. The 2010 film starred Julia Roberts and Javier Bardem, directed by Ryan Murphy, Columbia
Pictures; the book was originally published by Bloomsbury in 2007, and (somewhat embar-
rassingly) acknowledges the original edition of my book as one of its sources for a more
critical perspective on Bali, although sloppily referring to it as "Paradise Invented."

15. Hillary Brenhouse, "Bali's Travel Boom: *Eat, Pray, Love* Tourism," *Time* Thrusday, Jul. 22,
2010.

years, and it's very much a love-hate relationship." In her case, as in Gilbert's book, love, magic and inner spiritual improvement go together, but for Knight the downside was finding out that her Balinese lover already had two wives whom he had failed to mention. As well, he was a priest for the temple of the disease-bearing Demon God from Nusa Penida, whose name Balinese refuse to mention in case it brings misfortune—not exactly part of the New Age romantic dream.[16]

Another niche marketing success has been the Ubud Writers and Readers Festival. The village of Ubud, Liyer's place of residence, has been broadly successful in maintaining its cultural image, largely through the control of the wealthy Ubud royal family. Janet De Neefe, another Australian-born resident of Bali, built up a strong business in the Ubud area together with her Balinese husband and business partner, Ktut, through her Casa Luna restaurant and its various offshoots. On the back of these ventures, De Neefe has made the Festival an international hit that attracts leading writers. An important part of her motivation has been to draw people back to Bali after the 2002 bombings. Most of the audience comes to the island for these international big names, although Indonesian writers have been incorporated into the Festival.

All the diverse and contradictory aspects of the image of Bali have moved the island a long way from the appeal of trance dances, ceremonies and rural villages. As English cultural critic and long-time observer of Bali, Mark Hobart has commented, the problem for the island has not been so much the commoditization of Bali itself, since that happened long ago, but branding. Using standard marketing texts, Hobart analysed the problems of encapsulating Bali for tourist consumption: in the last few decades the selling of Bali has lost focus, or in advertising speak, is no longer "on message." Whereas once the promise was of a cultural experience out of the ordinary, the marketing of Bali has been spread too thinly. Along with art and dancing, the appeal to markets for "white water rafting to hang gliding and night life" (and one might add shopping, zoos,

---

16. Odyle Knight's *Bali Moon*, was originally self-published, but a huge success. Quotations from her interview with Kartin Figge, 8th June 2009, *Jakarta Globe* <http://www.thejakartaglobe.com/arts/on-life-love-and-mysticism/310819> read 7th May 2011.

Image-making and indigenous responses

and camel rides) has meant that Bali is trying to get into "markets in which other places are better qualified to compete."[17] Hobart, whose anthropological fieldwork on Bali went back to the beginning of the 1970s, delivered this incendiary message to an audience of Bali's leading cultural authorities and intellectuals in 2008. They were provoked, as they were by my own paper at the congress that asked whether Cultural Tourism had failed as a policy, but the reaction was a defensive one. Balinese with authority over tourism and planning find it hard to come to terms with losing control of the process of presenting themselves to the world.

Balinese culture is not necessarily in need of preservation, since it is dynamic and highly adaptable. Bali as a physical space defining cultural origins, however, is not in good shape. If there is to be a preservation of Balinese culture, then it needs to be a physical action as much as an intellectual one. If the once-pleasant Bali were to disappear, how would the island be able to survive on symbols

---

17. Mark Hobart, "Bali is a Brand: A Critical Approach," paper given at the Bali Culture Congress, Natya Mandala, Institut Seni Indonesia, Dénpasar, 14-16 June, 2008, see also Hitchcock and Darma Putra, *Tourism, Development and Terrorism*.

alone? The decline in quality of life for Balinese has been the cost they have paid for their relative prosperity. The range of problems and pressures that they are dealing with in the twenty-first century is perhaps beyond the ability of local or even national government. Bali's fate seems dominated by very narrow short-term interests. How will Balinese navigate the island's long-term interests against these? Paradise can be re-created only so many times before the raw materials—Bali's rich environment and the creative agency of Balinese—are over-exploited.

NOTES
Abbreviations used in the notes:
BKI: Bijdragen tot de Taal-, Land- en Volkenkunde van het KITLV.
KITLV: Koninlijk Instituut vor Taal-, Land- en Volkenkunde.
TBG: Tijdschrift voor Indische Taal-, Land- en Volkenkunde uitgegeven door het Bataviaasch Genootschap.
TNI: Tijdschrift voor Nederlandsch Indie.
RIMA: Review of Indonesian and Malaysian Affairs.

INDEX AND GLOSSARY

The Tuttle Story: "Books to Span the East and West"

Most people are surprised to learn that the world's largest publisher of books on Asia had its humble beginnings in the tiny American state of Vermont. The company's founder, Charles Tuttle, came from a New England family steeped in publishing, and his first love was books—especially old and rare editions.

Tuttle's father was a noted antiquarian dealer in Rutland, Vermont. Young Charles honed his knowledge of the trade working in the family bookstore, and later in the rare books section of Columbia University Library. His passion for beautiful books—old and new—never wavered throughout his long career as a bookseller and publisher.

After graduating from Harvard, Tuttle enlisted in the military and in 1945 was sent to Tokyo to work on General Douglas MacArthur's staff. He was tasked with helping to revive the Japanese publishing industry, which had been utterly devastated by the war. When his tour of duty was completed, he left the military, married a talented and beautiful singer, Reiko Chiba, and in 1948 began several successful business ventures.

To his astonishment, Tuttle discovered that postwar Tokyo was actually a book-lover's paradise. He befriended dealers in the Kanda district and began supplying rare Japanese editions to American libraries. He also imported American books to sell to the thousands of GIs stationed in Japan. By 1949, Tuttle's business was thriving, and he opened Tokyo's very first English-language bookstore in the Takashimaya Department Store in Ginza, to great success. Two years later, he began publishing books to fulfill the growing interest of foreigners in all things Asian.

Though a westerner, Tuttle was hugely instrumental in bringing a knowledge of Japan and Asia to a world hungry for information about the East. By the time of his death in 1993, he had published over 6,000 books on Asian culture, history and art—a legacy honored by Emperor Hirohito in 1983 with the "Order of the Sacred Treasure," the highest honor Japan bestows upon non-Japanese.

The Tuttle company today maintains an active backlist of some 1,500 titles, many of which have been continuously in print since the 1950s and 1960s—a great testament to Charles Tuttle's skill as a publisher. More than 60 years after its founding, Tuttle Publishing is more active today than at any time in its history, still inspired by Charles Tuttle's core mission—to publish fine books to span the East and West and provide a greater understanding of each.